Tenement Testaments
By:
Bertrand E. Brown

D1306387

My earliest memories weren't fond by any stretch of the imagination. That's not to say that my parents weren't good people. They were the best parents any child could wish for. It's just that they got caught up in the times. I had a college professor once who posed the question concerning President Kennedy and Martin Luther King. At the time I didn't think too much of his query but even then it was thought provoking. He wanted to know if the times created President Kennedy and Martin Luther King Jr. or if the men created the times. I'm not sure if I ever did come to a concrete conclusion but one thing I did know and that was that my parents were certainly a victim of the times. Both Kennedy and King stressed fair housing and integration and New York I fear was not much different than the rest of America in the early sixties and most of White America was not embracing change so when my
parents decided to flee Harlem in search of greener pastures I was forced to be their guinea pig in a manner of speaking. Oh, their was little doubt that they loved me but Queens, New York was still a bastion of poor Italians and they were not so quick to embrace Claudia and Frank's little golden child. Still, if we were to make any inroads and destroy the racism so inherent in American society then there was no way we could sit complacent in the rear ranks so it soon became apparent to me that not only were they embracing the struggle but that their only child, me, was to be placed on the front lines at four years old. It was almost like being drafted, as I had no say in the matter whatsoever.

Not long after that I found myself in full battle fatigue armed with only the notion that I was as good if not better than the next little White boy or girl and as both my parents were teachers they prepared me so aptly scholastically that I tended to believe much of the hype myself. I had to be the cockiest, most self-assured four year old on the planet. And I needed to be for when I hit the front lines I encountered the most lethal assault any four year old could fathom.

Enrolled in a little nursery school several blocks from the house I looked forward to the first day being somewhat naive about the inner workings of racism. I just thought that it was a smorgasbord of other little tykes anxious to play and put thumb tacks on the teacher's chair. What I found, however and

much to my discouragement was that I was the only little chocolate boy in a class of thirty-four.

My teacher, Miss DeWitt was an elderly White woman who appeared to be close to eighty and had one of those old sour, twisted up teacher faces that looked meaner than my mother's. Combined with a sternness that said you get out of hand and I'll tear your little bottom up I eased into the routine with some chagrin. School wasn't the way I pictured it to be at all. But still there were kids and as long as there were other children I knew there was still hope for fun or so I thought. Those hopes were dashed on the second day of classes when I returned to my little nursery school and found there was no one in attendance aside from Ms. DeWitt and myself, although I did notice many of my classmates from the day before walking in tight circles and holding their parents hand and large cardboard placards. They were all chanting something but being that Ms. DeWitt was so adamant about me paying attention as she taught, (as if there were a whole class in attendance), I couldn't hear what it was they were chanting about. I only wondered why my mom

2

*and I weren't out there chanting and walking holding big
cardboard signs and having fun like all the rest of them.
I guess we didn't get the memo.*

*Then it came to me that this must be what all the
hullabaloo is at night when mommy and daddy watched
the news. This must be that big thing they called
'racism'. They said it was when other people left you out
because of your skin color and mommy and me had sure
been left out from walking in circles and carrying big
signs so this must be that thing that would send my mom
into frenzy. This was racism. Still, I didn't see what the
big thing was. Walking in
circles over and over didn't look like too much fun and
after noticing a few of my classmates crying I was glad to
be inside with Miss DeWitt.*

*Mommy arrived not long afterwards and she and Miss
DeWitt left me to play with the toys in the corner of the
room and I guessed this was what they called recess or
lunch or something. Mommy tried to explain that it was
the time of the day when you ate, then played, then slept.
I think they called it recess and I was good at it although I
wasn't really feeling naptime or those hard mats they
threw down on the floor for us. They didn't have ADHD
in those days but if they had had it I would have probably
been the first ever diagnosed with it and so naptime was
out. Anyway, when I became a little bored with playing
by myself I turned to mommy and Miss DeWitt who were
in a very heated discussion about something or another. I
was afraid when mommy started raising her voice. She
was the daughter of a Pennsylvania coal miner from
Mississippi and a woman from Alabama and could be as
coarse and country as they came. She could talk a mile a
minute when she became excited and even faster when
she was angry. And right now she looked to be angry.
Combined with her Pennsylvania accent it was hard to
understand much of what she was saying. I did recognize*

3

a few 'hunkies' here and there and I was well aware by my fourth year that when I heard the word hunkie it was time to depart. I wasn't sure exactly what it meant but it usually coincided with the word cracker and was often heard when my parents were talking. At other times she'd use it in the grocery store and I now knew that it usually meant trouble as she had a very bad temper and whenever we were in public it usually meant that it was time to break camp and get the hell out of Dodge.

Funny thing though, I knew she both liked and respected Miss DeWitt so it was beyond me why she would use such language in her company. But then I'd long ago come to the conclusion that my mother didn't have all the bricks in the wagon and so I limited my queries and for the most part just tried to stay on her good side. It helped that I was her first born and she was crazy about me or else I probably would have been fair game and been called a hunky or a cracker too but like I said she liked me.

To make a long story short the two women started talking about racism and Ms. DeWitt said something about the smallness of people and my mom went on calling them hunkies and crackers and making gang signs at them through the window. My dad used to say she was giving them the finger but she wasn't giving nobody nothing but a hard time 'cause that's what mommy did and plus I know a gang sign when I see 'em. And anytime she threw that middle finger up it was a gang sign.

In any case, Miss DeWitt assured my mom that none of them ever had to come back to school but I would be taught there as right was right even if I were her only student. She and my mom hugged and my mom slapped me upside the head before putting my coat and matching cap on and walking me past all my classmates and home. According to my mom that was my first encounter with racism even though I still didn't have a clue as to what it was although it was beginning to take shape and form a

4

*little better and things were beginning to become a little
bit clearer to me. I had to be about five or six now and my
parents seemed to always be protesting about something
and from what I gathered it was always about hunkies
and crackers and for the life of me I couldn't understand
it. One day I asked my dad—you couldn't ask mommy
because the mere mention of the word hunky or cracker
and she'd go off and start foaming at the mouth like a
rabid dog in heat so I knew to avoid her.*

*My dad had a little more patience so I went to him and
asked him if we had any of these hunkies or crackers in
our house. To this he simply smiled and replied 'no'. I
figured they must be akin to having cockroaches or
bedbugs and I knew from conversations that they weren't
something you wanted in your house.*

*What I didn't understand was why there was so much talk
about hunkies and crackers if they weren't pests. But my
dad was if nothing else patient and explained that they
were pests of a sort and their goal was to make life
difficult for a Negro. When I asked why they would take
so much time to make life difficult for a Negro when
Negroes already had it bad he couldn't explain. All he
would tell me was that it was inherent. I didn't
understand inherent until years later and still don't
understand the dynamics of racism. But that didn't mean
I didn't encounter it on a regular basis. I just never
understood it.*

*The taunting of my parents didn't subside in the least and
those words became as common as bread and milk. And
when my parents took me to the small town of Uniontown,
Pennsylvania a hop, skip and a jump from Pittsburgh,
pennsylvania to visit the rest of my family I suddenly
became aware that the words hunky and crackers were
rather commonplace. It frightened me somewhat though
and perhaps that's why I was so aware of it. Every time it
was said there was shouting and screaming and someone*

5

*became very adamant about something or another. The
conversation usually went a little something
told him... or do you know what this cracker had the
nerve to say to me?' Funny thing about those words
though was that all my aunts and uncles used it but I had
never heard it once in the little Catholic Elementary
School I now attended back in Queens.*

*Things were no different when we returned to New York.
Not long after we got home a White woman walked her
dog passed our home and stopped there so her dog could
poop in front of our house. Now mom was as fastidious a
gardener and homeowner as there was and took pride in
the tiny yard around it. Everyday when she finished
pulling the weeds around her azaleas she'd sweep the
curb out and get her trusty shovel and scoop up the dirt
and gravel that had accumulated. So when she saw the
woman deliberately let her dog poop in front of her house
she very politely took her broom and shovel and
confronted the White woman, (they didn't have pooper
scoopers back in those days), and told her to pick the poop
up and take it home with her. (Only mommy didn't use
the word poop when addressing the woman.)*

*Now mymother wasn't what you would call a big woman
but she so intimidated that lady who was twice her size
that the woman picked up the poop in her bare hands and
scurried away looking back over her shoulder all the way
up the block. At these times, I'd find an old garbage can
or race to get under the kitchen table with my teddy bear
which I named Pinky and would clutch him with all
might and whisper to him until daddy got home because
like that scared White woman I was scared too of my
mother. And I knew it was only a matter of time before
she'd come in cussin' and sayin' things like 'that ol'
crazy cracker just gonna let her dog poop in front of my
house. I don't care what they say about Black folks white
folks are just nasty'. And then she'd get on the phone*

6

*and call one of her sisters who didn't live far from us and
rant and rave about these crazy hunkies all over again.
On days like these I'd just stay under the table until daddy
got home and would calm her down 'cause it wasn't
nothin' to say the wrong thing and get backhanded across
the room for something that crazy cracker had done to
upset my mother. Still, those crazy crackers were not to
be outdone by this crazy niggra lady who'd only recently
moved in. And I can remember daddy tellin' her that if
they'd kill one of their own and a man as good as the
president they sure wouldn't have any problem getting rid
of one little crazy ass Black woman. But did she listen?
Hell no. All she kept sayin' was that they all needed to
move. I can remember her staging her own private
protest march right there in the house shouting slogans
like, 'you move we improve'.
The next day that White woman or some of her comrades
took some poop and wrote 'Nigga Go Home' on our front
door and all hell broke loose but there was no chasing
mom and dad away since they now considered this there
home and that Martin Luther King Jr. man only
exasperated the situation with his daily rhetoric about
being free and citizens and being able to live anywhere
you chose to. Only thing I knew was that he wasn't from
Queens. The sad part was that my mother and father
truly believed him, which was okay for them, but it was
causing me hell and I really didn't want to fight for
equality everyday. I had a much simpler goal in life that
consisted of making mud pies, playing with my Leggos
and G.I. Joes. But for some reason Claudia wanted and
demanded so much more. And whereas normal children
went off to school each day hearing things like, 'Okay
sweetheart have a nice day. Remember mommy loves
you.' I went off to school with, 'Remember if anybody
calls you nigga you're allowed to beat them down and
don't come home if you let him beat you or if you let him*

beat you I'm going to beat you. I'm telling you it was like preparing for war each and every day and here I was all of six years of age combat trained and ready.

By this time I pretty much knew what a hunky and a cracker were but unlike my mother I didn't see the need to use the words much being that I'd made friends with a good many of the kids I was now going to school with. And according to mom most of them were hunkies and those that weren't were crackers. It was funny though because my classmates had become friends and had all gotten to know and respect me so there was no need to call them names.

And after several beat downs they knew not to call me anything but Bert since my mother had given me a virtual license to kill and so did I enjoy pummeling those nice little White kids who couldn't fight that every time they uttered something I swore they had called me nigga. In little or no time we had a pretty amicable arrangement for the most part. They either liked me and we became friends or they simply didn't speak for fear I would hear them wrong.

My dad used to say that New York was known as the melting pot but wasn't nothing melting in the pot I saw. Blacks were in Harlem. The Chinese were in Chinatown. The Jews were in Forest Hills and the Italians were in Little Italy. And they didn't like us moving into their neighborhoods despite what the Constitution said about us all being free and equal. I'd go to school with my friends and we'd play and get along during the weekday and then on Sundays we'd meet again at church and their parents, (you know the role models), would snatch their kids away or turn their heads when they'd grin and try to speak. It was all very confusing to me. These people who called themselves devout Catholics and who were draped in rosary beads and worshipping a God that professed love for all mankind were teaching their children to hate.

8

I couldn't understand but my parents were seemingly taking it all in stride. I, on the other hand, kept asking myself why these adults kept acting so childish but they did and they took their hatred to new levels each week. One Sunday my parents and I went to church. My parents seemed to be doing okay despite the racism and constant harassment and all I could say was that they were fighters. My father explained that Blacks had been fighting to stay alive since they were first brought to America and little had changed in the four hundred years since they'd arrived and being that my father was the next closest thing to Jesus himself in my eyes I tended to believe him. Still, something in me told me that when I went uptown to Harlem to see my aunt and my cousin Michelle they didn't seem to be fighting the same war that we were. And despite the war going on I also noticed that my mother was the one that seemed to be the one that enjoyed the skirmishes most. Sure my father would back her up but he didn't look for trouble whereas mom would seek out injustice gather her storm troopers, her small army and be ready to take to the street at the drop of a hat.

I can remember the Sunday we went to church and a group of teens were hanging out in the church parking lot the week mom and dad bought their first new car. I'll never forget that car. It was a 1965, burgundy, Chevy Belair with no power steering. It was a huge monstrosity but someone had told mommy that it was cheaper if you didn't get things like power steering, and air conditioning and so forth. And she believed them so the car was basic. (I'm surprised she got the radio). Anyway, it was hilarious to see her tugging and pulling this huge car with no power steering but this she did. Anyway, the teens standing in the church parking lot died laughing when they saw this tiny woman trying to maneuver this huge truck in this tiny parking place.

Well, being that they fit her description of poor White hunkies and crackers she resented them laughing at her. Before my dad grabbed her she had given them all a piece of her mind. When we came out of church we found the battery gone and had to get Triple A to replace the battery. It was always like that and I can remember later the same week mommy raise some hell about little Black Sambo adorning the walls of the bank where our school had us open our bank accounts. I'm not sure if mommy's the one that brought it to everyone's attention, (I wouldn't bet against that), or if someone brought it to her attention but nevertheless she had us along with her small army out there with our cardboard picket signs marching in circles in front of Jamaica Savings Bank on Jamaica Avenue shouting slogans like, 'Hell no! Sambo's gotta go.' And there on the wall of the bank was a White couple in horse and carriage being led by a short Black man with a lantern. That was Sambo and before mom was going to let a dime of her money be invested in my five dollar savings account Sambo had to go. I enjoyed that and couldn't for the life of me understand why if she liked picketing this much she hadn't joined the picket line at my nursery school instead of staying inside and talking with that ol' boring Miss DeWitt. When I asked her about this after leaving Jamaica Savings Bank and making the world better for me and Sambo I was met with one of those good ol' slaps upside the head and one of those 'damn boy I don't know why I even bother'.

I was still pretty much in a fog about this racism stuff. It was starting to sink in but I still didn't have a firm grip on it. All of my relatives used to tease me and make me feel stupid when the discussion moved in that direction. Even my cousin Michelle knew about it and she lived up in Harlem where I was told they didn't experience racism

*half as badly as they did in Queens. And I hated when my
mother would tell Aunt Lo and Aunt Thelma and Uncle
Fred and the relatives I admired most just how stupid and
naive I really was when it came to racism.*

*I'll never forget the story of how when I was back in
nursery school and the only little skin darkie there how I
told my mom that we had to bring a baby picture to class
and how she couldn't put my name on it because we were
to pick out our classmates pictures without knowing. It
didn't dawn on me that they would have no problem
picking out the only chocolate drop in the group.*

*They'd all double over when they heard this and after
awhile I just felt really dumb for not being able to
recognize the fact that I was different.*

*Life went on like this for awhile but the neighborhood
began to change as White real estate brokers anxious to
make a buck started bringing in a sprinkling of Black
families from the inner cities resulting in White flight.
There was no plan and the Whites fled further out onto
Long Island to places like Wyandanch, and Freeport and
Nassau County.*

*Over the next ten years or so we saw a complete
metamorphosis and Queens Village suddenly became
predominately Black while just across the street on the
other side of Springfield Ave. still remained essentially
White. You would have thought this would have made
mommy happy but I don't believe that any one people
would have made mommy happy. What my mother
deemed to be the ideal situation was to have lived Martin
Luther King's dream of people of different ethnicities
living and existing together in perfect harmony. That
wasn't too happen in Queens though. Realtors knew that
if they brought certain ethnicities to a community that
Whites would flee giving up their homes for little or no
money to the realtor who would then resell the home for a*

small profit, turning it over quickly thus opening it up to public housing and not only
lowering the property value but the inherent value of the people who took pride in their homes.
In came Hazel and Lester and a host of Black folks from the projects of Red Hook and Bed Stuy in Brooklyn. The Vietnam War was coming to a close now and with it came the drugs. Mom said they were brought in purposely to quell the niggers burning down the cities. New York was ablaze and just across the river Newark was burning. But when heroin hit the city the fires stopped. And it wasn't just the fires that were squelched but the Civil Rights movement as well. Oh, there were people still out there struggling, fighting but it's a well-known fact that if you kill the head the body will follow and after the assassinations of King, the Kennedy's and Malcolm the leadership dwindled along with the movement.
Oh, there were leaders and movements but the Panthers were through, most of them either dead or behind bars. Me, well I loved the Panthers. There was just something about these Black cats that raised both the devil and Jesus in me at the same time. I don't know if it was the fact that they were strong and looked good in their black outfits with their black berets tipped to the side or whether it was the fact that Mr. Charlie controlled and ran everything there was to run where I lived and everyday dealing with him made my life torture. I saw him when I woke up and went to school, when I turned on the T.V., even when I went to church on Sunday. And no matter where I was or what I was doing the White man was always there to tell me what to do, how to do it and when to do it. And what could I say? Most of the things they commanded were things that both my mother and father told me but that was one thing when they told me to do something but quite another when someone else told me. I had a hard time believing that what they told me was good for me

12

*when at the same time they were persecuting me and
anyone that looked like me.*

*So, you see that's what made the Panthers and Muslims
so appealing to me. They were cool and they weren't
afraid and they set the laws for Black folks like me. And
best of all they defied the White man calling his laws
hypocrisy. I think I was a rebel anyway just by my very
nature and if I needed a map or a guideline they certainly
provided me with one. I watched them on the news,
bought their books, and newspapers and absorbed all
their teachings like it was the Bible or the Koran they
were preaching from.*

*I guess all the inroads I'd made in integrating nursery
schools and Catholic Schools in the name of Civil Rights
still left me lacking when it came to Black pride. Sure, my
dad was born a teacher and I can remember him telling
me of The Confessions of Nat Turner and Frederick
Douglass and John Brown and how these were some bad
men in their day but I needed something I
could relate to right then and there. And my formal
schooling—not that dad's was informal—shoot dad's
home schooling came complete with written tests and a
forum where I had to regurgitate the knowledge given to
me. But what I'm referring to were those halls of
Montezuma where they taught you or better yet
indoctrinated starting off with saying the Pledge of
Allegiance to America for forcing you to live under
substandard conditions, receiving lower pay and paying
more for being poor. They didn't stop there though.
They taught us that in 1492 Columbus discovered
America although there were already people residing
there, which never made an awful lot of sense to me.
They taught us that Lewis and Clark discovered the West
even though there were people residing there as well and
that Benjamin Franklin, George Washington and
Thomas Jefferson wrote a Constitution for a country and*

13

a people that had come here to escape persecution and they added freedom and equality for all men before instituting slavery. Well, I could think a little bit by the time I was eleven or twelve years old and none of this made a whole lot of sense to me. If it was one thing that Claudia and Frank instilled in me it was the ability to think and to be logical. And the more I thought about my whole situation in the scheme of things the more it failed to make sense to me. Malcolm X's teachings, however, brought the whole thing to light and I became an avid follower of his teachings. Of course I couldn't swallow everything he said in its

entirety and I soon came to realize that he too had a need for progandizing . It was especially tough trying to incorporate his doctrine of White people being 'devils' in lieu of the fact that I had incorporated a good many Whites into my circle of close friends. When I spoke to my father about this very same dilemma I knew in the back of my mind that his thoughts weren't very far from mine or mine from his being that I knew some of the men he most revered such as many of the great poets and writers were his idols. For example he named his only son Bertrand Eliot after Bertrand Russell and poet T.S.Eliot. So, I knew my father didn't and couldn't possibly embrace the idea that the White man was the devil. He may have accepted that there were certain White men who acted like the devil but to canvas all as devils was too far a stretch. And after talking to my father who explained that the same man that was persecuting me and causing me pain and heartache was causing Black people across the nation pain and heartache.

Malcolm was simply throwing an umbrella over the whole network of pain and misery bestowed on us as a people. It was sort of a rallying cry to educate poor Black folks who had difficulty making their way through the muck and mire we know as racism.

What Malcolm did was put a face and a name on it and since it was hard to identify and understand he called the reason for the Black man's unfortunate plight in America the White man or the 'devil'. I like to reckon it to Hitler's telling the Germans that the reason for their misfortune was the Jews. Or

Reagan's labeling Russia the 'evil empire'. It was a rallying cry for Blacks. And it worked. The Black Muslim population grew by leaps and bounds. The inordinate amount of brothers in prison became Muslim. Those who were on drugs got clean. It was amazing how much hope he gave the poor, the hopeless and downtrodden. So, what did the man do when he saw the affect this one brother was having? Why, he did the same thing he did to the Kennedy's and Martin. He had him assassinated.

I was both hurt and bitter after this and although my father and mother could put things into proper perspective I had trouble dealing with this. I wanted to hate everything associated with authority, the American way of life, and Whites in general. Yet, every time I decided to take up the mantle of hatred one of those Whites would do something to ingratiate themselves with me.

What was even more distressing was that I had two parents who were fighting racism and injustice at every turn and yet they refused to become bitter and embrace hatred. I did not, could not understand how they could embrace those most responsible for their pain and agony and I refused to for many years

after his assassination. It was somehow easier to simply hate. To me it was just simpler to distrust and hate those who caused me pain. And pain was almost constantly there as a result of their hatred for me. Just seemed sensible to hate those who hated you, especially when it was unfounded. But Claudia and Frank were Christians and believed in turning the other cheek and blessing those

15

who persecute you. This made absolutely no sense to me but for some reason it did to them. That was Martin Luther King's teachings but I was more inclined to follow Malcolm who said you have a right to defend yourself. I thought frequently of the little nursery school my mother enrolled me in where they refused to accept me and even went so far as to withdraw their kids because I was admitted. I remember the angry White father who came to school saying that I stabbed his daughter when I was in first grade when she brushed my sharpened pencils on the stairway on the way to class. I thought of the crackers that smeared feces on our front door and the words 'Niggas Go Home' and I asked myself how I could possibly turn the other cheek and bless those who were persecuting me. I didn't have an answer.

Life went on and I grew increasingly vigilant and militant. The Civil Rights Movement that had been so instrumental in shaping so much in my life and done so much to change the country as a whole had all but died out and drugs had replaced the struggle and brought about a new struggle. The neighborhood was predominantly Black now but my school somehow remained predominately White. Oh, I was no longer the only little Black boy in attendance but what ever they were doing to maintain the status quo was working. And by the time I reached the eighth grade there were a total of only two other Black boys and a Puerto Rican and Black girl in attendance.

Of course they only admitted five of us so we had to be the cream of the crop. There was Vanessa. I don't know where she was from but she was the most beautiful girl in the world. And then there was Caroline a tall stately Puerto Rican girl from the Bronx. Talk about ravishing. She was close to six feet tall in the eighth grade and had hips on her to die for. To this day I have never seen a woman as built as she was. Then there was Bruce a little fat nerdy Black boy who wore glasses and used to repel girls like insect repellant repels mosquitoes. And there was Roger Mauge a big, stocky West Indian kid with a lot of mouth and a knack for saying the wrong thing at the wrong time. I liked them all and welcomed them as classmates and friends. At least they took some of the heat off me being the only little skin darkie in Sts. Joachim & Anne.

I'd gotten accustomed to little White kids saying obnoxious things like, 'can I touch your hair, or it feels just like a Brillo pad'. The worst was when they tried to compare you with someone of a darker persuasion and the only two they knew were Flip Wilson and Bill Cosby. So, one day I looked just like Bill Cosby and the following day I reminded them of Flip Wilson. After awhile I grew accustomed to it and labeled them ignorant but I never liked it. Then there was their favorite line of how much they liked me because I wasn't like the rest of those 'niggas' and of course according to my mother's instructions that led to a thorough ass whooping.

The adults were no better and I can remember this old White lady named Anna who was somewhere around seventy-five or eighty. Everyday she would stroll past our house on her daily walk. I don't know if she was part of The Community Watch or what but everyday at the same time she would stroll by our house and stop for a few minutes to talk to my mother about the azaleas, the cherry tree in the backyard or me, her pride and joy. I guess I was the first little Black boy she'd ever come to know and well I guess she just sort of adopted me as her pet or something. Anyway, I was outside after school playing with my newfound friend Bridgette Gardner. I don't remember much about her except that we were sitting on the curb playing marbles or something and she was chocolate just like me with two big thick pigtails. My mom said she was adorable and said her mother and father were good people. Well, Anna came walking down the street and saw me playing with Bridgette and never said a word but she got those old eighty year old legs moving and damn near ran to my house and started ringing the bell like the house was on fire. Anna was sweating and all out of breath. My mother in an attempt to get to the bottom of the problem and calm Anna down asked her what all the commotion was about. To which Anna answered, "Ms. Brown, Bert's down the block playing with one of them niggas."

My mother and father laughed about this for years and my father always the prophetic one sought to explain. 'You know I've always said that racism is a system based on stereotypes but once people get to know each other and relate and understand each other they can then begin to communicate and once they can begin to know each other they find that most of us have more in common than we have differences. It all made good enough sense but the whole idea of Whites being part of a racist regime made no sense to me and so I stayed away from them as much as possible.

Soon after that I let go of the few White friends I had at school and was content to hang out with Roger, Bruce, Vanessa and Carol Vilmenay. Then there were the kids on my block who were newly arrived and who I had taken quite a liking to. Most of them had come with the second or third wave and hadn't had to endure the trials and tribulations of integrating Queens. They brought a flavor I had never seen and tales of ghetto life I had never dreamed of living with Claudia and Frank. They brought all that my dear parents were so intent on hiding me from. But they brought it just the same.

Still. I hung out with my school chums as much as possible. One of the reasons was that I was hitting puberty and being that my hormones were racing I had to

*have Vanessa. I liked Carol too but Vanessa was so coy
and unassuming and yet so knowledgeable about things I
knew little or nothing about. Oh, sure I'd race home and
tell my boys Danny and Todd what had transpired during
the day and get their feedback on what I should do or say
next but I was really in the dark about both how to
approach a girl and then God forbid if she said yes to any
of my queries then what?*

*Of course, my mom and dad never thought I was
interested in sex and though they schooled me on Black
history and other worldly items they never once touched
on the subject of sex. All I knew about sex was that my
body was on fire and I didn't have a clue on how to put
the fire out. I knew so little about the subject that I was
sleeping one night and had my first and last wet dream
and I mean there was semen everywhere and not having
the faintest idea of what had just transpired I ran to my
parents with the hopes that they could tell me what had
just happened. Looking back, I don't think they ever did
and I went on as if nothing happened although I tried to
recreate the event on my own several times after to no
avail.*

*Where I had questions concerning sex it was not my
parents who filled me in but the fellas on the block who
schooled me, though not necessarily in the right way. It
was also at this time that I began smoking. I believe they
were Winchesters and I took to them right away because
of the advertisement that featured a tall cowboy on a
horse. And though I usually favored the Indian in the
movies this particular cowboy really appealed to me. But
that's another story.*

*Getting back to sex though, I was really curious and as I
said previously my boys were my instructors. Most of
them were fifteen or sixteen and older than I was and they
were from Red Hook or Brownsville or Bed-Stuy so they
were more hip than I was and had crossed these waters*

before. Major, for example, was the coolest guy on my block. He was the best at sports. He had eight sisters and he knew about girls. He knew so much about girls that he even had a baby. And though I couldn't even conceive the idea of having a child I respected him because he did. At least he knew what it took to create one. I had no earthly idea. So, I listened and learned and picked up pointers here and there. That was not to say that the opportunity wasn't there. We were experimenting boys and girls alike so we talked about it almost every day on the way from school. And everyday I tried to woo Vanessa into being at the very least my girlfriend but like I said she was aloof or coy. You can call it what you like but it was no easy task and then I made the blunder of a lifetime. I invited her to come and visit my friends and I on 112th Avenue. That was my block and I was so proud of it and the fellas that I hung out with that I wanted her to see me on my turf. I had forgotten that everyday I told my boys about the good lookin' breezy I went to school with and sought their advice. Well, I'd created this queen and she came to visit and the fellas were on her like fleas on a dog. I could hardly get a word in as Froggy, Danny and Major and all the high school boys let their rap be shown. When she left that day they walked her home while I went in the house and covered my face with my hands and cried like a baby.

There were other opportunities that arose but in the back of my mind there was always this image of Claudia killing me so even when the opportunity did arise I was very cautious about taking advantage of it.

I can remember Carrie. I never knew her last name but the word was that she was a prostitute in Manhattan. I wasn't exactly sure what a prostitute did for a living but somehow I knew that they didn't exactly approve of her lifestyle. Anyway, Carrie was the sharpest, most statuesque woman I have ever seen then or now. And boy

*could she dress. Carrie came home everyday at about six
o'clock and would stroll down to the end of the block
where she lived my eyes stuck to her like glue. I'd always
speak since I played with her kids and she'd always nod
or speak and it would make my day. She had one
daughter named Toya who must have had eyes for me
because she was always trying to get me to go behind her
garage with her but for some reason and even as cute as
Toya was I never went. Some of my other friends did
venture back there and would always emerge with a huge
smile on their faces. Problem was as curious as I was
they would never tell me what happened behind the
garage. And being that most of them were hip and I
wasn't so I refused to go back there only to become the
laughing stock of my block. But I always wondered.
When the pressure got to be too much and I could never
get that night to happen again on it's own I sought out my
friend Carol Vilmenay and lo and behold we hooked up
and became a couple. The fact that she was a head taller
than me hardly made a difference but as much and as
intimately as we talked at school and on the phone every
night I knew that when the time came—and I was
pushing hard—that she would ultimately be the one.
When I tired of playing basketball, stoop ball and skelly
I'd somehow ease away from my boys and make up some
lie about having to go to the store for my mother or
something along those lines. Every now and then Todd or
Danny would come along but that didn't matter much
cause both of them recognized her as being mine and our
friendship meant more than some little old breezy. The
fact that Carol let them know that she was my girl helped
a lot too. So, I'd call her and walk around the corner to
her house where she'd be standing inside the fence
waiting for me. I never went in because she had two
Doberman's that were almost as tall as I was and they
scared me half to death.*

We'd stand outside talking until her parents got home or I had to leave and then spend the rest of the night on the phone. I can remember her professing her love for me and I may have told her something similar but the truth of the matter was that Carol had the body of a woman and I wanted to explore it. We went on like this for months and each and every day when I'd get home from school one if not all of the fellas would ask me if I hit it yet and then they'd all laugh at how Mrs. Brown's son was going to do it right and wait for marriage. Now I'm not going to lie. It bothered me. I don't know if they were telling the truth or if they were lying but all of them had had sex but Todd and I and I'm not even sure about Todd. I swear I saw him coming from behind Toya's garage one day. Still, the teasing was beginning to bother me and my hormones were at an all-time high and I was no closer to getting any than I was when I was two. Carol had her own agenda but it consisted of me coming to her house after school when her parents were still at work which I didn't mind since I was there everyday anyway. But there was no way I was stepping inside that gate with those two horses she called dogs present. She kept trying to convince me that they were friendly and wouldn't bite but I wasn't convinced. We'd come a long way Carol and I. We kissed on the regular and she taught me how to tongue kiss and as soon as we had I'd become aroused and she'd grab me down there and I'd feel on her and lose my mind. I would take as much as I could take before heading home drenched in sweat in the middle of January but it never got any further than that. I had become so desperate by this time that I suggested doing it in a vacant classroom after school or in a vacant car. (There were plenty of vacant cars in Queens back then.) I even suggested going up to Belmont Racetrack which was a five minute walk from school and kicking it under the bleachers but she had this thing about being in the

22

*comfort of her own home in her own bed. All I could see
was an angry father with a sawed off shoddy pointed at
my head for screwing his only daughter or two wolves
tearing me limb from limb because I'm bouncing up and
down on their master making her scream.
Needless to say Carol and I never fulfilled our wish and I
have regrets to this day. But losing my virginity was not
that far off.
I'm not sure if it was Claudia's intent to create a bad boy
but if it wasn't she certainly did a good job nonetheless.
As kids we all got into little scraps and squabbles with
other kids but I don't know of too many parents who
would stand by and watch their children fight and egg
them on. Claudia did. My first two or three years in
Queens we lived next door to a white family, the
McKane's. There was Frank McKane and Rosella
McKane who had four sons but only two I remember and
the reason I remember them was because the younger two
were my age. There was Peter who was a year older and
there was Timmy who was two years older. Now being
that Frank used to hit Rosella and the boys followed their
father's lead and resolved most issues with violence the
boys were constantly fighting either among themselves or
with basically anyone they could find and being that I
lived next door and was in close proximity I was the
logical choice. At first they had tag team matches. First
Peter would beat my ass then when he got tired he'd go in
the house and tell his brother Timmy that Bert's outside
waiting to get his ass kicked and then Timmy would come
out and beat my ass 'til he got tired then go in the house
and tell Peter that I was still out there. This would go on
'til they were both worn out or it was dinner time and
they'd go in to eat and promptly whip my ass some more
for dessert. I'd drag myself up off the ground and wonder
why my mother allowed this to happen to her only son
who she professed to love so much and there she'd be*

waiting with a belt in her hand to beat me some more. I truly believe now that I was suicidal at eight. I couldn't win. But after she beat me she would sit me down and talk to me. That's when I knew mommy had some mental health issues and I was confident it was only a matter of time before someone would have her committed. That was my only solace. But it didn't happen and instead of having her committed I was taught the art of war by this crazed woman.

'Bert, if you let them beat you I'm going to beat you. You get a brick and hit them upside the head. If you can't find a brick then you bite 'em or gouge out their eyes. But don't you let them lil White boys beat you. Do you hear me? You get a branch off of that tree right there and when you see 'em walking up to you smiling and before they say anything to you take that tree branch and hit 'em up side the head with it and keep hittin' 'em until you see their eyes roll back in their heads. I guarantee they'll think twice before they mess with you again.'

And so following this crazy woman's advice I went out the next day and got a log that I could barely lift. First, I found Peter and walked up behind him and cracked him a couple of good ones that left him bloody and crying. Then I found Timmy and did the same before going inside. My mother hugged me and said, 'You did well. I don't think you'll have to worry about them again.' And I didn't. It wasn't too long after that that the McKane's moved away like all the rest of the White people.

Claudia turned me into a fighter and kept telling me that I was fast becoming a man but for some reason and maybe just maybe she saw me becoming a man she refused to leave me home alone at night when she and my father went out. It was alright for me to fly to Pittsburgh alone in the summertime to stay with relatives or to take the subway alone all over the city but for some reason she wouldn't let me stay at home alone. Perhaps she knew of

24

Carol's Dobermans and figured this would give me all the opportunity needed. I laugh thinking about it because my mother would recruit Ms. Harrigans' daughters to come over and baby-sit me. Ms. Harrigan was a gorgeous woman in her own right and had three teenage daughters who were attractive as well. There was Karen who was thirteen and who both our families had already arranged the marriage. And then there was Mousy who was nineteen and Lois who was seventeen. Well. Mom asked Mousy if she would be interested in babysitting me and I guess they arranged a price and came to some sort of an agreement because lo and behold here was Mousy on Saturday night.

Now I liked Mousy but I was aware that she hung with a faster older crowd and here I was just getting my feet wet so I looked at her liked I looked at most older women. …with lust in my eyes and dejection in my heart. But Mousy turned out to be different. She was cool and came into my room and sat and watched some movie with me. It was nice to have someone to watch television with but an older woman. I was in seventh heaven. To make matters even better she asked if I wanted her to pop some popcorn. Afterwards she came and lay next to me on the bed.

I dozed off a few minutes later. I don't know how it long was but I woke up in a most beautiful world. I felt her hands stroking my genitals and it felt wonderful. I was erect and the best I could do was nod a resounding yes when she asked me if I was alright and so she continued. Moments later I erupted and saw fireworks. I had never felt like this before but I certainly was hoping to feel like this again and the sooner the better. It was wonderful and the concept of God took on a new meaning. Lord knows I knew I had been blessed. And all I really wanted was to recreate the moment over and over again. It wasn't long before my parents were going out again. My dad was moving up the career ladder now teaching at Medgar Evers University, in Brooklyn, a part of the city college system and as you probably know that Black folks have no problem meshing business with pleasure and you had to ingratiate yourself with the powers that be just to get ahead. So, mom and dad decided to go and got fly one night and of course I couldn't be trusted to stay home alone so they arranged for a babysitter to stay with me. I was tickled when they asked me if there was anyone I preferred and I said Mousy. But to my disappointment Mousy was busy on that particular night. She recommended her younger sister Lois. I was Now I knew from what I'd seen that the sisters were tight but I never expected them to confer notes on a thirteen year old that they were babysitting but I prayed that they would. But by the time Lois arrived I was sound asleep. I was smart enough to realize that what had happened with her sister Mousy was a freak of nature, an anomaly, and a sort of blessing of sorts. Nevertheless I was heartbroken. I'd been thinking about Mousy's return the entire week and to now know that she wasn't coming was traumatic to this thirteen year old who had no control of the flood of hormones which were taking control of my body. What made it worse was that I had no real outlet when it came to obtaining sexual fulfillment. And the more my boys talked about it the harder it became for me. There was no Carol Vilmenay now and it seemed that everyone in the world had a breezy but me. The days that followed were too short and I'd run and play with the rest of the young teens around my way until I heard that all too familiar call of 'Berky' and knew that this day was at an end for all intensive purposes. My days usually were routine and mundane for the most part. I'd go to school, come home and do my homework, before knocking on Danny or Todd's door and playing basketball in someone's backyard until the street lights came on and I heard the familiar voice of my mother.

Most of the time and depending on how many people were hanging out usually dictated the choice of sports. Sometimes, and these were the good days, we'd have anywhere from fifteen to twenty kids out aside from the little kids that played with their toys and had to stay on the sidewalk under their mother's watchful eye. At these times we'd play something where both girls and the fellas could play. Kickball, punch ball, and dodge ball were the favorites and when they weren't around we'd play two-hand touch, football.

More often than not my dad would get out there with us and we'd have a ball. And then once a summer he'd charter a bus and get all the kids to get permission slips and take us to upstate New York to Bear Mountains for a picnic. A lot of times the parents would go to chaperone or just have a good time and we'd cook out and go swimming and just have a grand old time until late in the evening when we'd return home. Then everyone would get off the bus dead tired and thank my dad for being the person he was. Truth of the matter was and in my opinion a kid couldn't have had a better dad but that doesn't mean he always did the right thing or made the best choices. As I said before he married Claudia who there was no doubt had some mental issues among them being she was militant to a fault. She was a card-carrying member of C.O.R.E., the Congress of Racial Equality under Roy Innis. And she had ties to the Panthers, Malcolm X who she always bragged about seeing on his soapbox up on 145th before he blew up and got his own mosque and was just speaking on the street to anyone who would listen. She dragged my father down to Washington D.C. for the March on Washington in '63 and if there wasn't an injustice or something to picket she'd create it and throw baby boy on the front lines. If you asked me she was the predecessor to Al Sharpton. But whereas Sharpton had an angle and would do it for the publicity and to keep his name in lights no one could figure out what her angle was. Or was she just trying to right every wrong she saw? She had four sisters and they were the same way. The two that lived in Springfield Gardens were the same way and one of them was a card-carrying member of the Panthers as well. The only thing that saved our family was that she truly loved my father and her sisters respected him so when he said that they had to pick and choose their battles they listened. Well, that is they listened somewhat.

One night I was sitting home with him and he was watching the news. I was sitting there on his lap and when I asked where mommy and Aunt Lo and Aunt Thelma he very patiently explained to me that the 1964 World's Fair was being held in New York City and the three had been there and hadn't seen a Black represented as part of the fair and saw no Blacks working there. They had then come together for one of their daily summits and come to the conclusion that there must not be any Blacks in the world according to the organizers of the fair since Blacks weren't represented there.. Lo' and behold the next thing I knew the house was teeming with Panthers, and C.O.R.E. and groups that I neither knew nor cared to know at the time. Anyway, there I sat watching the news with my dad who had refrained from going and decided to stay home and babysit his favorite son when the next thing I knew there were mommy and Aunt Lo on the news. There were these White cops beating my mother with billy clubs while Aunt Lo tried to beat the helmeted riot cops with her bare hands trying to free my mother who was being tossed in the back of the paddy wagon. My dad and I were in shock and after gathering his wits he put me down and prepared to go and bail my mother and her sisters out of jail. This had become a ritual and through it all he always remained calm. And all I kept asking myself was why this saint of a man had chosen to marry the devil herself. But he loved this crazy woman and I guess I did as well.

Still, acknowledging that one has a problem is the first step in addressing the problem and I knew there was something wrong even if my dad wouldn't acknowledge it. All I knew was that wherever she went there was trouble and if there wasn't any she'd create some. I figured it was a bad gene or something and just prayed that I didn't have it.

Yet, as much trouble as I stayed in at school it was soon quite obvious that I had inherited some of her genes. It was soon confirmed that I too had it. One day my father decided to take me to Bohacks on Hollis Avenue to pick up a few groceries. He took me on his bike and sat me on the handlebars. I'd ridden this way many times before and it wasn't anything new to me but having that bad gene I'd inherited from my mother coupled with just being naturally mischievous I waited 'til he'd finished shopping. He'd picked up a ten pound bag of oranges, a loaf of bread, some can goods and a few other odds and ends, placed the bags in the basket on the front of the bike. He then put me in my usual place on the handlebars and we headed home. On the way, I watched everything including the front wheel and the blur of the spokes from my father pedaling so fast. And just as my father picked up speed that bad gene set in and I stuck my foot in the wheel to see what would happen and the next thing I knew my father went head over heels and was on the ground alongside of me. There were oranges and cans rolling all over the place and he had a big scrape upside his head. Those watching the whole event rushed to our aid helping the two of us up off the pavement and chasing down oranges. I'm sure my dad was embarrassed as hell and when I looked his way he just stared at me. When he was finished thanking the people for coming to our aid and putting the busted oranges and dented cans back into the basket he turned to me and simply asked me why I did that. He wasn't mad or anything. I guess by this time and with mommy always getting into something he probably just realized what I already knew and that was that I'd inherited her bad gene.

Summer came. I always loved this time of year because it usually meant me going to my grandmother's house in Pennsylvania. I had cousins everywhere there. It seemed like there were thousands and being that our family was very tightly woven I had a smorgasbord of places to stay and things to do.

Of course, I would miss the city but my parents were firm believers in an idle mind being the devil's workshop and so off I went. My parents would often accompany me for a couple of weeks to paint my grandmother's house or just to get away from the city. Whatever the reason I loved it. My grandmother had a farm that sat on the top of this hill and thirteen acres of land where she had pigs and cows and chickens and cats and dogs. It was a farm in all sense of the word.

Now, I was from Queens and wasn't particularly fond of getting up when the rooster crowed. An alarm clock would have sufficed but here I was waking up to slop the pigs or milk the cows or hoe rows of string beans and potatoes. We'd end about twelve noon. But in the mornings it was all work. My parents thought it a good experience and I accepted it although I didn't see anywhere in New York's asphalt jungle where I could put any of this milking cows and hoeing weeds to work. But I understood there reasoning and anything that would keep that bad gene at bay was worth it if you asked my dad. What I liked most about those days is that I brought something new to the country and just being from New

York City made my stock rise among the girls. I was an instant celebrity and my bad gene made me even more appealing. By this time my favorite cousin Barbara and David had started hanging around with the Sims' family. Their family and ours were tight even though Mr. Sims wasn't really accepted because he owned and ran the Club Holiday and was a numbers runner. And my family, the Dantzlers, were in no way associated with anything illegal. No they were the upstanding members of the community—proponents of righteousness and anything that put a blight or gave the Black community a bad name was deemed taboo including Mr. Sims. Still, the kids loved him—well at least I did—because in my opinion Mr. Sims was cool. He dealt with thugs and gangstas and underworld figures and he handled himself. He had the only Black club in Uniontown and it stayed packed. Every November right around Election time the cops would pick him up as a matter of course and put him in jail to show that they were doing their job and a day or two later he was out and it was business as usual. Mr. and Mrs. Sims had seven or eight kids most of them girls and all of them around my age. I think I dated one or two of them but we were all tight. And then there was Danny and Clyde. Danny was a big guy and when I say big I mean big. He stood about six foot tall and weighed well over three hundred and fifty pounds but there wasn't a mean bone in his body and Lord knows he was talented. He was an artist second to none. Then there was Clyde. Clyde was a car junkie. He had a van that he was constantly working on. And when he was finished we'd all pile in, grab something to drink and ride and get high. Guess it was that bad gene coming out. But if there was trouble I was either heading it or right there in the mix. I'd sit in the back of that van and we'd drink a little wine or have a bottle of liquor he'd stolen from the club or his daddy's bar and smoke weed and listen to music I'd never

*heard like Slave and Graham Central Station and
Mandrill—you know stuff they wouldn't play in New
York. It was a whole new world to me and I loved it. And
at the end of the night we'd tip toe in to the Sim's house
and crash. At the end of the summer we'd all pile into
Mrs. Sim's school bus, which she and Clyde and Danny
had refurbished to look like the Partridges family's bus
and head down to Cape May on the Jersey Shore.
These were good times but the city was getting worse and
I knew my stay there was being shortened by the drugs
and killing now infesting our neighborhood. Almost
everyday someone came with the bad news that someone
that we knew had been killed in what my parents called a
senseless war. I didn't know of a war that made sense but
that was the way they referred to it. Meanwhile, mom had
gotten a job at the local junior high school and even
though everyone knew that Vietnam and the drugs
smuggled in were taking over and the repercussions of it
were beginning to affect us all it wasn't until a young teen
not much older than myself was stabbed and killed in
school that everyone's attitude changed about our
neighborhood. It was bad enough that Ralph the ice
cream man who came around everyday started selling
heroin along with his creamsicles from the back of his
truck. But when our next door neighbor started selling
drugs and New York City undercover came running up on
both sides of our house when mom and I and a bunch of
my friends were sitting on the front stoop that I knew our
time here was limited. But the final straw was the
following summer when we went to Pennsylvania and got
a phone call from my dad telling us our house had been
robbed. Talk about feeling devastated. My mother
immediately made plans to return home and I with her.
Not very long after I was there to share my parent's grief.
It seems the robbers had broken in through the side door
when my father was at work and commenced to stealing*

everything including the towels. They took my mother's jewelry, taking only the real and leaving the costume. We were by no means rich or even well-to-do for that matter but the pain from what I could gather emanated from their being and feeling violated and they decided at that very moment that they had had enough of Queens Village. I, on the other hand felt for my parents and me not having either the maturity or the temperament to put things in perspective was livid. After all, whose parents were out there talking to the kids, working with the kids and trying to bring something positive to the community? Who was out there taking the time to arrange bus trips, arranging football and softball games and trying to correct the ills of the world so that these little Black boys and girls wouldn't have to face the same societal ills that they had to face growing up in a racist America. And most people in the community were well aware of what the Browns brought to the community and respected this. But then there were those that would have robbed Jesus Christ given the need for a fix. And it was that that drove Hazel and Nester to that point. Our neighbors later told my parents that Hazel had been the ringleader along with Nester and the rest of her crew whose names escape me now.

Hazel was my friend Kevin's older sister and had a reputation as a bad seed. She was thug before BET made thug popular and could roll with the hardest of the brothers. Neighbors told us that she was the one who robbed us and when the police came to survey the damage she and her crew sat across the street and waited 'til the police surveyed and wrote their crime report and left the scene and then went back in front of all the neighbors still watching and carried out the rest of the spoils. Nobody said anything afraid that they'd be next but it was a turning point for my mother and father and they immediately began looking.

Not long after that a neighbor, Mrs. Reid who had only moved in a year or so prior and who like my mother played softball and other games with us started having marital problems. She like many of the women in the neighborhood were stay at home moms tending to the children and the home in a very traditional sense. Mrs. Reed was pretty much the epitome of this.

In her late twenties, early thirties she had every teens tongue hanging out. They all thought she was so fine. I just saw her as my mother's friend who didn't garner my respect in the least since she came to my mother to ask for advice. I figured that anyone who came seeking advice from the daughter of Satan couldn't possibly have that much going on. Still, I had to admit that I could see where she was spectacular in others eyes. She had two great Danes both of whom stood close to five feet high and both were puppies.

When she would bring them out to walk them she would clear the streets and the ease with which she could handle those monsters was the envy of everyone and this included me. Her husband Mr. Reed was a very quiet fellow, who just happened to be a New York City policeman and I gathered that the reason he was so quiet was because she was loud and boisterous and had enough conversation for he and she both.

Together they had four or five kids ranging in age from one to six and it was obvious if nothing else that he loved his kids.

Well, in time the life of a housewife wasn't quite enough for Mrs. Reed and she began frequenting my mother more often telling her of her utter disdain for being a housewife and the wife of a cop. My mother who was very good at administering sound advice but not the best at taking it or living by it told her to be patient and that it would get better. But at Mrs. Reed's age this was hard advice to follow and it was soon obvious that she had gotten married and started far too soon at being a mother and it wasn't really taking hold the way she had planned it.

She and Mr. Reed soon parted company and he seemed fine with the whole arrangement and was quiet as he always was while she let the neighborhood as she always did that she was the one putting Mr. Reed out. Mr. Reed was cool as usual and walked to his car and got in without saying a word aside from one clear directive and that was, 'don't bring anyone around my kids'. We all gave Mr. Reed his respect. He had had it all and did his best to satisfy a woman that wasn't sure what it was that she wanted. And when he finally came to the realization that there was no pleasing this woman he left with all the dignity of a man that had given his all when his all just wasn't good enough. Every weekend we'd see Mr. Reed stop by on Sunday morning to pick up his kids and there was little doubt in anyone's mind that this was when he was at his happiest.

Oh, they'd be running and jumping and crying for him to pick them up and as always he did the best he could sometimes having two or three in his arms at the same time. They were ecstatic and so was he and so it went. Mrs. Reed, on the other hand seemed quite miserable. She started running with some married man who lived a couple of blocks away that had seven or eight kids and was married. Every now and then one of his grown sons damn near Mrs. Reed's age would come around to look for their father. My mother stopped talking to her as did most of the neighbors because not only was she running with a married man but we had all heard Mr. Reed's only directive and that was not to have anyone around his kids. And not only did she have this man around her kids but she began to let him stay there which was a no no. After all, this man was married and had children of his own.

Now she was not only married disobeying her husband's last wish but she was a home wrecker as well.

Weeks went by and Mr. Reed oblivious to all of this continued to pick up his children every Sunday morning until that one fateful Sunday when he came by and found this man sleeping in his bed. We all had become used to the sound of gunshots by now but never this close and as soon as we heard them we headed for cover. When their were no more shots in what used to be his house the doors opened. And there stood Mr. Reed. He just stood there. Moments later, two or three police cars arrived on the scene. After speaking to two cops briefly he climbed into the back of one and was quietly driven away. I don't know what ever happened to Mr. Reed. He was never seen from or heard from again. But I always felt sorry for him. Funny thing is though I never saw or heard from Mrs. Reed again either although I'm sure she continued to live there for some time after that but I can't ever remember seeing or talking to her again. What I do remember from that day is her lover's children coming to identify their daddy's body and after they did walking back up the block and home to let their mother know. I was in high school now. My friends were all excited about going to high school. And they were all choosing their schools like it was the best thing since sliced bread. But high school was just the next phase in a life with little or no choices. Claudia and Frank had already decided where I was going and it wasn't Jackson, or The Bronx School of Science or August Martin or any of the high schools my friends talked about going so it really didn't make much difference to me. In the end they chose Delehanty High School in Jamaica, Queens.

I knew nothing of Delehanty or any other high school but one thing I did know. It had to be of the highest academic excellence if they had chosen it for me. For Claudia and Frank always insisted on the best for their boy. I can remember many a day when I'd hear my friends screaming and playing when I was six or seven. But instead of me enjoying the normal games of a six or seven year old, Frank would have me sequestered in the basement of his tiny home in Queens having me take the same standardized tests he used to give his high school students. When I would hit the eleventh or twelfth grade percentile he would race upstairs to my mother and tell her that test taking was just a matter of becoming comfortable with the test taking procedure. The following week it would be an I.Q. test and when I finally tested out at 141 I can remember vividly him racing upstairs and showing my mother the results. 'I told you Claudia! The boy's a genius. Now my mother listened to my father. But when she heard this she completely lost it.

There wasn't a person from Queens to Calcutta that she didn't let know that her first born child, who just so happened to be a man child was also a genius. If you ask me that was where my life, per se, ended. The expectations now placed on me were astronomical. The demands became almost unbearable especially for a seven or eight year old kid. When I brought a B and was looking for some praise all I got were dirty looks and snide remarks about me not applying myself and my God given talent and how the worst thing in life was wasted potential. And then to see if the potential was there I was bribed. 'Bring me an A and I'll give you ten dollars. Well, if it was one thing I was lacking it was Swedish knits, a pair of Playboys, a pair of Cons and Pro-Keds so I'd bring home the A's and get paid and then I'd slipped right back into my B, C mode where I was most comfortable at and be subjected once again to the wrath of Claudia who was insistent that geniuses didn't make B's and C's.

It got so bad that I made up a mantra and would recite to myself on a daily basis anytime she started with the genius bit. Of course, I could only recite to myself or I wouldn't have been here to share this with you now. It went a lil something like this, 'Oh how I wish she were dead. Oh, God please kill her. Oh, how I wish she was dead.' Now that I look back I know that I loved her to death although she'd probably disagree but at that time there was no question that my only wish was that she was dead. To make matters worse and I attribute this to her being from out of the way Pa. since she was so country and I was so intent on being cool. Oblivious of this, she would take you out and announce to everyone, regardless of my feelings or my embarrassment that her son was a genius. All regard for tact and subtlety were gone although I don't know how to this day someone could possibly weave my son is a genius into normal conversation. I never thought that I was but it didn't matter to her I was held in high regard by her and I spent years trying to downplay her accolades.

Some months later, I started Delehanty and hated it. I knew noone and the children I did know were White and weren't exactly friendly. Here I had been in a small parochial school having perhaps a hundred to a hundred and fifty children in first through eighth grade and Delehanty, which was formerly an old factory seemed to house close to a hundred freshman alone or so it seemed. In any case, I felt like a fish out of water and hated every second of every minute of everyday I was in attendance. But my pain didn't last long and before I knew it we were moving. I had a sister now and between the size of the house in Queens and the neighborhood we were forced to move. I cried when we moved. I cried for a number of reasons but most of all I cried because I was leaving everything that I had ever known. And in my eyes I was leaving the greatest city in the world. I told my parents this but what did a fourteen year olds opinion matter. I gave them every argument I could muster but to no avail.

I even tried positive manipulation and told them how they were the greatest parents in the world, all to no avail. And so we packed up or at least they did while I hid and cried and recited my mother's sacred mantra that now included my father too. 'Oh, how I wish you were dead.' Well, my wish hadn't come true and before I knew it I was standing outside this enormous house in someplace called Montclair, New Jersey.

My parents used to take me to Garden City, Long Island every now and then. Or they'd ride out to the Hampton's on Long Island and let me see how the other half lived and I must admit I was awed by the enormity of the homes but I wouldn't have traded the largest of them for my little home in Queens for what we had there was not just a home but a community. I couldn't get them to understand this and of course parents know best even when they don't. Things were so concrete in Queens. Everything there was clear and in black and white. There was very little that was in the gray area. Drugs were bad. Stealing was bad. And so on and so forth. My parents had instilled their values in me and the wrath of Claudia was worse than the wrath of Jesus Christ himself in my eyes. I remember my friends and I riding our bikes up to Jamaica Avenue to go shopping. They were going to purchase clothes but Claudia only gave me enough to get myself a couple of new records. I believe 45's were something like sixty-nine cents at the time. When we got to Mays Department Store I realized that my boys didn't even have money for records but that didn't stop them from shopping. They were shopping for the latest fashions with no funds and they were planning the whole thing as we locked up our bikes. I unlocked my bike and jumped back on. Call me a punk. Call me whatever but I knew that going in and stealing wasn't something that neither I nor my parents would condone and I would rather be chided by my boys than listen to my mother's scolding and so I refrained from this little jaunt and pedaled home alone. I never told my mother but I knew she would have hugged me for choosing to make good decisions. And she would have chided my boys if I told her and no one wanted to be known as a snitch so I kept this as my little secret.

Pulling up outside our new home in Montclair, New Jersey there was no masking my utter didain. I knew it was Jersey and a far cry from the mean streets of New York. I knew that if anything Jersey was a distant cousin to the world's greatest city and just didn't rate in comparison.

Now a New Yorker's attitude about life is funny but so many of us have it. Have us tell it New York is the greatest city on earth and those born and raised there are by divine right the greatest people on earth. There are New Yorkers and then there is the rest of the world. I carried this attitude over to Jersey and had no inclination to meet anyone from this God forsaken place. Still, I had to as my father a graduate of New York University and Columbia he was now working on his doctorate degree. Everyone seemed happy and were adjusting well except for me. My sister was just a toddler and Jersey was the same as New York as long as Barney was on television but I was angry. How could I be militant living in a two hundred and fifty thousand dollar house. How could I complain about racism and all the other ills of society from my vantage point?

I was soon enrolled in Montclair Hiigh School with its acre after acre of rolling campus. I was a freshman and was on the freshman side of campus. To get to the cafeteria on the other side of campus you had to cross a drawbridge complete with a rolling stream that ran underneath. It was by all means gorgeous but I was like a fish out of water and I had never seen so many kids in one area. There were close to three thousand kids in

40

attendance and I didn't know one of them. And they were so different than the fellas I'd grown up with. They looked different, they talked differently and to me they just weren't cool. And if I was a star in Queens I was literally nothing here but the new kid. At my old school we had a converted classroom that we called a gym. There were no locker rooms only a parking lot with a couple of basketball hoops. But here they had locker rooms and a football field and track. None of this impressed me. In fact, it had just the opposite effect and made me really uncomfortable. Just the fact that I was expected to undress in a locker room in front of a bunch of guys riled me and I refused to do it. In fact, I refused to do anything that made me apart of this little rich kid network and so instead of attending class and taking part in my parents plan for making a better life for their children I completely withdrew. I went out every morning and walked the half a mile or so to school and that's where it ended. I refused to enter the halls of Montezuma and stopped speaking to my parent's altogether. I rebelled against anything and everything my parents suggested. I hung out right in front of the school and watched as students went to and from class. I tried to go to class but felt so uncomfortable with the kids there and the teachers that after a few short weeks I stopped going altogether. It was like they all spoke a foreign language that I didn't understand. Every now and then I'd walk to the field with my gym class and stand at the far end of the football field with a few of the hoods that like me refused to attend school for one reason or another. Most of these were the older fellas who didn't attend school because either they weren't able to do the work or they were simply to cool to attend.

Instead they would stand there and smoke cigarettes or weed and chill. I smoked cigarettes but had never smoked weed. But on one of these days I smoked—I guess out of boredom and ran all the way home afterwards. Mom was home as usual and greeted me with one of those what are you doing home in the middle of the day. Well, being that we weren't on the best of terms she accepted the fact that I wasn't feeling well and allowed me to go to my room and to bed.

That was the beginning of my drug usage but hardly the end. Montclair was a drug users bonanza. All these kids with money and in close contact with New York made it a drug users paradise. In the mid seventies there were stores where you could walk in and purchase pipes and bongs and the people that worked there were quite knowledgeable in where you could obtain just about anything and everything you wanted. This was for the affluent. And next door to High Times was a delicatessen. On the other side of the deli was a liquor store.

When I was growing up in Queens my perception was that there were two kinds of people. There were the haves and the have-nots. The have nots drank and got high as a coping mechanism. These were the haves and they were doing the same thing and it made no sense to me. Wealthy white women in Mercedes would pull up in front of the liquor at ten or eleven in the morning already inebriated and would hit the liquor store and purchase a fifth of this or that and I'd see them again at around three or four. And much as I tried I simply couldn't understand how a people having so much could be so miserable.

I, on the other hand, was miserable for different reasons. I had been displaced in the name of progress. I'd done everything to tell my parents that what seemed like progress was often times not progress. Now here I was in a futile position trying my best to cope. The world which had seemed so easy had now become complex and I had no idea of how to remedy my situation or give it a semblance of normalcy. The kids had no ethics, no morality, no goals, and all seemed hedonistic to me. They didn't do things out of necessity or out of a lacking, or hunger. They did things out of boredom. They got high out of boredom. They stole cars for the same reason and committed other miscellaneous crimes for a lark. When they were apprehended it was simply a matter of 'Hello Officer Peterson. Nice night isn't it?' at which time the officer would reply, 'I'm fine Mark. How are your parents? Do you think they'd appreciate you out here stealing cars and joyriding at eleven forty-five on a school night?'

'No sir Officer Peterson.'

'And you've been drinking too?'

'Just had a few beers officer.'

'Alright, Mark. I think it's time you turn it in. By the way did you win today?'

'Yes sir, caught two touchdown passes in the fourth quarter. That's why we were out celebrating.'

'That's great. What's wrong with lil Stevie.'

'Oh, you know Stevie. Never could hold his liquor.'

'Alright, well give me a hand with him. Throw him in the back seat and I'll take him home.'

That's the way things were done in Montclair and it just seemed so far-fetched and didn't make any sense to me. It disrupted my whole way of thinking and I didn't possibly see how I was ever going to fit but after awhile I too became lax. Well, that is until my parents found out that I hadn't been to school in close to two months. I'd gotten used to smoking weed and would wile away my days on Randy's porch and smoke weed and drink Wild Irish Rose from eight in the morning until school let out at a quarter to three. Then I'd wander home go into my room, which I'd painted navy blue with black lights. It was easy on the eyes and being that I stayed high it was soothing. I'd turn on some Bootsy or Parliament and just chill until it was time to go to school again. I didn't have much to say to my parents during this time and was still quite angry with them for having taking me from paradise and placing me in this hell.

So, we had a big house and they were climbing the corporate ladder. So, what. There was no sense of community. There was no passion. There was no focus in their lives. Later on, I reached some degree of financial success and was asked if I wished I were born rich. I had to think about this for a minute and my memories of Montclair came rushing back. And I answered angrily.

'I have had the opportunity to live that lifestyle at certain junctures in my life and if rich takes my ability to strive and yearn for perfection and be focused as to my reason for being here on this earth then no I would loathe being born rich.'

The answer shocked the reporter conducting the interview but that's exactly what I saw in Montclair. I saw on a daily basis people with no earthly idea of why they were here on this earth or what their purpose was.

I, however, by the mere fact that I was born Black was by my very birthright endowed with certain inalienable rights to work hard and achieve, to be the best that I could be, to help others less fortunate than I, and to be by my very essence the best human being that I could be. Well, that was until I moved to Montclair and became confused. My focus now changed to making my parents life miserable. How dare they up root me for the sake of prosperity? The very thought angers me to this day. What I failed to realize at the time was that that they too were human and didn't know or have all the answers as much as I thought they did. A few years ago I went to Montego Bay in Jamaica and was shocked to find the people so poor. I was there for a reason I'll share with you later but I also was poor though not what you might call destitute. I enjoyed my week long stay but I's one thing I remember more than the food or the women or the sights it's what one of my Jamaican friends told me in reference to a statement I made. I said I never realized that Jamaicans were so poor. He was not in the least bit insulted. He took my remark in stride and simply stated that Jamaicans unlike Americans don't have two cars and five televisions and yes they are poor according to your standards but they are rich in spirit whereas you with your cars and your televisions have monetary possessions but are poor in spirit.

That was Montclair. They had the wealth but were oh, so poor in what really counts. They were soulless lifeless entities who smoked and drank all day because they were lacking in what mattered most.

In rebelling against all of this and my parents choice I set a precedent that has followed me throughout my life. I became introverted. I read constantly to ease my boredom. I tried to concentrate my readings on the struggle although it was difficult to stay on point with the assassinations of my heroes.

That coupled with me being in flux and that my hormones were in constant overdrive and that there was always the remote possibility that I would get lucky I'd do the crime knowing full well that I had to accept the time.

My only reprieve was that there were two brothers across the street that were close to my age and George the younger of the two was my boy. His older brother Frank was cool too but he had assimilated so much that he wasn't sure what he was and by the time he was seventeen he'd become as White as any White boy I knew. He used to laugh at us for trying to maintain our heritage. He was into playing the guitar and listening to Bob Dylan, The Doors and the Grateful Dead and bragging about how many Dead concerts he'd been to.

Frank and George had an older sister who went by the name of Lavinia or Lolly who I thought was fine as hell but would never look my way to give me the time of day. She was about eighteen and already starting to club and date men. I had a crush on her but no more than or less than I had on anyone else. She had a shapely behind and not just beginner breasts, (which made her a woman in my books), but as I said before there was no attraction at least on her part. The most we had in common was our musical taste and whereas George was into Chick Corea and Return to Forever, and Frank the Dead, Lolly and I were more into Donald Byrd and the Blackbyrd's and things like that. But what we had most in common was the fact that we all got high. And since I spent so much time lock downed at least I could go across the street and get a reprieve every now and then.

After awhile mom even put a constraint on me going across the street and so I took it upon myself to purchase a little weight to sort of tide me over until after my sentence had been commuted and I was on parole if that were to ever happen. But I was sixteen and my life like so many of my comrades consisted of no more than going to school and coming directly home and doing my homework—nothing more—nothing less. My mother was happy with this arrangement because in all truthfulness my father was seldom there between his work, working on his doctorate and spending time with his mistress. So, mom enjoyed having me there to keep her company and run with her as I did when I was younger but she failed to realize that I was getting older and seeking my own life and independence. Looking back I guess the worst thing a normal teenager wants is to be tied to his mothers' apron strings and I was certainly a normal teenager. I made James Dean look like he had a cause. I rebelled against anyone in authority and that included my parents, my teachers, the system and that included the local law and government in general. I was oppositionally defiant to no one thing but everything. Emerson and Thoreau became my idols and Civil Disobedience my bible. I had minor brushes with all of the aforementioned and dared anyone to try and harness me. I walked out of class when I did attend and cut school at the drop of a hat. If a friend said let's... I was leading the way as long as it was something that I knew would upset Claudia and Frank. And after awhile I had the two of them muttering and questioning themselves as to whether the move to Jersey had been the right move when it came to me. There was no doubt that I loved them I just wanted some distance some ability to grow and make some decisions for myself and to them I was still Berky their little boy. I fought long and hard to break away, to unshackle the chains that bound me and refused to let me gain my independence. I never took it into consideration that this was their time first raising a child or that they were only trying to protect me from the world and myself.

I think the culmination of our battles came the Saturday morning I came to breakfast with my sunglasses on. They were used to seeing me high so this was really something unusual for them. By this time, they'd come to the conclusion that I could not be left on my own to abide by the law and stay in solitary confinement while they left me at home for one reason or another and so now I had to accompany them wherever they went. And being that I literally loathed being around them I would make sure I would take one of my mother's seconal before sneaking down into my father's bar and drinking as much as I could to set the seconal off and then climb into the backseat of the car and sleep for six or seven hours straight. They'd commenced to put a lock on the phones so that I couldn't dial my cousins in Pennsylvania but no matter what they would do to inhibit that bad gene from acting out I'd do my best to find something else to make

47

them miserable and change their mind's about Roe vs.
Wade which remained in the forefront of the tabloids. I
think that by the time I was sixteen they'd become avid
supporters of a mother's right to choose much to the
chagrin of their Catholicsm.
Anyway I came to breakfast with my sunglasses on one
full day after finally making parole for good behavior.
The night before there had been a party at Frank and
George's house and I'd attended. I'd noticed a cute little
breezy at the party and was considering talking to her in
another vain attempt at alleviating my swollen hormones.
Only problem was that when I'd finally come up with a
viable game plan and went in the backyard to talk to her I
found her and my boy CoCo kissing like there was no
tomorrow. Incensed I did what came most natural to me
and with the addition of a few drinks lit into CoCo like
there was no tomorrow. We tussled, tearing up Mr.
Burrough's tomato patch before retiring both of us
exhausted by the melee. And since all my boys came to
me telling me how I'd kicked CoCo's butt I was willing to
let him have the girl since I had my dignity and the win.
Some older cats were calling me from a car out front and
so I went. They wanted some coke and being that I
always knew where to cop and they knew I was a stand up
guy they gave me a hundred and told me they were
looking for a gram. Well, I knew I could get a gram all
day for eighty and could keep the twenty for myself I
gladly obliged when I felt a sharp crack against the back
of my head. And then again… And again until I lost
consciousness… I awoke the next morning with not one
but two black eyes and threw on a pair of shades I had
lying around and headed down to breakfast. Now the last
thing I wanted to do was alarm the warden that she'd
made a mistake by granting me parole and I get in an
altercation as soon as I was released from prison but it is
what it is and when she asked me to take off my glasses at

the kitchen table I had to oblige. Both she and my father gasped at the sight of my swollen eyes and my sister Valerie just stared. When they regained their composure they looked at each other and then held up a large zip locked bag full of some of the best thai stick I've ever run across. I'd had the opportunity to run across a quarter of a pound of what used to be known as some primo shit and cashed in some of my bonds when the opportunity came to purchase some. In my undertakings I must have been slightly high or inebriated and left it out in the open where my parents could find it and they had and now were confronting me about this. Well, I admitted it was mine and I couldn't blame it on anyone else. But I became a bit testy when they started comparing me to Pablo Escobar and some of the biggest drug barons in the free world. Somehow a hundred and twenty-five dollars of marijuana didn't put me on the world stage when it came to illegal drugs. I had a few friends by now, most of them females. A few of them liked me in more than a platonic way and I enjoyed the camaraderie. But when it came down to sex there was still a lull and this time it was on me. There was Debbie Alves, who was one of two Black females in my junior class and we were good friends. We were both a little naive when it came to sex but she was ready to delve into the unlimited possibilities. I, on the other hand, was a little leery about delving with any one short of Angela Basset, Dionne Warwicke or Cicely Tyson; the epitome of Black women to me

There was also a little Irish girl named Cathy that tickled my fancy though and she was quite different and didn't fit into any of my principles or ethics but she wore heels and would put my libido on high every time I'd see her. Her father just happened to be police chief of the Montclair police department and though this should have sent up red flags I chose to ignore them. The bottom line was Cathy said she'd let me in , said the possibilities were real even though she had a boyfriend and since I wasn't considering marriage at the time this appealed to me. We exchanged barbs and I'd practice my rap on her. She was receptive and welcomed my love lines and we became fast friends. I saw a reason to abide my parent's rules when she told me she and Andrea or Christine would stop by in the little beige Volkswagen and pick me up. My parents seeing that there was no feasible way to keep me in let loose the reigns somewhat and I intent on getting me some abided by their curfew now as much as possible. We'd ride around Newark, New Jersey till one or two o'clock in the morning lips glued to each other and my hands roaming as much as a seventeen year olds could with two people up front in a Volkswagen doing their best to ignore what was going on in the backseat and me trying to be as discreet as possible since I'd know we be sitting next to each other in class tomorrow. And she was ready. I didn't know her boyfriend Jimmy but was indebted to him as well for teaching her as much as he had. But I always smiled when I thought of the image of Jimmy in the hospital when she gave birth and he wondering why his little Irish baby had brown ears and kinky hair. Still, for the year or so I rode with Cathy and Andrea and Christine we had never had occasion to go all the way and this bothered me. Still, this was better than nothing and I glowed with the fact that I was making out and getting my feels on a regular basis. Cathy seemed content as well and so all was well.

Cathy was in love and was juggling Jimmy and I and had eventually come to the decision that she was ready to go all the way. I'm sure she had already but when she made it apparent that she was ready to give herself to me I was wordless.

My parent's were hardly ever home. Both were out there hustling, working and doing everything to pay the mortgage on this monstrosity they called a home. And at the same time I was maintaining and coordinating things to make things copasetic when Cathy came by to give herself to me. She came and of course I had raided dad's bar but he was low at the time, (I guess I'd drunk up most of his good stuff.)

The only thing that I could find could calm my nerves was a bottle of vermouth, (whatever the hell that was), and when she came I offered her that and after the initial discomfort of welcoming her to this monstrosity of a home we picked up where we always left off kissing, loving, wishing but today was different. Today was the day when we took it one step further and the fact that I didn't know what that one step was didn't really matter because Cathy loved me for what reason I did not know and would take me there. She was fast, and I'm sure she'd experimented with sex long before I knew what the act consisted of. She could teach me, and all of my Black militancy was put on the backburner when it came to just getting me a piece. I was hungry, no better yet starved and it didn't matter that she was White. She could have been Chinese or Mongolian. All that really mattered was that she was going to be my first. She could have been Rush Limbaugh's mother. If she was going to give me some I could forget all the extenuating factors such as color and race, or whether she was English speaking or ambulatory. As long as she had that good-good and I'd felt it enough times to know that it was intact. And so here was Cathy and I was ready. We sipped a little and no matter what or how much I drank I was so anxious, so hype that when it came time and she'd lost her clothes I tried to force it in her. Now I'd always put being cool at the top of the list as being one of my top priorities. It was the characteristic that I liked best in myself. But today after all attempts at being cool were an afterthought. And after several grunts and attempts she and I both grew frustrated and withdrew our attempts. I was never so frustrated in all my

51

*life but I guess the Good Lord was looking out for me.
Her father was a bigot and the police chief for Montclair
and I'm sure had he known his daughter was seeing me
that it would have been the closest thing to a modern day
lynching that Montclair had ever seen. She was already
not allowed to receive phone calls or call me. She did
anyway but Lord knows what would have happened to me
if he'd found out. And I'm sure my corpse would have
been found somewhere in the Jersey swamps. But my
little sixteen year old behind was interested in one thing
and one thing only and the consequences didn't concern
me. Well, after that we never met again concerning sex.
We still remained friends but never quite got this far
again. But it didn't concern me. I finally came to the
conclusion that it just wasn't meant to be. And so I went
on with my life and eventually got to where I had to relax
my view on race relations being that I was once again
thrown into a school where I was the only Black male in
my class. There were three Black girls but in my
loneliness and in my attempts to remain social I began to
intermingle with my White schoolmates and was opened
up to a whole new frontier. I was forced to go to summer
school for geometry. I went to the afternoon session and
on my way I'd meet Fat Kat better known as Robert
Katzenson and we'd exchange pharmaceuticals. He'd
give me some marijuana and I'd pass on some of my
mother's seconals. Fat Kat was a year older than I and
lived only a block or so from me and he kept weed. We
attended the same school so he and I became fast friends.
But the whole affair was strange to me. Whereas I spoke
to my mother with the utmost respect, Fat Kat didn't show
his mother any respect whatsoever. He used to treat his
mother almost like she was there for no other reason than
to serve him. She fed him, washed his clothes, and took
his younger brothers to football and soccer practice. But
he treated her like she had to, like she was supposed to—*

and not just because she was his mother—but because he was a White male and like Black folks she was subservient. This was all new to me and strange to me but I still liked this little fat white boy. I guess what made it a little more acceptable was the fact that Fat Kat treated everyone in the same manner. He had a Napoleonic complex and you would have sworn he was one of Hitler's generals put in charge of Prussia, Poland or Czechoslovakia during the II World War.

I remember him commandeering us; his boys like he was some Wall St. tycoon and we were just a group of his high school chums. Well, he made plans for us, ordered us and generally ran things for his crew like he was some type of Mafioso godfather or something. He drove one of those beat up paneled station wagons that had seen better days years ago and many miles before. But to him it was like the latest model Mercedes. And whatever he told us no matter how outlandish we believed it.

One day we were all sitting around his room in his house listening to some Led Zeppelin, (that's all he ever listened to). I even grew rather fond of a few of their songs but always wondered why White folks always listened to White musicians trying to sound Black instead of just listening to Black musicians. They never sounded quite as good as the original so why bother? I never understood.

But anyway Kat always kept us moving, in the mix, and in the middle of something. One week after a long week at school in the early spring Kat planned a sort of a get-away for us where the lot of us could get away from the family and go to upstate New York on a sort of retreat where we could lean back smoke some of that good good Thai or Buddha or ses and lean back tell a few good lies about one of the or better yet the newest breezy in our stable. We would share our tales of our recent manhood, our conquests, our women. You know—we would lie.

So anyway, we all crowded into this ol' piece a station wagon and headed to God knows where led by our fearless leader who unbeknownst to us knew little more than we did but his utter braggadocio had us believing that he was all-knowing and that we were on our way to heaven. We drove for close to two hours that day before stopping at someplace that looked like all the other places we had passed on the way up there but Fat Kat said this was our ultimate destination and so we all lumbered out and gathered our backpacks and began our long trek to who knows where. I fell in line like the others behind King Kat and his long staff like he was Moses and I was following him out of Egypt. I half-expected to come upon the Red Sea or pharaoh's army at any time but neither of those appeared. Instead only the clearest of blue streams with the coldest of cold waters rushing through it. All this was something for a little Black boy used to little more than the pavement of big city streets. I was enthralled and amazed and sat by the waters edge and stared. I wanted to be that water, understand that water, understand that God that had created that stream and made it flow. I wanted all that was, that is to be made clear to me. I wanted to understand a God that could make hidden streams so beautiful and allow people to be so ugly. I just wanted to understand. And meanwhile while I was lost in trying to make sense of the world and trying to understand the nature of my savior who was as complex as well as the world he created, and which was so beautiful and yet so simple my boys led by their leader were pitching their tents. Working under Kat's watchful eye they were all completed within minutes and were now seated alongside the stream next to me passing the reefer among them and commenting on just how lovely the whole thing was. Kat was beaming being that he was the sole reason for it all and I suppose he should have felt some sort of pride for bringing us and introducing us to such a beautiful piece of God's creation. We were all in to becoming closer to God and his creations but not in the normal sense. They were experimenting with the likes of John Lennon and the Beatles, seeking out gurus, transcendental meditation and means of accessing him other than in our parents more traditional ways. We sought Him through the message in our music; music so wrought in social messages that spoke of God's works and his preaching's that we were constantly being inundated with His words though in a practical way which was more applicable to what was happening in the world around us than a teaching that was distant and disjointed and neither reflected life as we knew it nor paid homage to it becoming a better place for all. And so I listened reflected and let our artists pontificate on the road in which we traveled. These men and women, these artists were like me, wrought with human frailties and so I only took what they composed; the best of them and incorporated it into my religion, into my teaching, into my way of life. And here next to this stream this cold spring day I listened and reflected on all that was good within us as human beings. Like Henry David Thoreau I was more and more beginning to take these times alone to reflect on that which was good and evil and try to evaluate what was more than Black and White but what more so was right in God's eye. I don't think my comrades were viewing life in these terms but my initial plight in life wouldn't allow me to abandon my heritage or those screaming imperialism and injustice to end around the world.

My father had me reading Dostoyevsky and the Diary of Anne Frank and William Shirer's Hitler when I was ten or twelve. And he made the very profound comment that probably affected me more so than any comment he'd made up to this point in my life or maybe I was simply starting to become receptive to this brilliant man that was my father. In any case, he told me to read these. He was

always giving me something or other to read and I having
an insatiable appetite for knowledge would devour almost
anything that would broaden my horizons. So, I read
these three books with the sudden realization that Black
Americans were not the only people that had been dealt a
bad hand. And from what he began telling me the Jewish
people had suffered almost unfathomable atrocities since
the history of man. His overall thought to me though was
that we as Black folks were not alone in our suffering.
Man's inhumanity to man spanned the globe and
spanned history since the beginning of time. I thought
about this and after doing quite a bit of reading I realized
this to be true and although I could hardly let go of how
the Black man's plight had come about in America and
taken prominence in my forefathers lives since their
inception in this country it must be noted that my
viewpoint and my thinking still remained in large part
with my people but it came to also embody those
everywhere who had been or were still the subject of
persecution and injustice.
I'd always been a caring, compassionate soul but my life
had always been a microcosm of a larger world.   I guess
my parent's move to Montclair, New Jersey had been in
large part to expose me to a larger world; a world larger
than just lower poor Black folks trying to put food on the
table for their kids and hoping that their children could
somehow
escape the muck and the mire that had become the reality
that was their life among the mean streets of Queens, New
York.
Montclair was, on the other hand, a smorgasbord of new
ideas and untapped potential still waiting to be tapped.
Montclair had a varied, mixture, a more far reaching
intellectual base which needed to be accessed still further
when the subject of persecution and injustices suffered by

all and especially when the subject of Black people was brought up.

First of all, you had Montclair State College with some of the best and brightest Black minds in the country right there. There were the Black newscasters, (another source of wealth for us), who resided there along with a number of Black writers and historians. My dad, (an accomplished writer in his own right was also in league with the likes of Betty Shabazz, (Malcolm X's widow), noted author John Oliver Killens who he hired and other such heavyweights such as Ralph Ellison, author of The Invisible Man who he was in constant contact with and who was one of many who made up his stable of intellects. There were other Black writers and noted academicians he was in league with and this made for quite a knowledge base for an inquisitive teenager such as myself to frequent when there were queries and quandaries I sought answers to.

More often than not though I was lost in a myriad of thoughts and questions about life not unusual to a young teenager.

I, like my mother was particularly sensitive to the struggles of Black folks in this country but in lieu of my lily White surroundings I had no one aside from my parents to talk to. Still, my father told me that I could travel, learn and answer most of my queries vicariously. And that's exactly what I did. I had a voracious appetite and I spent a good deal of my idle time reading Emerson, Thoreau, and Malcolm X and those who thought as I did. I, therefore likened my trip to upstate New York on this cold spring day to Thoreau's around Walden Pond. Although it was only a couple of days it was more like a retreat, a time to think and reflect and this I did. I wondered about everything. I wondered why slavery had evolved into what I deemed almost a racist caste system at the expense of Black folks and what matter of thinking

57

with us being a Judea Christian country could possibly rationalize racism. These things puzzled me. I understood it from an economic, imperialistic point of view whereby the masses had to be subservient to a ruling class in order for the ruling class to benefit. But from the standpoint of a Judea-Christian belief system and aside from those whose main thought process was purely economic I couldn't understand it. From the doctrine though that we were all brothers and the emphasis was on loving thy neighbor so the adherence to racism did not make sense to me. To me this belief system did not coincide with the atrocities of racism and I wondered how and in what manner man could co-exist with himself when he could put his fellow man through such utter hell and not only condone it but live with it.

I believe most of my beliefs were inherent in that bad gene I inherited from my mother and I knew it was an abnormality because so few had it other than she and I. I questioned everything but mostly authority. I guess that's why I had such an affinity for Thoreau and Emerson. I especially liked Thoreau and his writings on Civil Disobedience. Thoreau questioned the government on a number of items. For instance, he questioned why he was required to pay taxes for living on Walden Pond when he asked for nothing from the government and was more or less self-sufficient. He

grew his own vegetables, hunted for his own game and asked for nothing. Yet, the government levied taxes on him. When he refused to pay he was threatened with imprisonment and eventually incarcerated when he refused to pay. In a way, he was a little like the modern day Republican. The only difference being that he didn't take advantage of the highway system, Medicare, and social security and then complain about the government levying taxes. I guess for a better analogy he was more

58

like the Boston Tea Party participants, (or 21st century Black folks), who protested taxation without representation and called it tyranny.

My being out there in the woods by this fast-flowing stream reminded me of Thoreau's Civil Disobedience but I didn't really have anything to be disobedient about. Still, I liked the fact that he had the unmitigated gall to stand up to this behemoth that had in the name of Christianity stolen a continent from an indigenous group of people by simply labeling them savages because they chose to believe something other than what they or so that was the pretense. What gall? But that was hardly the end. No, in fact that was only the beginning of the atrocities that our great nation was founded on. They would then go on to steal another wholly and distinct group of indigenous people from their land and use them as forced labor under the guise that they too were savages for not conforming or believing in a like manner and then completing this tryst by saying how they had civilized the free world.

I liked the fact that Thoreau and many others had taken a stand on the side of righteousness and so eloquently stated it for essentially what it was and opposed it. To take on such an evil and oppose it with the full knowledge of what the repercussions could ultimately be and accept it thrilled me.

Bob Marley was on the rise at this time as well and he quickly became one of my icons, my idols, one of my heroes. The fact that he was disciplined and followed a religion where the prophet shared my pigmentation also helped and I spent a great deal reading and studying as much as I could about Rastafarianism. The fact that ganja was said to help gain greater insight into one's inner-self didn't hurt either. And so I read and smoked and read and smoked some more. I read about every resistance movement in America and felt a certain kinship to all of them. I read everything I could get my hands on from Geronimo, Sitting Bull, and Chief Joseph of the Nez Perce who held off the greatest army in the world with a few dozen warriors in the lava beds of California to Nat Turner and John Brown's slave insurrections. Where other kids were reading Superman and Fantastic Four comics I was reading about those who opposed the very fabric of America. I had no outlet for my bitterness but I felt a need to stay abreast of America's atrocities against her own or as Malcolm X would say 'the victims of America'.

My life however wasn't consumed with these thoughts or as my dad would say it would have engulfed me. Yet, I was aware. The problem was that I was quite consumed with this part of our history but could by no means find an avenue for it. Still, I continued to seek answers.

In the meantime, I wasted away my days with Kat and Kevin Hoey and some of the local fellows. And I guess that's how I found myself in upstate New York that cold spring afternoon. We were all pretty bushed that night and after sitting around sipping some Southern Comfort and a few beers we called it a night. I hadn't bothered to pitch a tent and so Kevin and I shared a tent. It was close to fifty-five or sixty degrees when we went to sleep that night.

But when I awoke I awoke to the sound of roaring, crashing, waters, and cold like I had never experienced before which would have been okay in itself, but when I opened the tent flap I found myself being jostled to and fro, teeth chattering as I rode each wave. I was like one of those white water rafters you see on The Outdoorsman on Saturday morning T.V. Only thing was there was no raft, no kayak, nothing. There was just me and pieces of my tent speeding downstream. I believe they call it a flashflood. I don't know. All I know is I was freezing and after grabbing a branch and pulling myself up on the

60

muddy shore I noticed my boys reaching and thrashing just as I'd done moments before. I rushed to help pull them out shaking and shivering as I did so. The temperature had dropped into the thirties by this time and a slow, steady flurry of spring snow drifted down adding to the chill. There was little or no conversation as we gathered what was left of our soaking wet belongings and made our way towards the car, which now seemed like it was a million miles away to our shivering asses.

Seeing the car we all seemed to light up although no one said a word at this point. Getting in we all rejoiced as Kat started the car. It was several minutes before we felt the heat. Slowly we began to thaw but when Kat put it into reverse it refused to move. In the end, we sat there for more than three hours until a tow truck towed Kat's hunk of junk into a service station. We then waited half the night until Kat's father found us and drove us home.

Much of my high school years went pretty much according to plan. I remained an average student, which seemed to eat at my mother. Her son the genius refused to accel and she eventually gave up hope. My dad, who was much more patient or so it appeared, seemed much more understanding or maybe he was just so caught up in his own pursuits that he didn't have time to try to figure out why I chose not to succeed when he himself had to fight adversity every day of his youth just to eat. His favorite line when it came to me was 'everybody finds his God in his own time'. I really didn't understand at the time but I guess it was his way of dealing with a son who chose for whatever reason to be a chronic underachiever. To tell the truth and this is by no means a cop out but I was in over my head. Sure, I may have had the brains to succeed but my self-esteem was in the toilet. I wanted to achieve and make them proud but I was so busy fighting just to belong or better yet to prove myself in a White world where I was always Flip Wilson or Bill Cosby—a

61

good nigga—that I just grew tired. I'd given up long before I'd reached Jersey or high school.

I'd leave the confines of my home and step out into a world where I wasn't down because I didn't come from the projects of Red Hook or Bed-Stuy and was looked at as a bourgie little sheltered nigga. And when I arrived at school I was viewed as a nigga—different and a good nigga—but nonetheless a nigga. I was in a quandary and by this time knowing full well that I didn't fit in anywhere I simply snuggled up in a drug induced cocoon oblivious to a world I hardly understood. With the help of my street corner pharmacists who prescribed everything from weed to heroin I nestled in good or at least until I had a better handle on the situation.

That is not to say that I gave up on the brothers altogether. They certainly looked like my heroes but I guess at the risk of making excuses they didn't act like the men I'd come to know. Perhaps it was my generation. Perhaps it was the fact that in every race there are those that don't quite meet the criteria. And my expectations were that as a Black man you stood strong and tall and persevered in the name of race, in the name of all those that had fought the good struggle in the face of insurmountable odds. There was no other way. You just did so and when you had your seed and it sprouted it was his duty to continue struggle just as you had done. But the young Black men I came into contact hadn't gotten the same memo and didn't seem to have any cognizance of this mantra that governed my life.

I remember countless times smoking a little weed together, sipping a little cheap wine and just hanging out in the park looking for some type of mischief to get into to pass the time. And on one special occasion jumping in Solomon's van and heading to D.C. to hang out with my cousin Barbara at Howard University for a day. By the time we got there we were so ripped that Solomon ended up sideswiping several cars on the way there. Barbara as always was glad to see me and put us up for the weekend. You think these Negroes would have been appreciative. Instead, they tried to talk to Barbara and her roommate Vicky who was a real showstopper and when these thugs couldn't make any headway with Vicky they decided to rob her instead.

Me, being the naive upstanding soul I was didn't even realize what had happened until they started pulling out the booty halfway back to Jersey. My stomach dropped but there was little I could do now. All I could ask was who were these so-called brothers? The brothers I'd grown up in Queens would never have thought of doing anything like this. But that wasn't the straw that broke the camels back. The straw that broke the camels back happened sometime later but first let me tell you how things proceeded from there on out.

My parents were moving now. At least my father was. As bright as he was, he never saw or really had any real insight on where his only son was as he was climbing the corporate ladder in leaps and bounds. He was now Chairman of the English Department at Medgar Evers College, (a branch of the City University of New York), in Crown Heights, Brooklyn, was working on his doctorate degree at Nova University in Philadelphia and was trying his best to get acclimated to his new home in Montclair, New Jersey. He was also having an affair with one of his co-workers at the university.

It was nothing to wake up on a Saturday morning and see him hosting an educational TV show on television called Sunrise Semester. Oftentimes, during his more or less down time he was hosting some kind of get together for his co-workers at the house with a few members of the new entourage from Montclair.

One particular evening, he held just an event and of course I was locked down but I remember I met a pretty young girl and her parents although for the life of me I can't recall their names now. But I do recall hers. Her name was Cynthia and like me she had been the victim of Black folks escaping the horrors of New York City and being caught in the throes of upward mobility. She lived about a block and a half from us and although I'd been there for the better part of two years I'd never seen her. That's the way it was in Montclair. You may see the car in front of the house and may even see the car move from time-to-time but you never saw the inhabitants of the house. But thanks to pops doing his best to ingratiate himself in the community here I was face-to-face with Cynthia.

She was a cute little girl and though a bit too light in color for my taste she was still rather well endowed for a seventeen year old. She had nice round buttocks and ample breasts and though I still wasn't sure exactly what to do with them when I did find out, I knew she was rather well endowed when the time came. We hit it off from the very start and after mingling and getting through the uncomfortable silence of our initial introduction we settled in with a couple of drinks I manage to swipe from the bar and we relaxed into our own world. I was later to find that our lives paralleled more than just a little. She was also from the city and was having a difficult time adjusting to this aborted way of life they called Jersey living. Her parents had also enrolled her in the name of upward mobility in a Catholic high school after a short rendezvous with Montclair High School. She also found the transition difficult and admitted that she felt like a fish out of water. The only difference was that her parents had taken the whole upward mobility one step further enrolling her in East Orange Catholic, which was an all-girls school. She hated it and was rebelling in the worse way.

I enjoyed her company that evening and she made what had come to be a terrible test of my patience as a show dog for my parents, (who still touted me as their little genius), a fairly good evening. I still didn't have the playa game down though and when the evening was over I still hadn't gotten her number and so in the following weeks I would go out of my way to pass her house to catch a glimpse of her. Funny thing was I never did. Well, at least I never caught up with her where I could get her attention although I did see her several weeks later. What I did see left me sick to my stomach. You see I'd been hanging out with Solomon, Randy and Chris blowing smoke when they started looking for some mischief to pass some time. As always this was my cue to get ghost. Despite my rebellious attitude I still valued my parents love and trust. And I knew that as hard as my parents worked I wasn't going to be Public Enemy # 1 and make them in any way look bad while I was under their roof so on most adventures concerning the law I deferred and as most of the activities of my crew were fraught with breaking the law in some way I refrained.

They were just as contented with robbing a liquor store as sticking somebody up but between the Good Lord and Claudia's well-known penchant for a good backhand I declined and so they went their separate ways.

As I passed Cynthia's house hoping to catch a glimpse of her, later that day after going on an adventure of my own, I was shocked to notice Solomon's van pulling up in front of her house. As usual they were high and I stood a fair distance away oblivious to them and watched as they carried something away from the van. Much as I strained to see I couldn't make out what it was. Later, my boy Randy told me that what they had been carrying was no other than Cynthia. It seems they'd gotten her drunk, taken her to his house and raped her, each taking several turns with he while she was unconscious until she couldn't walk then driven her home and laid her down on her front steps. I immediately became sick to my stomach at the thought. This was the price for upward mobility. It's funny though we poor kids who came from the poorest parts of the city still had values and these kinds of things were just not acceptable. I cried for Cynthia, cried for myself then just cried. A few weeks later my parents told me what had happened and I responded like it was news to me. 'No, I hadn't heard. No, I didn't know anything about it. No, I didn't know anyone so sick that they would have done anything like that.'

I never saw Cynthia again. It was not long after that I heard that her parents' sold that big, pretty house on Grove Street and moved away and I wondered if they had gone back to one of the ghettoes where life was safe and people had values.

I hated Jersey and by my junior year in high school I'd decided that by hook or by crook I was going to get out and being that I had no way of writing my own ticket out of this cesspool of swampland I'd do something that was totally against everything I believed. I'd join the service. Of course, I hated guns, war, and the idea of man killing his fellow man, (although I could almost justify it in certain aspects), but being that Jimmy Carter was in office and he appeared a peaceful man I thought that there could be no better time to enlist and so I did when I turned seventeen. However, the recruiter who I enlisted with failed to let me know that I couldn't enlist without my parent's consent until I turned eighteen years of age and so I was once again at the mercy of my dear parents who naturally refused to sign. And so I spent my junior and senior year waiting for the chance to leave them, to escape Jersey and to see the world.

My mother's youngest brother, Uncle Fred who was the epitome of cool in my book had been a Marine and so that's what I'd become. There is no other reason. I had *the faint hopet of going to Duquesne University in Pittsburgh to study journalism. I'd entered a few writing contests and always done well so I decided to pursue my writing career. And with my father being a prolific writer I knew or at least thought that perhaps a gene or two had been disseminated onto me, his only son. But when I wasn't accepted immediately I became dissuaded and decided that time was of the essence after all I was fast approaching eighteen and had no plan, no future to speak of and no time to waste. So the day I turned eighteen I signed up and with the recruiter's help and his assurance that I would become a TV cameraman I joined the few, the proud and well you know the rest. I was due to leave Jersey on the Fourth of July and so I went to Pennsylvania to say goodbye to my relatives and enjoy the holiday festivities.*

My cousins David and Barbara made sure my sendoff was a little less than spectacular. Both were taken back by my news. But after becoming acclimated they both took it upon themselves to make sure I had the time of my life. I remembered arriving a couple of days before the 4th and not sleeping for the next two days. I went to barbecues and parties and more barbecues. My cousin David, who had a mean streak second to none, (another gene pretty prevalent in our family), fixed me drinks of straight alcohol with a pinch of cola for coloring. Being somewhat naive I gulped them down eagerly, with him chiding me about manning up and being Marine tough, Bogart tough, Ram tough. I was so damn egotistical and so intent on proving myself successful on my new venture that I downed death quickly and with out caution.

A few hours later, I found myself climbing through my Aunt Annabelle's kitchen window and just barely making it upstairs and to the bedroom, (although I have no idea of how long it took me to get there). What I do recall is throwing up all in David's bed and then sleeping in it. I later learned that people have died, drowning in their own vomit. My cousin David awoke me from my drunken slumber and decided that scrambled eggs were just what the doctor order. Just seeing them made me start throwing up all over again and I wondered what it that made him so devious and evil.

Two days later I was back in Jersey awaiting the Marine van to pick me up. I said goodbye with apprehension and more anxiety than I'd ever known. Truth of the matter was that I was scared stiff when that white van with Marines painted on the side pulled up. I was leaving the comforts of my home and my family to go on a quest like none I'd ever been on before. I had no idea what to expect and had never been away from home for this long a period of time but here I was kissing mom, dad and Val goodbye and climbing into the van with ten or twelve frightened recruits. That's not to say there weren't a few hard core street thugs from Paterson, Newark and Jersey City who weren't at all afraid but were looking forward to it like it was the best thing since new pussy but then everyone didn't come from a home like I had. For some in that van I think the Marines proved to be a respite, a saving grace. At least now they weren't on the mean streets of some of Jersey's worst ghettoes. Here they wouldn't have to worry about where their next meal was coming from or who they had to rob and steal to get it from. The Marines was a job and would supply all that and would give a young man an opportunity to travel and if one were smart would even provide one with tuition to attend school should he choose to pursue his education. Those were my reasons for enlisting but what I found was quite to the contrary.

We took a plane to South Carolina and then a bus to Parris Island, and to this day, close to thirty-five years later, I still have no recollection of where Parris Island is except that I have no proclivity to ever go back there. I was later to learn that it was rather close to Buford wherever that is but all I know is that I have never had any desire to return. I remember getting off the bus to people yelling and screaming for us to get on the painted footsteps. We were pushed and slapped and cursed 'til we found a set of footsteps to stand on. I was one of the fortunate ones and quickly found a pair to stand on but some of the fellows had difficulty and fought each other to find a spot. One not so lucky recruit in his haste fell and broke his leg trying to find a spot. I smiled at my own good fortune and at the fact that I'd never envisioned grown men playing musical chairs but that's what it amounted to. Things only got worse from that point on. Our head's were shaved and we were renamed. No longer was my name Bertrand but was quickly changed to Big-Lipped Motherfucker or New York on good days. We were awakened at four a.m. in the morning not by mom's tender loving voice but to the sound of aluminum garbage cans rolling down the middle of our concrete squad bay and the sound of our drill sergeant's voice calling us shiftless, lazy ass motherfuckers. After two or three weeks I was convinced that motherfucker not Bertrand was my Christian birth name. We'd then line up and march to chow where we'd be commanded to sit down and no longer than it took us to sit down and pick up our forks we were just as quickly told we were done at which time we left an entire plate of food and got into formation outside the mess hall. This was what they called first phase of boot camp and the purpose was to break everyone down before building them into lean mean fighting machines. I didn't see the point in any of this. The only thing I saw was a waste of good food and push ups, sit-ups, chin-ups and every other kind of up you could think of. I hated PT but what I hated even more were our morning runs. I'd run before but after a few weeks they had me running three to four miles every

69

morning before six a.m. When we finished that we had classes and then more PT but mostly we just stood at attention and waited. We were always waiting for something. And while we waited we stood at attention. Some days we'd stand for three-maybe four hours at attention. And as if that isn't a painful display of discipline in itself, South Carolina has an annoying little critter called a sand flea that was attracted to hot sweaty Marines like flies to shit and being that temperatures were constantly in the upper nineties and we were constantly sweating in the heat those sand fleas loved us and they had a nice little bite that would keep you slapping yourself silly when the drill instructors weren't looking. You see the drill instructors had a certain affinity for these little buggers and used to say that 'anything you do to my sand fleas I'm gonna do to you'. And after seeing a few of my comrades get the piss slapped out of them for slapping one of those ol' sand fleas I thought it better to endure their bite than the wrath of the drill instructor. Now I'd pretty much grown accustomed to life as a Marine recruit after about a month, (but that's not to say I liked any part of it). Still, I hung in there, keeping my mouth shut and my eyes open. Every night we'd have mail call and receive a few letters from loved ones. Barbara and David wrote more than anyone and kept me in pretty good spirits but the Dear John letters were flowing. A lot of guys received them but on one particular night one of the recruits, (a big White boy), received one and was particularly distraught over the fact that his girl had found someone else in his absence. That night as we all slept he took his M-16 put it in his mouth and proceeded to blow his brains out. I understood his pain, as I had gotten a Dear John letter not more than a week before. Of course, I was fairly used to diversity and things not happening as I planned but that was hardly a reason for me to take my own life. It was just time for a new plan.

Guess everyone didn't look at things the same way though and we were put on high alert and security was doubled up. We were in a crucial phase and it was probably the most difficult phase of boot camp and the most dangerous. We were on the rifle range and were in contact with live ammunition on a daily basis now. I don't know how long we were out there; something like two weeks and had to qualify with both the M-16 and the .45 before moving on in training. We'd spend any extra time we had in the barracks breaking them down, cleaning them, and putting them back together before heading back to the rifle range. Now coming from the follower's of Martin Luther King and a home that championed non-violence I hated guns, detested them. Everything I'd heard and seen that was connected with guns I hated. And here I was about to make this my sweetheart for the next four years or so they said. Not only didn't I like guns, I was deathly afraid of them and anytime I'd get near one I'd break out in a cold sweat, my palms would get clammy and I'd just go to pieces. And yet here I was. The same thing happened to me when I'd get near water and here I was in the Marines. The very word meant water life but do you think I drew the connection when I enlisted? No, not I, not my dumb ass. Now here I was lying flat out on my stomach in the sands of South Carolina waiting for the command to fire my M-16 at the bulls eye some two hundred feet ahead of me. I was firing round after round off with the easy squeeze of my finger and when they pulled the target down to look at the hits and where they scored they had some difficulty with mine. Each time the target appeared empty and each time they appeared more and more confused but not I. I knew it would have to be either a blessing from God or the luck of the Irish if they were to find a single bullet hole in my target since I'd committed to closing my eyes and just squeezing off shots like the other recruits until I heard the firing stop at which time I would cease to fire as well. It seemed to me like this was a plan and all seemed to be going well even with my eyes closed when I felt three or four officers grabbing me. It seemed that my plan hadn't worked as well as I'd expected and I'd continued to fire when they'd called a cease-fire and the Marines who changed the targets were standing doing just that. Of course I knew there was a huge penalty to pay for my disobeying a direct order but I also knew that despite their claims that I was trying to shoot somebody that that was totally untrue, unfounded and if they'd only check my scores they would have found that me shooting or coming close to hitting anything was highly unlikely.

Still, as in all things in life there was a price to pay and no matter how much I pleaded my case I was recycled which meant that I have to do that two week phase on the rifle range all over again which was hardly to my liking. I was placed with another platoon and sent back two weeks as was protocol but in those two weeks I actually learned to shoot and earned my marksman's badge and was returned to my platoon.

Following my little debacle at the rifle range I went back to my normal platoon which was now doing the obstacle course and marine training which was swimming and the slide for life training two more things that exposed my phobias. Another of my many phobias is my fear of heights and the slide for my life combined my fear of water and my fear of heights. You see we were expected to climb to the top of this huge tower where a long cable was attached. You were then expected to throw a sort of rope over it and slide down til you were maybe twenty or thirty feet over the water and let go then swim to shore. I wanted no parts of this charade either and each time the line would get shorter to make the jump I'd find myself back in the last spot. For the first part of the day this worked to perfection until one of little those little bastards

72

decided to squeal on me. The next thing I knew there were three or four Marines escorting me up this ladder meant for one and doing everything to persuade me to put aside my fears and ascend this ladder to the top and jump off. I had thoughts of the fellas back in New York climbing to the tops of buildings and then jumping from one rooftop to the next. I wasn't doing that then and I wasn't doing this shit now.

After a half an hour or so of tugging and pulling me they eventually got me to the apex and when they felt they had me secure they pushed me off. I held on for dear life and cursed them and their mother's, wives, and offspring if they had any and wished them all to a flaming lot in hell when I finally hit the water and started thrashing and gasping for air.

I hated the Marines and everything it stood for but it wasn't long before I was proficient enough to be assigned the rank of platoon leader and started making some of the decisions. It was about this time that we started our training where we'd repel off the sides of small mountains. But there were no such things as small mountains and if my foot came one foot off the ground it was entirely too high. But I was in charge now so I lined 'em up and had 'em repel off the side of that mountain while I orchestrated the whole thing. And those White boys that squealed on me only days before were now firmly committed to a new career of cleaning out the men's urinals in the barracks.

The days and months that followed were uneventful and I wrote my parents with pride that my graduation was fast approaching. I soon received a reply that said they would be in attendance and I was both thrilled and proud. I wanted them to see me in my Marine uniform and to know that I'd accomplished something and accomplished it without their help and support. I guess they were feeling more or less the same way when because when

73

they came to see me walk across that big old parade deck
they cheered and were louder than all the other family
members combined. And despite my reservations about
the whole purpose of the Marine Corps I had to admit
that I was proud to be a member.
My next duty station was Camp Lejeune, North Carolina
and I received that news at the same time I received the
rather unsettling news that I wasn't going to sunny
California to become a TV cameraman as I had been led
to believe by my trusted recruiter. In fact when I brought
it up it seemed like the whole base came down with a fit of
hysteria. They laughed. A TV cameraman? Boy where
do you think you are? Your first and primary position is
to be on the front lines, hit the shores first and take out s
many as you can possibly take out before they do you.
This was all a revelation to me and I insisted that they
look over my contract again because it was obvious
someone had erred. When I insisted it was pointed out
that the fine print states that if a job is not open or
available at the time of a recruits graduation then he
would or could be placed in a place where needed.
I ended up being made a GRUNT or basic ground troop.
Everyone in the Marines was first and foremost a
GRUNT but my bourgie, intellectual ass hated being
defined s something as commonplace as a GRUNT. To
me it sounded like a big, burp or someone with flatus and
I didn't appreciate the connotations. What I hated more
was what was associated with it. I was expected to force
march a minimum of twenty miles every other week. With
a full pack that consisted of a change of uniform, sea
rations, (canned food), toilet paper, and whatever
essentials one could carry that would constitute life out in
those North Carolina woods. By the time we'd packed
everything into those backpacks they'd usually weigh
anywhere from forty to forty-five pounds and along with
the ammo bag and my rifle it was close to sixty pounds of

gear I was forced to hump. I cursed the Marines and everything associated with it. I now understood why they were the few, the proud…

It was November now and cold. We were forced to go on these forced marches every other week and the way they worked was that we'd fall out in platoon formation as we did every morning, full packs at the ready lying in front of us. I was a machine gunner so either I carried the machine gun, which weighed about thirty pounds or the ammo bag, which weighed about the same. Most of the time when we got into the forced march you were with your machine gun team and you'd take turns carrying either the machine or the ammo bag. And I didn't mind this at all. What I did mind were these big, tall, lanky, cats that would go hard in the barracks talking 'bout who they screwed back in the hood and how they weren't gonna have this or that on the block and then get on a force march and start crying about this was too heavy or that was too heavy and start lagging behind. What would happen on a forced march was everyone was humpin' in single file at a steady pace and your platoon leader or sergeant would walk up and down this file and yell, 'Asshole to belly button. C'mon keep it moving'. And that's how we were expected to march as quickly as possible without running and at an even pace. But what would ultimately happen is I would get behind some six foot twelve nigga with legs for days and no heart who would start crying about this or that and start slowing down and falling back which in turn would force him to then walk twice as fast to catch back up. And that's when I found out why most fools in the Marines shared my name, 'Motherfucker'. And I'd name him right then and there. 'Motherfucker if you don't step the pace the fuck up I'm gonna load this motherfucker up and shoot you in your punk ass…you sorry ass piece of shit.'

75

Aside from some water and some height I wasn't afraid of too much and especially these simple ass motherfuckers who called themselves Marines.

I really began to appreciate my parents during this time in the service. I was now able to see the importance of good education and more importantly the ability to think. And believe me I thought. I thought about what trumpeter Branford Marsalis said about how teenagers don't think they react and how this very thought is what had thrust me into such an illustrious position. Here I was marching out to the middle of nowhere as fast as my short, stubby little legs could take me and for what. One North Carolina tree was as good as the next. But there was no thought process at involved in being a Marine. If my commanding officer had a particular affinity for this group of trees twenty miles to the south of Osh Kosh B'Gosh then that was our destination. There was absolutely no thought process involved. And my only thought process up until this point was to get me out of Jersey and away from Claudia. Only Claudia didn't appear half so bad now. I'd sit around the campfire, feet sore and aching and wonder how the hell did I get involved in some shit like this. Sometimes after a long day of marching up one hill and down the other side we'd sit and talk of our experiences that had brought us to the point of enlisting and in all the time and different campfires I never heard of a kid coming from my background like mine signing up. Still, it was what it was but whereas I hadn't been thinking before my brain was in overdrive now and every conceivable thought came to mind now. Why for one was I lugging a thirty-pound M-60 machine gun around the woods in North Carolina with an ammo bag and no ammo? Had or was there a terrorist threat in the backwoods of Fayetteville? And why was I walking back and forth between trees, (they called it a

*perimeter), at two a.m. in the morning on so-called guard
duty? What was I guarding against?*

*These and more thoughts clouded my mine and
sometimes I used to daydream and wonder what mom was
fixing for dinner as I dug the spam like meat from the
cans of sea rations.*

*On weekends we'd march back to the barracks and most
of my co-horts were so exhausted from the twenty-mile
trek back they'd just fall across their racks and call it a
day but my boys would be damned if we'd give those
motherfuckers two weeks and then the weekend following
too. So, we'd shower and throw on our double knit pants,
knit shirts and some platforms and grab us a cab and
head for the closest city, which just so happened to be
Jacksonville, North Carolina.*

*Jacksonville was the equivalent of Andy Griffith's
Mayberry R.F.D. with the only difference being that
Camp Lejeune with it's sixty thousand Marine's was only
a stone's throw away. And I guess that's why it was next
to impossible to find any girls there. Guess parents with
daughter's knowing the personality of Marine's who had
been cooped up on base for who knows how long wasn't
what you wanted your teenage daughter exposed to. So,
there were few if any what you might want to call nice
girls around although there were women.*

*My sole concern when it came to women was not fat or
skinny but simply the one who was gracious enough to let
me in. As I said nice was an afterthought. But even with
that I still believed that I was God's gift to the world and I
would never demean myself to purchase sex from any
woman on God's green earth for I knew it was free and
some woman someday would recognize my worth and give
it to me freely and of their own accord. I even had some
contempt for the women dancing in strip clubs for selling
themselves so cheaply while men gawked and pawed over
them. Still, this was the center of Jacksonville's nightlife*

*and where the fellas chose to go when we had the night
off and since it was better than sitting in the empty NCO
club pouring down drinks and shooting pool 'til two in
the morning I usually tagged along content to sit and
stare at some half-naked female gyrating on some pole in
a cage.*

*On one such evening while I stood staring up at a female
in a cage, a drink in one hand, oblivious to everything
around me when a young woman sidled up next to me
and began talking. It was just friendly talk at first and me
being me thought little of it until it got a little more
personal and I turned and looked at her. She was slight
in build but I immediately knew that she had several years
on me and although she was bundled up for those chilly
North Carolina nights it was obvious from the bumps and
bulges that she had everything and it was in the right
places. We talked some more and after some time she
inquired as to who I was there with. I told her a few of
the fellas. I think there were four of us and I began
wondering where she was going with this. Her answer
shocked me. I thought I'd come across a lot in my short
life but what she said next really and truly threw me for a
loop. What she said was that if I brought the fellas to her
hotel room she'd let me go for free. Talk about a brother
being shook. The thought of sex flashed through my mind
faster than a meteorite through the earth's atmosphere
and I immediately went about rounding up my boys. They
were all in the same predicament I was in and we grabbed
a cab and headed for the hotel. When we got there they
all argued about who was going first and so on and so
forth. There was no question who was going first since I
had arranged the whole thing and so they spent their idle
time figuring out who was going second and third.*

*Maria, as we came to know her had a tray of reefer out
and a bottle of Richard's and everyone sat around and got
loose while Maria got comfortable. When she was ready*

she had them go in the bathroom and wait. I was a little high so I guess I wasn't quite as nervous as I'd been in the past and she was patient and guided me through each step as if I were a newborn baby. When it was over I knew I had died and gone to chocolate heaven. I was cool though. I couldn't let the boys know that it was my first time and so I went outside and sat on the bottom step of the motel and thought about what had just happened. I still hadn't paid. My boys paid for me and I was good with the arrangement. By their going it allowed mine to be free. To top it off when she summoned me to come back upstairs to cap the night; blowing smoke and rehashing the evening with me sitting quietly in the corner just listening, Maria went through the performances like she was Siskel and Ebert rating our performances. My boy C.C.Criner from Ohio was always the loudmouth and he just knew he was the shit and inquired about who had been the best of course knowing he had been. 'Well, what's your name?' she said turning to my man. 'Cicero', my boy from Jersey said. 'You were all right. And what's your name', she said turning to my man Wise. He answered and she told him the same. They both smiled and I guess they were glad not to have been embarrassed. When she got to Criner she asked his name. 'James Criner but everyone calls me C.C.Criner. You can call me C.C.' "Well, C.C. I'll tell you this. You've got a big dick but you can't fuck. Now that little nigger over there he can really fuck.' Nothing more ever needed to be said. I have never been more grateful to anyone on this earth than Maria. She was my first and although I didn't have the faintest idea of what I was doing she made me feel like Jesus Himself had come down and christened me His own son. Of course C.C. wasn't all that happy but in the weeks that followed he was right there with me each and every time shelling out his hard earned dollars trying to convince Maria that he

79

was every bit as good as me. She took his money and everyone elses I brought with me and we'd sit there and smoke and drink and have a grand ol' time. And I'd keep her supplied with clients.

In turn I became her pet or pimp depending on how you looked at it and she kept me dressed and fed. In essence she took care of me and there was nothing I didn't want for. Life was good for me during this time and Maria made the Marine's almost bearable.

If there was one thing that made the Marine's less than bearable it was this one kid in my platoon and it was like he was sent to make my life miserable. His name was Kevin Lutz. Lutz was a seventeen year old White boy most of us had chosen to call Klutz instead of Lutz because he stayed in trouble. While most of us had our own agendas and were just trying to stay cool he had his own agenda and that included seeing who he could fuck with now. I'd made it pretty plain to him and everybody except my partners and already lost the little rank I had from fighting and so if you weren't a true partner you kept your distance but not Pvt. Klutz. He'd come over and sit and join in on the conversation like he was one of the brothers. I think he was from Tennessee or some backwoods state where they see sheep and goats as a good piece of ass and drink corn liquor and bay at the moon and call it choir practice. I don't know. But what I do know is that the boy was country and for some reason he was attracted to me and used to tell me I was the coolest brother he knew before tryin' to give me some dap and huggin' me. He had this thing about calling me 'cuz' which disturbed me although everyone who knew me knew we couldn't possibly be related because I prided myself on being cool and he was one of the uncoolest, country bumpkins I'd ever met. Still, I didn't like him calling me 'cuz' simply because I knew that hillbilly from Appalachia probably believed incest was best so I wanted

*in no way for him to think that we were kin in any way.
And no matter what I did to show my utter disdain for
him he made it a point to be up under me. I remember
one time when my sergeant who along with the rest of us
had had his fill of Pvt. Lutz suggested he try some Nair on
his face instead of shaving to help him avoid razor bumps
and how Pvt. Klutz ran through the barracks one night at
about two o'clock screaming that his face was on fire.
After the initial shock we all sat there laughing 'til we
cried about this fool. But the one thing I remember most
about Pvt. Lutz was when he came to join me one night.
The fellas and I were out in the field in our second week
and everyone was pretty anxious to head back in to the
barracks. I was thinking of going to see Maria and just
hanging out with her for a little while when he came to
join me around the fire where we were warming our sea
rations. He like the rest of us was always trying to trade
something he didn't like out of his package for something
he liked better but no one seemed the least bit interested
in swapping anything and we were all into our meals and
dreaming of better days and frustrated about our lot in
life when he took the whole packet of five or six cans and
threw them in the fire. It was a typical Klutz move and
after cursing him out for throwing cans into a fire we
went on enjoying our meals as best we could.
About five or ten minutes later we heard a couple of
minor explosions and then it felt as if I'd been shot and
my face was on fire. A can had exploded and hit me right
below the left eye and basically attached itself under my
eye. I'd never felt pain like that in my life and whereas
my boys held me down and tore the hot metal from my eye
and made sure I was okay they made one mistake. They
let me up. I immediately knew who was responsible and
was in hot pursuit. But Pvt. Lutz had done more than
gotten ghost and the next morning at formation he was
marked AWOL. Still, I knew that before it was all over he*

81

would turn up and when he did his ass was mine. I was still upset, my eye still hurt, and all I knew was that he was the cause. Later that night someone told me that they saw him going into his tent. After confirming this I proceeded to get one of those small shovels used to dig trenches and snuck up on his tent and proceeded to beat the hell out of his tent and him. Fearing for his life some of the fellas grabbed me and pulled me off of him. There was no movement from the tent but I didn't care. From what I came to find out later I chopped his face up pretty good and knocked him out and of course I lost a stripe but that was only the beginning and a trend that would continue to last throughout my career in the Marines. I didn't care much about losing the stripes. I had Claudia's gene and was adamant about being right, doing right and standing upright. And whenever I saw something that didn't appear right or correct I spoke on it and after I spoke on it I usually lost a stripe.

But that wasn't the end of my relationship with Pvt. Klutz. Several months later and after apologizing for his fau paux he came to me one Friday night asking what I was doing. I told him that I was going into Jacksonville with some of the fells for a couple of drinks. He asked if he could go and not to be mean I told him he could tag along if he hurried. And as soon as he turned to go gather his things I bolted jumped into a cab and was gone. I'd been in the club a couple of hours when who did I see heading my way. He was beaming talking about how'd he looked all over but he'd finally found us. I was not quite as overjoyed but enjoyed myself nonetheless despite his presence. A few minutes later I heard a loud shattering and saw the huge plate glass window shatter and realized that the person who'd gone headfirst through it was no other than Pvt. Lutz. My boys looked at each other, shook our heads and grabbed our belongings and headed for the door. We knew that was the end of leave for that weekend and probably the next couple. That's just the way it was. If there was trouble in town we were reprimanded and our leave was taken. We were restricted to base until the townspeople had calmed down and the brass were sure that we had learned our lesson. It happened but the funny thing was and I don't know if it's a cultural thing or not but the brothas rarely if ever got down like that but give the White boys a few drinks and they'd cause havoc and fuck things up for everyone. Not to be apart of the whole cluster fuck we grabbed cabs and headed back for base hoping to get there before the word did and we almost did except there was more than just the fight at the club happening on that particular night. It seems some brothas had robbed an officer on post and everyone was up in arms. The cab stopped at the entrance to base and the MP's were all over it asking that we get out and show I.D. Well, me in my rush to leave and get away from Pvt. Lutz had forgotten mine and so they arrested me and took me away and the whole time the MP's driving he has the .45 pointed at my head.I'm pleading with this fool to put it away but he keeps telling me that an officer's been robbed and the nigga looked just like me.

Fifteen minutes later we arrive at the jail and who's their in the same holding cell as I am—no other than Pvt. Lutz. And here he is too drunk to even recognize me. Obviously being held for his involvement at the club I didn't bother to acknowledge him. All I wanted was my phone call so I could get one of my boys to bring my ID down so they could release me. I sat down and waited my turn at the phone when Lutz gets to stirring and talking all kind of crazy nonsense. I ignored him but then he sits up and starts throwing up before lying back down or better yet passing out. Well, I've never had a strong stomach when someone's vomiting and if I even get a whiff of it I'm right there alongside of them throwing up to so I moved to the farthest area away from him and closed my eyes.

However, when the young MP comes back to tell me the telephone's now free he has a fit and blames me for the mess that's his holding pen and demands that I clean it up. When I tell him that I'm not the one responsible for the vomit all over the floor he explains to me that Pvt. Lutz couldn't have possibly done it because he's been sleeping since they brought him in. I guess it's a fairly good guess what I did to Pvt. Lutz when he eventually got back to the barracks.

A couple of years later I was shipped to Twenty-Nine Palms in southern California right outside of the Mohave Desert where I spent some time sleeping with the rattlesnakes and scorpions. At night we'd go to bed with the order to keep our boots on so as to avoid rattlers and scorpions from nesting inside and all night we'd hear their rattlers shaking. It didn't make for a very restful sleep and if that wasn't enough the White boys would kill them and cook them and eat them. Now I enjoyed and marveled at all that God provided in terms of nature but this was a little too far-fetched for me.

While here in San Diego I had the opportunity to visit Tijuana, Mexico. There was a direct order for us not to go down into Mexico but for most of us this was the closest we'd ever get to Mexico and so when we got leave we jumped on a bus and headed for Tijuana. When we arrived all of us noticed that Tijuana was no more special than any other military town we'd come across. There was a main street with strip clubs lining both sides of the street and people, Mexicans outside trying to usher us into them. The difference aside from the fact that everyone spoke Spanish was that they had live acts unlike any I had ever seen before. Instead of girls dancing or something of that nature they provided live acts with women and donkeys. I guess you can guess my stay in Tijuana was not long.

*Now they had me following tanks around the desert.
They were riding and I was on foot and again I
questioned why I had enlisted. The temperature in the
daytime sometimes reached a hundred and forty degrees
and dipped to forty degrees at night. It was hell in the
daytime and frosty as fuck at night.*

*After a month or so though I was shipped to Fort
Fairbanks, Alaska for cold weather training. By this time
I was sure that they were trying to kill me. There was no
doubt that I'd run my mouth and caused too much
trouble for even the few, the proud to stomach and so the
ultimate plan was to kill me dead. Instead of it being a
hundred and forty in the daytime and forty degrees at
night it was forty below at night. Here where the
residents had to plug their cars in at night just so they'd
start the following day they stuck me out there at two in
the morning to walk guard duty around the perimeter of
the camp. Now if I had been a foreign country intent on
taking over America this is one place they could have
kept. And here I was. The only positive I had was that
my boy Pete was there with me. We'd both been assigned
to Ft. Fairbanks. He'd had some marijuana dipped in
formaldehyde. We used to call it angel dust and we took a
chance getting it aboard the plane at LAX which was no
small task with all the dogs they had but once we were on
board we blew some smoke in the bathroom and
proceeded to be even higher than the flying altitude of
thirty thousand feet. And I'm glad we did too. Coming
down in that frozen tundra was no joke and after a day we
decided to pool our pay and get the first cab we could
convince to take us back to Newark. We weren't there a
week when Pete came down with pneumonia and being
that there weren't ample beds and rooms we ended up
sleeping on the floor of a room already occupied by four
other Marines who just happened to be all White. Well, I
wasn't feeling the arrangements and let it be known. I*

85

also couldn't understand why with six of us Pete and I were the only ones constantly chosen to do guard duty during the wee hours of the morning and I let it be known.

During this time the only thing working in our favor was that sick bay gave away syrup like it was water and we stayed warm from the codeine in the cough syrup. Liquor was out because they were worried that one would lose his senses out there in the cold and would suffer frostbite and lose a limb so liquor was outlawed but syrup worked just fine where I was concerned. Didn't work well for Pete though and like I said he came down with a pretty severe case of pneumonia. I ended up not only pulling my shift on guard duty but Pete's as well—well at least until he got back on his feet. But after a week and he faring no better and me not getting any sleep I went to this young corporal who resided in our room and made a plea for both Pete and myself. But the fact that Pete was a proud Puerto Rican from Paterson and I, a New York nigga we had a hard time convincin' this red-neck peckerwood that we weren't trying to get over and he denied our request to get Pete transferred to a hospital. And it would have been all right if he denied my request but when he tried to pull rank and say that 'you people are always trying to get over', I pulled my knife grabbed him and put it to his neck. Of course you can guess the rest. I was threatened with court martial, charged with attempted murder and lost a stripe. Pete used to tease me that I was going to be the first Marine to be discharged at a lower rank than when I enlisted. By this time I didn't care and we were both told that we would be transferred to our next duty station somewhere in some Cracker town in Jersey. We were assigned to a reserve unit to do the last six or seven months of our active duty and went home to stay except for one weekend a month. We were now weekend warriors but they might as well given us dishonorable discharges since on those weekends we were supposed to be there for duty we ended up in some club in Newark, Paterson, or Jersey City.

I was hanging out now. I'd just bought a new car and spent six out of seven days in the streets and when I couldn't stand it any longer I'd go home and crash 'til I had the energy to start running again.

When I first got home everything was wonderful—well almost everything. It soon became clearly evident that I, (as much as I fought not to let the Marines brainwash me), had been conditioned like one of Pavlov's dogs. When my mother would come to my room to tell me breakfast was on the table I'd jump up and run looking for the line in front of my rack and try to stand at attention. My mother would just watch before shaking her head and turn around, shake her head again and leave. I noticed something else that bothered me somewhat during this time. My parents who had always had an open and trusting household began locking both their and my sister's door before going to sleep at night. It was disturbing but they didn't know this person they had raised and I didn't help my cause any. I was afraid to speak when I returned home. My vocabulary that my parents had become so proud of had now been relegated to a bunch of expletives and I was afraid that if I spoke it would end up something like, 'What up motherfucker?' so I stopped speaking because I was afraid that I would say something inappropriate. Of course, in the streets what I'd learned was acceptable and so that's where I made my new home.

The Marines had shown me a lot. I was aware of it but had been sheltered and protected as much as possible. The Marines showed me a grimier seamier side of life where people didn't always have the best of anything if they had anything at all. I can remember arriving at Camp Lejeune and entering the barracks where I thought

87

*I was supposed to reside. Not being familiar with Lejeune
I entered the wrong barracks. A platoon of Marines were
lying around in different stages of dress. I was later to
find out that these were Marines awaiting discharge for
drugs. Most were heroin addicts. And I must admit that I
was appalled. Going home was no different and life was
not so pristine and innocent as it once had been.
Everything seemed grimier now. The innocence of youth
was gone.*

*I hit the streets hard and was in Paterson a lot now. I
enrolled in William Paterson College now but spent most
of my time in the student union drinking pitchers of beer
with my boy Spider. Spider was about the worst person I
could have come in contact with on a college campus. He
had no interest in college and I have no idea why even in
enrolled but here he was. We started off blowing a little
smoke together and he had a dorm room and so when I
was either broke or it was too damn cold to just hang out
I'd go up to his room and drink some wine and listen to
some music or just rap about this or that. He always had
some hair-brained scheme about this or that and when I
met him his whole thing centered on making money. And
being that he didn't have any skills that were marketable
he chose what every non-thinking soul chose to do
around that time and that was to sell drugs. Everyone I
knew had seen Scarface and every young brother saw
selling drugs to be their saving grace. Well, as you know I
had no particular proclivity for guns or violence after just
having done a stint in the Marines. And though I wasn't
sure where my destiny lay I knew one thing for sure it
wasn't in guns or drugs. Still, I knew everyone in Jersey
who sold drugs and being that he was from Paterson and
I had a few connects from there I hooked him up and
faded from view just as quickly as I faded in.*

*My boy George, a Puerto Rican kid I had grown tight
with decided to front him a half a pound of some pretty*

good weed and Spider jumped at the chance. I did the introduction and sat in on the meet and made it clear that this was my only connection and George made it clear when and where he wanted his money. He kept prompting me to go in on deal as if I was the assurance he needed that he would be able to collect his money on time and there would be no mishaps around the money or the drugs but I wasn't buying in. I didn't know Spider that well and knew that wasn't my forte.

When George and his boys were gone I told Spider all I knew about George and made it clear that George as nice as he seemed was nobody to be played with and Spider told me he understood perfectly. He was in a prime place to unload it and guaranteed me he had everything under control. And badly as I wanted to believe him I knew he was in way over his head. George and I had boxed and trained together for a spell and he'd brought me to his home to meet his family and we'd even hung out together on occasion but there was just something about him that could be rather unnerving and since I couldn't pinpoint it I kept my distance.

In the coming weeks I saw less and less of Spider in the student union and on campus and I knew that if he should have been anywhere it should have been right there unloading the product and letting the word get out that he had some of the best smoke on campus but Spider wasn't to be found anywhere and I grew worried. About two weeks later and it was coming closer to the time George was supposed to come collecting I made my way up to Spider's dorm room and after knocking for some considerable time he finally opened the door.

And it soon became obvious to me that he was high as a kite and from the looks of the place hadn't seen daylight in a month of Sundays. No Spider had been holed up smoking the very product he was supposed to be selling. I didn't know how long he'd been there but I suspected he hadn't left since he'd been given the package. I continued on at William Paterson picking and choosing the classes I wanted to attend and not attending the rest when one day I was waling towards my car in the parking lot when I saw George and one of his henchmen. I never worried about George but the kid with him was notorious around the way for being a stick up kid and well just for being a gangster. He was young, probably my age if not a little older. When George approached me I could see he was more than a little angry. Still, I wasn't worried since I had made it plain that I didn't want anything to do with the whole charade. The first thing out f his mouth was 'Where's Spider? Don't know' I replied. But his boy not knowing me or our relationship went up under his long overcoat and came up with a sawed off shoddy that made me gasp. 'What's up', I said looking directly at George now. 'Put that shit up. This is my nigga fool.' George said smiling at me. I guess it was more than a little obvious that I was scared as a bitch. I didn't roll with guns or people who rolled with guns and I knew that with this crazy fool there was bound to be trouble.

'You know what room he stays in?' He asked knowing full well I did. 'You know that nigga been duckin' me,' he stated. 'I ain't really seen Spider' I commented now regaining my composure and stating the truth. 'Well, I've called him and stopped by and niggas been duckin' me.' There wasn't anything I could say. Spider had been duckin' everybody. I don't know whether it was intentional or unintentional but the fact remained that he had lost touch with the gravity of the situation and was about to be brought back to an earth shattering reality and there was nothing that I could do.

We took the elevator up to Spider's dorm and I knocked. I felt bad, almost as if I was setting him up but I knew that crazy motherfucker would have used that shotgun on me just as easily as he would have Spider and felt no

90

remorse about it whatsoever. When Spider peeked through the peephole all he saw was me and although it didn't take him as long to answer as it had previously it was still too long for George and as soon as Spider cracked the door and took the chain off they were all over him. First, there was the shotgun blast that tore up half the room, then my boy beat Spider half to death with the stock of the shotgun while I stood there watching Spider beaten within a half inch of his life while George chastised him for everything from smoking up the product to not calling him and telling him that he might need a little more time to get the money together. Granted it was all very disturbing to me and taught me a great lesson about the streets. Never ever write a check that your ass can't catch.

My lesson although thorough was still not enough to keep me from the streets altogether. But and although I was always attracted to the streets I had the good sense to only dabble on the fringes of it. I soon dropped out of William Paterson with a no point '0' grade average and decided to work for awhile although finding a job was not quite as easy as it appeared. The Marines had promised adventure, travel and a skill and here I was back in the world wondering where I would be able to apply my skills. Each day I searched the classified section of the newspapers and let me tell you I searched for months. But not once in all those months of searching did I once find a position as a machine gunner. I eventually took a job as a bagger in Shop Rite supermarket in the working class town of Bloomfield, New Jersey. Bloomfield is the next town from Newark and most of its inhabitant are Italians and they reminded me a lot of Blacks so naturally I fell right in here. I didn't like the job much but found a nice little crew to hang out with. Montclair was right up the block and I still had a lot of connections there but whereas Montclair was typically bourgie Bloomfield was what everyone referred to as a Greaser town. Most Whites looked down on the poorer middle class Italians with their hair slicked back like they'd just stepped out of the fifties. They were cool to me though. They reminded me of the brothas walking around holding their dicks and hanging out without a care in the world. So, I felt right at home here. The money was okay and I guess I just felt glad to be working again but having no patience I contacted my Uncle Fred who lived over in Harlem to see what he could do for me in terms of a second job. In about a week or so he called me back and before I knew it I was employed with Inman Construction working in downtown Manhattan. I'd get off at around three-thirty and head back to Jersey change clothes and head to Shop-Rite where I'd bag groceries to nine or nine thirty at night. I'd listen to put my eggs on top and don't smash my bread all night and then push the carriage out to their cars at which times little White ladies would thank me and hand me a nickel tip. Most days I would take it and say thank you. On other days, and depending on the customer I'd turn and simply say I think you need it more than I do. On these days they'd go back and tell my manager about the uppity nigga who refused their nickel. He'd in turn give me a stern reprimand for their sake and we'd go back to business as usual. My mother shopped there and she spent so he didn't fire me as she was one of their best customers and my job security.

We'd go out every night after work and I made some good friends during my time at Shop-Rite. There was Brian Frerichs. He was a good kid. His mother was an alcoholic and it used to just eat at him. He had an older brother, Roger who was crazy as a tsetse fly in December. The boy drove a new gray cougar and invented the very saying of 'driving dirty'. He was following in his mother's footsteps, kept cocaine, and stayed in a bar with a drink in his hand and talked of nothing but going skiing *in Vermont. That's all he talked about but he had a good soul and was always offering to buy me a drink but after a couple of times of hearing him talk of his adventures of skiing in Vermont I avoided him like the plague. It was a funny thing about Roger. He refused to work but he kept money. I can honestly say that I have never seen anyone who profited from his misfortune more than Roger. It had gotten so bad that he was ready to write a manual on how to sue and collect. He used to tell me of the times he'd been in accidents and of course it was never his fault and he'd collect. He was quite the character. What was really interesting though was that as nice a guy as he was the Bloomfield Police had him pegged. If there ever was such a thing as racial profiling when it came to a White boy it must have started with Roger. Roger would enter a bar or a club in Bloomfield have a few drinks, just enough to have him slightly inebriated and they'd wait for him to start his car and zoom in on him and arrest him for drinking and driving. I mean he wouldn't have to do anything anymore than start the car and the sirens would be a spinning.*

Brian never got in any trouble and was a beautiful kid but between his mother and his brother he suffered. He tried to keep his home life as normal as possible but it was an almost impossible task. His dad worked constantly and hardly spoke at all so disenchanted was he by the whole home situation. Brian supported the family as best he could and brought home the groceries while his mother stayed plastered and Roger was in and out of jail. He tried going to school too when he wasn't working and he worked all the time. But when it came time for an assignment he'd pay me to do his research papers. And because he was a friend of mine I didn't charge him too much. I charged him twenty-five or thirty dollars if he made an A and less depending on what he made. So confident I was in my writing skills that anything less than a C and he didn't have to pay me. This worked well and it was funny but what bothered me was that even though I could write his papers and get him through school when we went for the same job don'tcha know he was the one who ultimately got the position. We talked about this on more than one occasion and he felt for me. Still, he didn't make the rules or call the shots anymore than I did so we relied on each other for strength. He had his situation and I had mine. We smoked together, hung together, cried together and loved each other dearly despite being as different as the seasons of the year. I loved women and he loved fast cars. I remember he bought a Pontiac Trans Am that I refused to get into and brought it by the house to pick up my little sister to ride in it when I refused. She loved Brian too. And he acted more like a big brother to her than I did; babysitting her when I had to work and my parent's were busy. They loved him too. About the only thing I regret Brian ever doing was introducing me to Dana. Dana was a cute little Italian girl from Bloomfield who had five older brothers. Dana and I met and instantly fell in love. Well, at least she was in love. We hung out, blew a little smoke and became closer and closer over the next few months. My mother who wasn't particularly fond of anyone with her pigmentation was never really fond of her but put up with her because her son seemed to like her. I guess you could say she tolerated her. Anyway Dana and I experimented with damn near everything including sex. Looking back at the relationship in hindsight the relationship we had was little more than two people on the same path at the same time finding that we had something in common, a need, a compulsion that drove us and demanded that we stay together to feed our hunger and our needs. That along with a certain trust and bond drove us. We needed each other at that point and time and the trials and tribulations we faced as a young Black man and young

White female kept us together far longer than if we had been of the same skin color. We were friends first and foremost and hung out in virtually the same crowd. And our relationship, I venture to say was the same as Brian's and mine or her girlfriend Carol's, (who lived a couple of doors down from Dana). As long as I was stopping by to pick Carol up to go out with the rest of the crew and there was no romantic tie or interest everything seemed fine. Her mother and sisters welcomed me with open arms but had I shown I had some type of romantic interest I'm sure there wouldn't have been a problem. But the minute I would have shown some sort of romantic inkling I somehow doubt I would have been met with the same reception. The same was to be said of my parents although I am certain they felt some discomfort for me dating a White girl for different reasons. My parents both born in the late nineteen twenties had grown up with Jim Crow. They'd witnessed the atrocities America had bestowed on its darker brethren for no other reason than the hue of their pigmentation. They'd been around during the times of Emmet Till and countless other lynchings and it's safe to say that each of them had experienced enough due to racism that for all of their beliefs in equality and firm belief of how far they had come as a people. They still had doubts about how far the other man had progressed. My father was quick to say that you could legislate laws but it was entirely different matter when it came to legislating a man's mindset. So if anything, my parent's were afraid for their son. And after a year or so of me dating Dana and looking back on the whole affair, I can now attest to the fact that their fears were well founded. Still, when you have a seventeen year old and a nineteen year old in love there are little problems in the world and what problems that do exist are all conquerable.

*And the fact that we'd both found sex at the same time
and were now loving each other regularly, (at least we
thought it was love), we knew there was nothing that
could keep us apart. Yet, I was not as naive as she and
though I was rather well known in Bloomfield and
Montclair we still encountered problems when we stepped
outside of our normal haunts. And being that we were
both young and adventuresome we were constantly
stepping outside of our normal haunts. We were fond of
the city. She because it wasn't often that she got to
frequent it and I have to admit that Jersey could get
stagnant very quickly. She also fashioned herself a rather
free spirit—you know the self-styled hippy or an eighties
Bohemian. Whatever it was that she considered herself
Greenwich Village suited her better than any place else
and she loved it. Perhaps with all the artists and persons
outside of the loop we fitted in better. Dana related better
with Janis Joplin, Jimi Hendrix and The Doors than she
did with Bloomfield and all the John Travolta, Saturday
Night Fever look alikes. Me, on the other hand, had no
problem hanging out with the crowd listening to Bootsy
and Parliament, or Janis Joplin and kind of liked The
Bee Gees and the Saturday Night Fever crowd that was
Bloomfield. I think we hung out in The Village more
than we did Jersey. And she insisted we go to every
concert we could get tickets. I saw everyone from
Jackson Browne and Joni Mitchell to Roy Ayers although
my preference was always jazz I couldn't say no to her
rock-n-roll when she so readily agreed to anyone and I
mean anyone I wanted to see. We really enjoyed each
other's company and in many ways she seemed much
older than her years in many respects. The only problem I
had with her was that she had no idea of danger. She
lived in a perfect world and hardly understood racism.
We usually ended the night with me dropping her off a
block or so away from her house so her overprotective*

brothers wouldn't get outraged by her not making her curfew, (and she never made her curfew). Dana would be out at night and someone would ask her what time she needed to be home and she with her very flippant attitude would shrug them off and say 'when I get there' but none of us would drive her to her house knowing full well that she was due home at sometime around twelve even though we could never get a straight answer out of her. I enjoyed her company so I never rushed her and we usually arrived back in Bloomfield sometime around two or three in the morning and the next day she'd call me as if nothing happened and be ready to roll again. When she did get hit with some type of reprimand she'd simply go to work and then go to stay at her girlfriend's house and tell me to pick her up from there. She kept weed and we both stayed high in our attempts to deal with a world not ready for an interracial couple and everything was working fairly well when we went out one night and at the end of the night we found ourselves in a truck stop, pants down, both of us sweating up a storm after around the third round. It was always good and neither one of us ever got enough when we were both aroused, (even more than we already were), by flashlights pointing in the car. I can't remember what town we were in now but it was somewhere Negroes were definitely not in large amounts and the White cop who ordered me out of the car let me know it in no uncertain terms. Throwing me up against the car pants still halfway down to my ankles I didn't say a word. But Dana who saw no problem making love to a man she loved was appalled and let the cop know it, screaming and cursing about her rights and the fact that she hadn't done anything that normal people don't do when they're in love. And all the time I'm as quiet as a church mouse thinking that if this had been two White teenagers the cop would have told them to zip it up, find a room and move along. But I wasn't White and I had my

Black snake up and deep as far as it could go in this cute little White girl and it was obvious that as far as we had come he didn't approve. I could hear my mother telling her girlfriend that Bert was dating a White girl and her girlfriend saying 'don't worry Claudia we ain't down South and my mother replying, 'we're south of Canada'. And if at no other time I knew she was right. The cop was growing more livid with each of Dana's protest and if I could have I would have thrown a muzzle on this crazy bitches mouth but I did what I thought was the right thing and said nothing. I watched as he slammed her up against the hood of my car and I guess this woke her up a bit because for the first time since he appeared she shut up. He then emptied her pocketbook which set her off again. 'You have no right to go through my belongings' she yelled and I knew under the law that she was right but who was I to say. He quickly found the weed and her pipe and began asking me if I smoked. I said nothing and he scooped out a bowlful and held it down by his penis and told me to smoke. I refused and felt the back of his hand against my jaw. It stung like hell and I could feel my eyes water but I did nothing. I was used to the stories every summer of young Black men in Newark and New York reaching for a shiny object and every summer some kid getting shot and killed. The shiny object was never found. The community was in an uproar and the cop was usually suspended for a week or so with full pay until there was a complete investigation. When the investigation was completed and the community had quieted the policeman was usually reinstated. No, I wasn't playing this game. The cop not getting me to bite took the weed dumped it out at my feet before tossing the bowl and telling us to get the fuck out of there. It's a humiliating thing but I was grateful he hadn't done more. Meanwhile Dana bitched and moaned all the way home about how her civil rights had been violated.

*That wasn't our only experience with racism in north
Jersey as a result of dating someone not of my race and in
all honesty the experiences have been far too numerous to
write upon but I will tell you of two other experiences
rather briefly that still trouble me to some degree.*

*Dana being several months from her eighteenth birthday
was by law still considered a minor in the laws eyes and
being that I was nineteen or twenty or somewhere in that
age range I was for all intensive purposes considered an*

*adult. And being that I was her boyfriend Dana would
just naturally ride with me when we'd go out. Sometimes
there would be three or four cars and maybe twelve or
thirteen people on a good night. And Dana would do her
own thing when we'd go out. One night she decided she
was going to drink Southern Comfort the entire night and
this she did with reckless abandon and without caution
and passed out. Now on this particular night I left early
and I was later told that she was upset and this in part led
to her over indulging. I don't know. I wasn't there but
my crew brought her home, placed her on her doorstep,
rang the doorbell, and drove off. This was common
practice in Jersey and though I'm not condoning it or
saying it's a good practice. All that I'm saying is that it is
still pretty common practice.*

*White kids were good for that in Jersey and as bad as it
sounds there are worse things that can happen. Not to
stereotype, but in Newark and the Oranges if one was to
get inebriated to the extent that they couldn't make it
home and would pass out where they were then chances
were and it's been documented that you could wake up
naked. There have been instances, not in Jersey, but in
North Carolina, where I watched someone shoot some
heroin and o.d. and before the other niggas at the party
thought to give him mouth-to-mouth they robbed him of*

the rest of his drugs and then revived him. And don't you know this idiot whose lips had literally turned blue and was as close to death as I've ever seen anyone come after being resuscitated sat back up and wanted to know who had stolen his dope. So, to drop this woman off on her doorstep intact aside from what she did to be in her present condition was no crime as far as I was concerned but her mother and brothers seemed to think so and I received a summons to appear in court for contributing to the delinquency of a minor. It didn't matter that we were only a year apart. The fact of the matter was that I was a Black boy sleeping with a White girl.

I didn't bother to tell my parents because integration and equality were both good and correct and the Christian way to act; except when it came to their son. And I know they truly believed in those principles that King espoused. But this no longer did they apply to their son. Recognizing that I was now at that critical age where I could be lynched and castrated for committing one of the most heinous of all Black crimes; sleeping with a White girl all of a sudden King's teaching were no longer applicable. This worked on both side of the color line. Liberal Whites who called themselves progressives and readily embraced King's non-violent approach to change and equality all the way up until it was their son or daughter who was actively instituting the change. So, I refrained from telling my parents and instead took my boy Leon to court with me in Bloomfield, New Jersey. She was there with a few of her brothers and mother and all made their case while I stood silently awaiting the judge's decree and was astonished when he simply said that I was banned from the town altogether. I was so glad I wasn't in the Deep South. Banned from a town for dating someone of another race... Wow!

I took it all in one ear and out the other and proceeded to go down the block and have a drink with Leon, where we

*laughed about the whole incident. She called me that
night and we went out as usual.*

*But that was not the end of Dana although I was tired of
going through hell because of skin color. Still, it seemed
that the more that people tried to break us up for
something as ludicrous as pigmentation the more resolved
we became in keeping our relationship afloat.*

*Still, things were getting worse and despite how much we
professed our love to each other, the rest of the world
wasn't quite ready for us and we knew it. If at first we'd
been naive we weren't anymore.*

*We were coming down the Garden State Parkway one
night on our way home when a red Ford pickup truck
rode by and gave us the finger for no apparent reason. It
was around one or two in the morning and I'm thinking
that the guy probably just had a little too much to drink
and so I sped up, pulled ahead of him and got ready to
exit when he speeds up and exits as well. I pull to the
light at the exit and stop and notice a cop car facing me.
The next thing I know is that the guy in the red pickup is
getting out of his car and rushing up to my side of the car.
My windows cracked slightly and he's just a ranting and
raving and carrying on something awful. Now I'm going
to tell you, I grew up in New York City and have seen a lot
of things in my life but I have yet to see someone so angry
over who knows what. But not knowing what the problem
was other than this White woman sitting next to me I
turned to her and told her to get my gun out of the glove
compartment. But being that she was in full panic mode
and was being held victim by her own emotions she could
do little but scream which didn't help the situation any.
Anyway, he's trying to stick his hand or arm in the
window in an attempt to get to me so I started rolling the
window up on his arm. And I'm rolling and I see his arm
being pinched and turning red and he's still cursing but
now he's also dancing in the street trying like hell to get*

101

his arm free and I'm still yelling for her to get my invisible gun hoping to scare him and she's still in panic mode screaming her fool head off and all the while the cops just sitting there obviously waiting for the light to change and acting like he doesn't see a goddamn thing. That was the longest light. And it seemed that just when the light changed everything came to a head. The cop made a left as if he didn't see us. The irate fool outside of the car then took both hands and gripped what he could of the driver's side window and yanked as hard as he could and the glass flew everywhere. At that time I roared through the intersection all the while glancing in my rearview mirror to see if he were following or not. To this day I cannot explain motive or reason for that man's actions other than the White girl in the front seat of the car.

My patience almost gone now, I knew it wouldn't be long now before I'd have to give up the good fight and let her go. A few weeks later she stopped by the house to speak to my mother. She had a rather good relationship with my mother despite the fact that my mother wasn't particularly fond of her.

Still, Dana believed that she was a warm, wonderful person, (and she was), and if someone didn't particularly for her then they had to deal with their issues but she was going to continue to be just as sweet and thoughtful as she was. And that is how she dealt with my mother. On one of my mother's weaker moments she invited Dana and my friend to accompany me up to Jackie Robinson's home for his summer jazz benefit in Connecticut. The benefit had become an annual event and we'd go up sit on the lawn in the backyard and listen to the likes of Dizzy Gillespie, Jon Faddis, Grover Washington Jr. and Gerry Mulligan. There were so many people there that you had to park a few miles away and then take a shuttle bus to the house but there was plenty of room in the backyard and one could literally walk a few feet and be at the stage. Anyway, Dana took Claudia's invitation as a sign that they were finally on good terms but she soon found out that she was sadly mistaken when she came to the house and asked mom if she could sit down and talk to her. (It would have been better if she had addressed me around the whole situation but she for some reason decided to sit down woman-to-woman and have this talk). Dana and I weren't on the best of terms at this point and I ushered her in and left to handle some business and told her I'd be back to drive her home in an hour or so since she told me that's what she needed.

When I got back Dana still sat in the living room but no longer was she the confident, self-assured young lady I'd left there. It reminded me of the time I took her with me up to 145th Street to the Dunbar apartments in Harlem where Uncle Fred lived. I ran upstairs to pick up my check and couldn't have been upstairs for more than fifteen minutes. When I came downstairs she looked like she'd been hit by thunder. She looked the same way now. When I asked her if she was ready to go she jumped up like a jackrabbit in heat and was out the door. I threw a glance at my mother and could tell she had some words of her own for me when I returned. I had no idea of what transpired when I left but the air told me it was not good at all. On the ride taking Dana home I inquired but couldn't get a word out of her and being that it was payday and I had a date and was trying my best to free myself of her completely I let it go. Besides I knew that if it was that serious Claudia would tell me when I got home. And I was right. No sooner than I got home my mother took my hand and led me into the living room and sat me down.

'Bert, I guess you know Dana's pregnant.' It was my first hearing of it and being that it was I sat there a little embarrassed but more in shock than anything else. My

mother recognized my surprise right away. 'You didn't know?' 'No I didn't.' 'Well, she is and wants to have the baby. I don't know if you know it or not but the girl really loves you. She wants to have the baby and has gotten you a job with her brother in a corrugated cardboard factory at night. She's proposing that you get married, get a little apartment for the three of you while she waitresses and you can go to school at night.' I sat there dumbfounded at the thought of these two women making plans for my life without either touching base with me or asking me my opinion. I knew they both had my best interest at heart but the bottom line was no one had asked me how I felt. My mother, however, had already closed the deal. She told Dana that she needed to be at Planned Parenthood bright and early on Friday morning. It's just how Claudia was when it came to her son. She saw me with all the potential in the world and she saw Dana as a distraction and deterrent from all that I could become. Claudia saw Dana as not only a distraction but as a problem too. She made it clear to Dana that as much as she professed to love me the world was not ready for us. And the world certainly wasn't ready for a bi-racial baby. And being that she was older and wiser her decision was final. She was going to put the money up for the abortion and I was to pay her back the following week on payday. There was no argument from me, as I had already grown tired of the trials and tribulations of dating someone not of my own persuasion. Dana proceeded as directed but our relationship was permanently altered and we both went on to date others of our own ethnic background. Still, she stayed in touch even when I moved to Queens some years later.

Life in Jersey following Dana grew old and mundane and I was tired of busting my rump working two jobs and still not having anything to show for it. Looking at the alternatives there was little for me and the home situation

*was not getting any better. I'm not saying that there were
any altercations or anything but Claudia had gotten me a
full time job at Foster Wheeler Energy Corporation where
she worked so we rode to work and rode home together
everyday. I wasn't doing much of anything around this
time. I was dating this cute sista who was about eighteen
and was dealing on the*

*Weed and heroin but I didn't see any future for us so I
wasn't pushin' up real hard. My parents never met her
and I knew better than to bring her home. She was
straight street and I knew they wouldn't see her as being a
good match for their son. My mother recognized that I
was growing more and more despondent about everything
set me up on a blind date with her friend Marie. She had
a daughter Val's age and my mother had met her at one
of Val's school gatherings and they had become fast
friends. Marie had me by about seven or eight years and
was one of the finest women I've ever come across if not
the finest and she was smart as a whip but she was Italian
and by this point I had had my fill of White women and
the high cost of dating them. We had a lot in common
and when she told me she dated Walt Frazier of the New
York Knicks she had me hook, line, and sinker. That and
because my mother was so worried about me I took her
out to The Living Room, (a little private Black club in
East Orange), that provided the best live entertainment in
the area. They had a lot of local talent and a few notable
jazz bands that would perform there every so often.
Marie turned out to be congenial, good natured and she
really turned out to be a lot of fun but all I could think of
when I took her home was how close I'd been to being a
father not more than a month or so ago and much as I
wanted to stay the night I left after one night cap and
called it a day. Still, 'til this day I regret not getting to*

105

know her better. The worst thing in life is missed opportunity and Marie despite all her baggage was certainly a missed opportunity. My dad always a connoisseur of beautiful women looked at me almost as if I was crazy when I returned home that night. He asked me how my night was and I replied matter-of-factly that it had gone okay. And he half expecting that I'd be seeing her again remarked that she was a hammer. I never saw Marie again and continued on with my little humdrum existence.

I was still very much in contact with my family in Pennsylvania and always tried to stay abreast of what they were doing. David had been killed while working in Florida. The murder was unsolved but when Barbara went down to identify the body the coroner's office told her that he had both arms broken and both legs as well and had gotten hit while crossing a highway. The one discrepancy that stood out like a sore thumb was that David had been wearing all white and there wasn't any dirt or other indication that he'd been hit by a car or anything else. His mother, my Aunt Annabelle had a private investigator look into it and they seemed to think that he was stripped naked by Florida cops and beaten to death. 'Til this day no one knows exactly what happened but all will agree foul play was involved. Barbara was attending Howard University now but her whole demeanor changed. It's almost as if she'd lost her innocence, her whole reason for living. My cousin Michelle who was from Harlem and used to join me every summer on my grandmother's farm was now at Ohio State but Marilyn and Chris were still there and so I contacted Marilyn who informed me that she was attending California University of Pennsylvania which was previously a teachers college and since I saw no future in working a dead end job and getting high all the time I asked her to send me an application which she did.

106

And having nothing better to do I filled it out and sent it in. About two weeks later I received a letter back saying I was accepted and I couldn't have been happier.

The winter semester was to start in about a week and I packed a couple of pair of underwear, an extra pair of pants, a couple of sweaters, my stereo system and I boarded Greyhound. California University of Pennsylvania was nothing like the brochure I'd been sent. It was tucked in the mountains of western Pennsylvania with nothing more than a few buildings, maybe ten in all and a population of maybe two or three thousand students. The town itself was maybe another thousand, a far cry from the hustle and bustle of Jersey and New York with its Main Street complete with its bar, laundromat and fire department. There were a couple of restaurants set up for the college students but no fine dining institutions where you might consider taking the family. Most of the businesses catered to the college students but other than that there was a paucity of business and activities. And I guess that's what I liked most about it. It was barren of everything I was used to. There were no distractions. There was nothing. I'd purposely left my car at home so I couldn't just up and go when I had a mind to escape the boredom. I guess it was a sort of self-imposed exile. I'd been running for the last five or six years, smoking and sniffing all the dope I could get my hands on and I was tired. I knew my grandmother and Uniontown were just a hop, skip and jump away but with no car and no public transportation or mass transit system there would be, could be no distractions. And I knew that even this far away from everything because of that bad gene I could find something to alter my course. I always did. And nine times out of ten it was women that I'd succumb to.

Like my enlistment in the Marines, however, my sole motivation was not an education per se but resembled more of a Republican ideology. It was not a progressive mantra but a more reactive ideology. It was not to actively pursue and education but to instead get away from the stifling, domination of a mother who was adamant about her first born being not only the best he could be and pursuing his own dreams but pursuing hers as well. The pressure she bestowed on me was too great. And that's not to say I ever doubted her love, devotion in wanting the best for me but at times, (most of the time), her love could be so overwhelming that it never gave one a chance to expand, to spread my wings and fly.

California gave me the opportunity to do that and after a first semester of for the first time finding out how to manage my time and social life that came with it everything seemed to fall right into place. My grades weren't great but I was learning things that I had no earthly idea about and I was intrigued. It helped that I picked my own classes and had some leeway as to what I filled my cerebrum and cerebellum with. And it just seemed that anything that I had the faintest notion or interest in there appeared a class to fulfill my lack of knowledge and some knowledgeable professor to answer my questions. I loved it. I loved the school, the area, everything about it. I loved everything about it except the weather. I have never been in an area so cold in all my life. The cold front that used to blow off the three rivers was nothing short of blistering.

My first semester I was relegated to the dorms. I knew that because I was a little older and more mature than most of the entering freshman that this arrangement was not going to work for me. My initial roommate was a White kid from Johnstown, Pennsylvania who had obviously not been around a lot of Blacks if any. This was obvious almost immediately and what he did know of Blacks he must have gotten from television or his parent's limited knowledge so he a plethora of questions for me

108

and it made it difficult to get any peace when he was
around. For a time I had to ask myself if I wasn't having
some sort of déjà vu and wasn't back with Private Lutz
again. He wore cheap K-Mart shirts that were plaid with
the cowboy snaps on them along withLee jeans and brown
suede shoes that shouted nine ninety nine every time I
saw them. As far as stereotyping goes I hate to do it
because we as a people have always been stereotyped but
if there is such a thing as a red neck country bumpkin he
was the definition. I think he was about eighteen, had
never been anywhere but Johnstown, knew little about the
world outside of his rural environment but still felt that he
was superior because he was White. To make matters
worse he was arrogant in his ignorance. I lived across
the hall from a couple of brothers I took a real liking to.
One was Charlie Earl from the Braddock section of
Pittsburgh and Derrick who was from Philly and this was
my clique for now. Neither of them could stand my
roommate, Craig and Charlie Earl who was a not too
bright but good-natured soul would actually sit down and
try to talk and understand Craig. But Derrick who was
from a real city, (sorry Pittsburgh), and had interactions
with Whites on a daily basis knew how the interactions
between Blacks and Whites went down didn't have time to
talk and try to educate. His tolerance level was nil and
anytime Craig would foster a negative remark concerning
Blacks Derrick would get ready to beat Craig's ass I
don't know how many times I intervened to save that
White boy.
I tried to be patient, tolerant even but he was so ignorant
and arrogant that I lost my patience and took it to him the
only way I knew how to after every avenue was closed. I
beat his ass every which way I could and all the time
asking where his White superiority was now. We came to
an understanding after that and Craig monitored most of
what he said. He still wasn't cool but then you couldn't

ask him to elevate his whole game in a matter of weeks that made up a semester. I think we'd both made up our minds that we'd find other housing arrangements for the upcoming semester but Craig wasn't finished yet.

One night I purposely told him that I was having company prior to his leaving so he knew too make other arrangements for the night. And so I thought nothing when I invited this cute little chick over to the room that night. I'd been peeping her and we'd been chatting briefly over the course of the last couple of weeks and I guess we were feeling each other because she agreed to come over at around eleven that night. Eleven was when the yard would come alive. Most of the normal people were asleep by this time and only the bad boys and girls were out at this time of night. We called it Creepin' after Luther Vandross' new song. Anyway these were the kids that had boyfriends or girlfriends or weren't committed but needed a taste and had found something or someone that stirred the good good in them. And I had found one who thought I was worth her braving the cold to come up to my dorm room. I was waiting and welcomed her into my bed with the quickness. She was as cute as she could be and had skills I hadn't dreamed about and was more than willing to put in some work. I wasn't really considering a relationship or anything of that nature but she still marketed her skills as if she were trying to win the account and I was more than willing to let her present her sales pitch. I was all but won over although I still didn't see propositioning her the following day for anything remotely resembling a relationship when Craig walked in, turned on the light and lay down on his bed ending ol' girls presentation. I was fit to be tied but I let the whole affair go with firm consternation that I would move just as soon as the semester ended.

The following semester I followed through on my resolution and found a place as far off of campus as I possibly could. I found an old hotel that was being renovated. There was a lounge and bar downstairs and this suited me well. Here no one could just stop by on their way to and from class and the bar and restaurant were perfect since I didn't have to brave the Pennsylvania winters to eat and drink. I was on the top floor in a studio apartment with no frills but it suited me fine. I was doing better in school now and my goal was now not just to not go home but to make deans list. I still wasn't sure what I wanted to major in but the mere fact that I was achieving was enough for me. By this time, I had amassed a nice circle of friends. They were an older crowd most of them being in their mid twenties and like me had experienced a little bit of life and had finally resigned themselves to the fact that minimum wage jobs were not an end in themselves and perhaps college was the answer so they were serious about their undertaking whereas those that had come fresh out of high school were still deciding whether college was the answer. We'd already been through that and so it wasn't a question of whether we should be here but how well we were going to do while we were in attendance. It's funny but we were different from most of the student's in attendance. I didn't know if it was just our age or the fact that we were all just special in our own right. I can't pinpoint what it was that made us different and unique but that we were. There were only about four of us in this unique little clique but we basically ran things on the yard.

My best friend, and confidante Beatrice was years older than the rest of us and quite a bit wiser, (I'm thinking this was due in part to her being quite a bit older than the rest of us). Anyway, Bea lived right at the end of campus and perhaps even a bit closer than even she desired. She had a cute little place. I'm not sure what you'd call it. It wasn't quite what you'd call a studio because she had a full kitchen but I believe that's the only thing that was full.

111

You see the living room; bedroom and dining room were all in one. I called it headquarters, others called it the B Hotel, while still it call the Information Center while still others referred to it as CVS simply because all the best drugs in California passed through her apartment. Not only did the best drugs pass through there but almost every Black on campus. At that time I didn't have the introspect or perhaps the intellect to understand what the attraction was with Beatrice. Men came by in droves, single men, men in relationships but in general men came by.

They came by to talk, to listen, to share their dreams. And when they had shared and listened and allowed her to share their dreams they thanked her and some even blew smoke with her in thanks and appreciation. I never understood her allure or the relationship with all those poor wretched souls seeking guidance and it wasn't until some years later when I went to her with the same type of thoughts and longings and desires that they did in the early eighties that I began to understand some of her allure.

Bea had the unique gift of always putting others before herself. She sat with almost eager anticipation as men came up to her apartment to seek advice on their relationships and anything else that came to mind. If anything Bea, a psychology major was a good listener. And I think that's what made her so unique. At twenty or twenty one years of age young men and women are usually so wrapped in themselves and their dreams that they hardly have time for mates or anything else. Most men in my impression are merely little boys grown up. These young men, miles away from home are looking for the same support system they got from their mothers. The women they chose though may have resembled their mothers in physical stature with their thirty five year old asses and breasts. You know the ones that had just begun

112

to sag a little and been replaced with the wisdom of having experienced a little about life and could now share it with their offspring with an air of knowledge. But the only thing these young girls could afford the brothers on campus was the physical stature.

When it came down to the wisdom and direction that was needed for these young men to grow in maturity they could not provide what was necessary and so they sought Bea for advice. And this she did, always listening, rarely giving advice and for the majority this was good enough. And that was what made Bea unique although I don't think most of us recognized her rather distinctive qualitities at the time. To me Bea had these qualities and others. I saw her as bright and open. She had the ability to admit that she wasn't all knowing and readily accepted new information and sought it freely.

I like most of the other brothers had a woman. In fact, I'd met her the previous semester and after making the decision not to go home for the summer I hid out in her dorm for the summer. We'd made love every day but it wasn't in the traditional sense of love. What she did was sex me any way she could think of. She was quite well adept. But like all of the other brothers I spent any leisure time I had at Bea's house although I wasn't there for the same thing the rest of them were there for. I didn't need advice on much of anything and especially relationships. I lived with A.B. but had no intentions of it going any further than a semester or two. To me A.B. was nothing more than a creature comfort, more or less like a fixture that made my house more livable, more comfortable. She supplied my needs and I supplied hers. When she needed an escort for a function at her sorority I was there. And when I needed a bed warmer on those cold, bitter Pennsylvania nights she was there. And though we never openly acknowledged it was no more than that. She kept her dorm room on those days that we weren't exactly feeling each other. We liked each other, maybe loved each other but I'm not entirely sure we were in love. And you couldn't tell from Allison who wasn't ever one to openly show her emotions. It really made it hard on me because I never knew how she really felt and I wasn't going all in with someone that wasn't all in herself. When I look back I think Allison had been so badly abused by the men she fell in love with that she was extremely cautious when I met her and simply couldn't or wouldn't allow herself to be hurt again. I do believe the only man she truly trusted was her father

So, I wasn't at Bea's for the same purpose as the rest of my brothers. I was there to absorb all the knowledge I could acquire. She was a plethora of knowledge. Sometimes we would just chill and listen to music and talk of life and the events of the day or anything that would come to mind. I became so enamored with her that I began seeing her in a different light and one evening we sat and blew some smoke and drank some wine then decided to try a Quaalude apiece. After setting them off with a little more wine we sat back and let the music move us. We talked for hours and I do believe that we shared something quite uncommon to men and women. What we shared was a friendship not predicated upon sex but one based solely on admiration and respect for each other's view, values and insatiable thirst for knowledge.

A.B. and I were still cool although she despised Bea and the time I spent with her but there was little she could do and though she speculated she like everyone else could never exactly pinpoint any one thing that said we were intimate but that was the common belief. Why else would a man and woman be around each other as much as we were if it weren't for sex?

We went places that meant something to us as we shared the same tastes. We shopped and upgraded our wardrobes at thrift stores where Blacks were not visible

*and found quaint little stores like Gabriel Brothers where
imperfections were at a maximum. But if you looked you
could find a treasure here and there for little or nothing.
We loved scavenging through Gabes and for ten or twenty
dollars we'd come out with shopping bags full of goodies.
When we'd go back to campus and head to class in our
new gear we'd be inundated with compliments but like
most of what we did our peers had no clue as to what we
were doing. It's funny though they wouldn't have been
caught dead in a thrift store but we had different values.
Being a little older we'd been out there in the world and
knew the value of a dollar and to save was to be wise.
Our relationship hardly ended there. She was a
psychology major and I a sociology major our courses
sometimes overlapped and intertwined and at times we
ended up taking the same classes. And being that both of
us were extremely competitive this made classes even that
much more enjoyable.*

*She and I were in our were in our own little world and
whereas most of the other students would sit in the back
of the class and pray that the professor wouldn't see them
or call on them Bea and I would take the first two seats up
front and monopolize the discussion oblivious to what the
other students thought. When the professor had a
question she or I would answer it and then spend long
hours after class was over discussing the lecture. We had
other friends too who were apart of our small clique.
There was Gary G. who we simply called "G" who
enrolled sometime after I did. Seemed his mother had
passed and the only way for him to stay eligible for social
security was to be enrolled full-time and this he did never
really considering the thought of attending class. Gary
"G" was from New York and his family lived within
minutes of my grandmother's farm and his parents had
the same intentions as my parents and sought to get Gary
out of the city every summer and would send him out to*

Uniontown in hopes of keeping him out of trouble. But Gary was much more streetwise than most of us. His mother died when he was only a small child and as much as his father tried to protect him from the streets of New York he was still unable to do so in large part and Gary being who he was found himself hanging out anyway. School was not a high priority and although he was accepted to California University as so many were he neither had the discipline nor the desire to attend classes. A self-proclaimed dj he and I became fast friends. I liked him simply because he was from New York and reminded me so much of the city. We had the same mentality for the most part and were always quick to pick up on some new money making venture and when it came to music we were like two old men when it came down to the evolution of R&B music in America. Music was his forte and my hobby so we enjoyed each other's company immensely. But as much as we enjoyed each other's company there were profound differences that separated us and kept us at odds on many a day.

We certainly had different philosophies on life and as militant as I was I had come to the realization with age and maturity that it was tough to fight the powers that be as much as we may have detested their ways. I often thought of King and Malcolm and their strategies and eventually decided that neither would have been nearly as successful without the other.

In reality, though and as much as I loved Malcolm for what he did to instill pride in Black folks his tactics sometimes bothered me. If there was any thought of resisting the man in anyway other way than non-violently it had to be ludicrous to even put any faith in that tactic when the largest arms dealer in the world at the time was the White man and for me it didn't make any sense for him to sell you or me the gun that would be responsible for shooting him. And when you ran out of the bullets—

116

then what—please Mr. Man would you sell me some more bullets so I can shoot your ass some more. And that's what it was like for me to see Gary resisting the White man at the game he invented, arranged, and set up the rules to. Here was the deal. If you wanted to survive in White America as a Black man there were very few avenues in which to do this.

The law of averages plainly stated that although there were millions of little Black boys running around trying to throw a basket into a hoop and embodying themselves as Michael Jordan or Lebron James that in truth there are only two hundred players in the NBA so there's not a whole lot of future in that. And the world of entertainment can be classified as minimalism.. There are only one or two great rappers, one or two great singers, one or two great actors, and as we all know only been one African American president so these are hardly fields that we should be aspiring for. However, when we speak of survival and the masses of Black people we have to speak of where they can thrive in numbers. And there are few places. But one of those places designated where Blacks can thrive is in education and to see a young Black man look a gift horse in the mouth and decline the gift bestowed upon him truly bothered me. Gary's social security payments were dependent on his being enrolled in school but the mere thought of him taking advantage of a free education and perhaps learning something and graduating with a degree exhibiting his new found expertise or skill in a field was beyond his comprehension. Education is the foundation.

Gary was dating some skinny, little light-skinned filly from Pittsburgh named Carrie. She and I had his best interest at heart and would escort him in the front door of the classroom and this fool would walk straight through and out the backdoor. As if this wasn't bad enough Gary would go right to my apartment and lie across my bed and

117

pick up a book and would lie right there in that same position until he completed it. Just seemed to me that if could have just had the discipline to force him to do something other than what he chose to do he may have been walking down the aisle with the rest of us. Still, Gary "G" brought a flavor that we all enjoyed. Driving a white Cutlass with a red vinyl top he was always flashy and game for anything. Now Gary was like the ret of us and blew a little smoke every now and then but he was no drinker. Problem was he was a follower and was always down for anything. One day out of sheer boredom, Gary, Bea and I made a couple of calls looking for a quarter pound of weed. He and I had been selling weed for a couple of months now and though we never made a lot of money we could at least stay high for free and take care of our crew without always having to run out searching for the good good. Well anyway on this day we found ourselves a little low. I think we were down to our last ounce and decided to re-up. Hanging outside downstairs waiting for Bea I pulled out a bottle of Bumpy's, (Seagrams Extra Dry Gin), and offered Gary some. He declined as usual and I went through our ritual teasing about him not really being from New York and not being able to hang. And he not having a strong consternation eventually took the half a bottle and finished it in one swell swoop. There was no doubt that we were all quite nice when we got in the car and Bea of course had a little something something and so on the way out into the country we blew some smoke and were on our way. Gary who always drove like he was qualifying for a spot on the NASCAR circuit was driving to fast as usual on one of those narrow roads way up in the mountains when he hit a curve too fast and the back side of the car skidded off the road and hit the guard rail. It was the only thing that saved us from going over the embankment and as I caught my breath and looked out the back window I saw

*cows in the pasture below us that looked like ants and I
sat there holding my breath praying that neither he nor
Bea shifted their weight the slightest bit or we would have
been down there in that pasture. Somehow Richard Petty
eased the car back on the road and we were off again.
This time he drove more slowly, obviously aware of the
near death experience. A little later we found our way out
to some little country patch with maybe thirty or forty
houses. Pennsylvania had plenty of these patches
whenever and wherever they found a new coal vein. But
what surprised me was that the composition of these
patches was always Black and it just wasn't Pennsylvania
it was everywhere I went and I'm convinced that the
United States Census Bureau must be comprised of little
scared White kids not willing to frequent places such as
these or this may just be another ploy to under represent
Black folks in America. I don't know but I do know that
everywhere I go whether it is in a major city or the
backwoods of Pennsylavia or North Carolina they are
there in droves.
Anyway after finally arriving at our destination Gary
introduced Bea and I to some backwards fool they called
Cutty. I wasn't aware that they had the Beverly Hillbillies
in Black but then what did I know. He got in the car with
us with his quarter pound of reefer and stuck his hand
out for the money after going on and on about how his
product was top notch and the best thing going and how
he had it imported straight from Taiwan to this coal
patch. I sat there listening to see what he was gonna
bring new to the sales pitch I'd heard so many times and
when he didn't I asked him to try it. But being that I was
already high as hell I couldn't feel a thing after smoking
and told this young brotha that his product wasn't shit.
Well, that's the way I felt but my delivery must not have
been too correctt because the brotha wanted to fight or
shoot or something that backwoods people always resort*

119

*to doing because of their limited communication skills. I
don't remember if the kid made the sale or not but I do
remember Bea and Gary chastising me on the way back to
Cal for my being crazy and damn near getting everyone
killed but I had no fear of danger and it must have been
Claudia's bad gene flaring up again but I simply loved to
fuck with people.*

*We went back to school and after a couple of days or so
we were sitting and smoking after class and I realized it
was pretty good weed. Everyone else thought it good too
and everything was lovely for a while. We were smoking
more than ever now and we eventually ran out with no re-
up money left and it was okay with me 'cause I was
beginning to worry about school and my grades. (I was
always worried about school and my grades right through
here). Whereas Gary wasn't worried about anything
besides selling weed on campus and having a reputation
as a gangsta. Still, he was my boy and so I tried to support
him but it became clear to almost everyone that the only
PHD he wanted was in street crime. And so when he had
depleted our money and drug supply Gary refused to let
that be a deterrent and decided to rob some football
players of their stash and then stay right there on campus
and sell it right under their noses.*

*What made it worse was that they had some light blond
shit that I hadn't ever seen and haven't seen since. And
being that it had such an unusual color it was easy to
trace and of course when people were asked where they
got it from they were quite happy to turn the next person
on and so Gary "G"'s name was thrown out freely. A
couple of these boys were in my classes and being that
football players, in general, are not some of the brightest
stars in the sky they often came to me for help in their
studies. I gladly helped them and in exchange they'd pass
on to me some weed but mostly coke and we'd
consummate our transaction. We interacted on a rather*

limited basis and every now and then they'd throw me a tip or a hook up on something I was interested in but we were cool until Gary decided to rob them. I'm not sure whether they had a game or what when Gary broke into one of their places and stole like a half a pound of this blond weed and there was no surprise when word got out that he was selling it. And being that they like every other college student living on campus were trying to augment their income they weren't too happy about this latest development and after busting down his apartment door and coming in with shotguns intent on blowing him away they naturally stopped by my place next. I was breathless, speechless and scared shitless when they broke down my door and searched my apartment. After convincing them that I had no weed and was taking time off from selling and smoking and had no idea where Gary was they finally gave up their search and left to find him. It was the end of Gary's college career at Cal even though he would pop under the cover of darkness to see Bea and me from time-to-time but for all intents and purposes he was forced to cut all ties and ended his short stint with us. I was still living with A.B. though she only had a month or so before she graduated and though we'd never really committed or made plans to continue seeing each other after her graduation I knew I'd miss her. She was a good cook and used to have dinner ready everyday when I got home from school or work and at night when the lights went out she'd make a man feel like a man with her screaming and moaning about how good I was and how I was the best she'd ever had. And she'd been taught well when it came down to having a lady in the daytime and a ho at night. She could say things under the guise of darkness that would make a man jump through hoops when the dawn broke through. But she was ready to move on and start her life and I couldn't much blame her. And so with all pomp and ceremony we said our farewells and she moved on.

I spent most of my time at Bea's house now that I didn't have to be interrogated for being there or felt some compulsion to go home because there was someone waiting for me. Our relationship grew but never once did she ask anything of me other than that we remain friends. In fact, she never asked me that or even mentioned it and we sort of just remained whatever we were and we were content. I even had old girlfriends visit Bea's house while I was there and we'd talk about what had transpired that made it or didn't make it work. But there was never any discussion or jealousy. We just did our own thing and kept on stepping. I was intent on graduating after my three years there and went to see my advisor one day to see if I couldn't quicken the pace and although I didn't have an appointment was surprised that he'd left his office open. I was even more surprised that he'd left an open checkbook on his desk. And being an opportunist or better yet a fool I scooped it up and hastily mad my way to the closest bank down on Main Street. I had to pass it on my way home so I made a check out for two hundred dollars cash and promptly cashed it and continued home. I had four hundred dollars in my pocket and really didn't need the money but it had been there and so I with that bad gene coupledwith that ol' fucked up New York mentality took it with no conscience or remorse and kept it moving. That was Thursday. Friday evening Allison was to arrive for some formal dinner event that I really wasn't interested in attending but I figured ours had always been a symbiotic relationship based on contingencies and if I wanted to feel her and freak her all night long then perhaps I should suffer through her little AKA event she was so adamant about me attending. One thing was for sure though and that was I wasn't spending my money buying an outfit or two to attend her

*event in. So, I cancelled buying and outfit for the Friday
night affair and decided to buy something for the
Saturday night affair instead which was informal and if I
bought something for this one chances were I could wear
it again. Friday evening Allison arrived and brought her
silk dress and the pressure was mounting---at least on me
it was so I crossed the street and walked over to Bea's
house to see what she had that would lessen the pressure
on me and make my evening flow that much smoother.
As usual my girl was holding and as we were tight she
never charged me, (that's not to say that she always was
kind with me, there were days when I could be especially
obnoxious when she would just put me out and other days
when she wouldn't let me in at all), but on this particular
night she let me in, (I think she felt sorry for me), and
gave me a Quaalude to calm my nerves. Now most of the
time you sip a beer or have a wee bit of wine to set the
Quaalude off but I was never one to do anything in
moderation so I drank a pint of Seagrams Gin and then
took the Quaalude and proceeded back down the hill to
get dressed with Bea telling me she'd be down in a little
while to see how I cleaned up after her girlfriend Evelyn
arrived. I had my outfit laid out days before and all I had
to do was take my shower and get dressed. I don't know
where A.B. disappeared to but the bathroom was
steaming, I took the 'Lude and was sitting on the bed
waiting for it to work and while there I finished the bottle
of gin and then stepped into the shower. Two minutes
after getting into that hot, steaming shower, the
introductions were made. And I'm guessing this is what
transpired. My body must have said, 'damn this hot
water's soothing' and I relaxed just a little. And then I do
believe that's where Mr. Seagrams and Mr. Lude met
because the next thing I knew I was lying flat out on the
floor with half of me in the shower and half of me out.
I'm not sure who picked me up, dried me off and put me*

*in the bed but I do remember hearing Bea's voice and all
was good. At least I knew that I was in good hands and
remember telling all those voices, (I heard lots of people
but couldn't really separate the faces and voices), that I
didn't want anyone to touch me but Bea which must have
been really awkward and uncomfortable for A.B. whose
voice I could now make out as well. Needless to say I
didn't go anywhere that night.
The next day I took the bus into Pittsburgh as I didn't
want to frequent the same bank I'd been to before to cash
another of the dean's checks and arrived in Pittsburgh at
about a quarter to three. The bank closed at three but I
made it inside in time and handed the teller my check and
stood there and waited for it to be cashed. I saw her get on
the phone and even watched closely as the clock struck
three and two bank personnel went and stood on either
side of the bank doors and still it didn't dawn on me that
they were trying to detain me until the police arrived.
When it finally did I burst through the doubles doors
damn near trampling the woman trying to obstruct my
path and made a quick left and headed down Smithfield
where the cops had parked and were waiting patiently. I
did my best to elude them and the next thing I knew I was
bent over a squad car, a woman cop, had me in some kind
of hold that I'd never experienced before. I'll say this for
her. She was efficient. I can't tell you what transpired
after that but I do remember being transported to the
Allegheny County Jail on Ross Street. It was a huge gray
granite building and looking at the building I was already
suffering remorse. As I climbed each solitary step to my
cell I felt like I'd lost my very soul and wasn't sure what I
was going to lose up in here with these criminals and
sexual deviants. That's when I heard, 'ooh baby's got
nice ass, I can't wait 'til I*

get some of that' and I knew at that point that I wasn't a criminal and I didn't want to be hard. I also knew that Bea, Gary, Fast, Moses and Gerald and everyone else that I was tight with was going to have to dig deep but they were going to get me out of here with the quickness. I had a phone call coming and I knew who that would be and so after calling Bea and informing her I walked back to my cell confident now that there would be a dead soul or two before anyone got next to me in this den of sin. Still, when it was time for dinner I was still in my cell. I stayed in my cell. I did go out on the tier to joke with some of the niggas who'd been in the holding pen with me and came to the quick conclusion after hearing everyone's story that everyone but me had been falsely imprisoned. Everyone in there was innocent except me. We talked for hours standing outside of our cells. What else was there to do?

The jail was so crowded that mattresses were thrown on the floor of each tier and a good many of the inmates didn't have cells. I was one of the fortunate one's that did but after listening to my cellmate, (a young White boy about nineteen), who went on and on for days about how he'd bought some parts for his car and didn't know they were stolen I sort of wished I didn't have too be locked up with him. I eventually told him to shut up and go to sleep at which time he decided to talk to our other cellmate, (a brother a little older than both of us who never uttered a word being that he was a heroin addict and was crying because he was going through the agony of withdrawal). In any case this White boy felt compelled to talk to someone, anyone and after he came to the conclusion that he wasn't going to elicit conversation from either of us decided to talk to the people on the outside of the cell. There was a new crew there now but it didn't matter that he didn't know them he still continued his idle chatter

*telling everyone how he had been falsely imprisoned and
how all he really wanted was a cigarette.*

*Well, the brothers sized him up very quickly and he let it
quickly be known that this was his first time being in lock
up. Seeing fresh meat and the large diamond studs in
both ears they decided to trade him cigarettes for his
earrings which he agreed to and being that he was so free
and nonchalant about his earrings I guess they thought
he was free about everything else as well and asked him if
he wanted to get out. He, not having the sense he was
born with agreed and they told him if he pulled hard on
the cell door from the inside while they kicked it it would
pop open. I wanted to grab him at this point and slap him
for being so goddamn stupid but it wasn't any of my
business so I watched as he pulled and tugged while they
kicked and the door or the bars eventually gave way and it
slid open. I damn near pushed his ass out and watched as
he stood outside and smoked and laughed and carried on
with his newfound friends but I had no inkling to join
him or them for that matter.*

*Moments later I heard my name called and I was told to
prepare to leave because my bail had been posted. On the
way downstairs I shouted to the punks who had made the
remark about getting some of this sweet ass that, 'you'll
never get none of this you punk ass faggots'. But after
sitting downstairs for about a half an hour I was told that
they hadn't made my bail in time and it looked like I'd be
spending the weekend there at which time I was marched
right back up to my cell with my tail between my legs
listening to those punk ass faggots tell me that there was
still a chance and how good it would feel. I'd never felt so
down or depressed in my life. The White boy was still out
there laughing and joking and aside from asking me what
had happened went ahead shooting the shit with his
newfound friends. I was tired, nerves wracked, and leery
to say the least of having to spend another day or two here*

126

caged up with these sick individuals and I swore to God that I would never transgress in anyway again. I didn't dare leave my cell and though I wasn't on a hunger strike or protesting against anything other than my own stupidity I had no appetite that it made it worth me putting my ass out there in general population and in jeopardy. I wondered how this little White boy could get along so well with these fools he had never met or even had the opportunity to meet other than today and yet co-exist so easily and well. I didn't have answers for any of these questions but followed my intuition and went nowhere those bars for fear that they might open. My suspicions proved true later on that evening when I heard him scream out as they raped him continuously throughout the night in the next cell.

I stayed in that cell for the next two days while everyone ate and showered and did whatever it is people do while their locked up but I guess you can say that I was neither an active participant nor had any inclination to want to be. What I was was 'scared straight' and like Richard Pryor said when I got out all I could say was 'thank God for prisons'.

Bea and Gary picked me up on Monday morning. Bea had arranged my bail, which I believe, was ten percent of five thousand dollars or five hundred dollars. Both apologized for leaving me in there over the weekend but I was so grateful that I was once again a free man that any apology fell on deaf ears. I was truly grateful and happy to see Bea but in that short time I had changed. And the fact that Gary walked down the long corridor of the courthouse with a quarter pound of weed hanging out of his inside coat pocket only made me see clearer.

I had no sense of what constituted good upstanding friends who were not only going to have my welfare at heart but would help me to grow as a person. No longer did I see Gary in that light and I knew that he wasn't

127

seeing the blessings bestowed on him. My dad would tell me later on in life when teaching me patience and tolerance that everyone finds their God in their own time but after such a harrowing and sobering experience I needed no further guidance in how I wanted to proceed with my life. I was traumatized and it was a good hour into the ride before I could even speak. I saw and heard things in the short time I was there that I neither wanted to hear or see ever again in life. And where I saw it as humbling but learning experience Gary saw it as a pronouncement that his boy, his main man had become a true "g" a gangster when my only thoughts were to go back to school and apply myself and become the best student possible. I shared my thoughts with Bea who understood completely and only laughed at the sharing of my short stint in jail. As short a stint as it was it was certainly long enough for me to understand that I wanted no parts in the future. I shared these same stories "G" but they had no effect. He too laughed but for different reasons I'm sure.

School became an afterthought after that as I worked diligently to finish up and get out of there. As much as I enjoyed the hiatus I was ready to leave and get along with my life. And then out of the clear blue I received a letter offered me a grad assistantship. My schooling would be paid for along with my room and board and in two short years I could obtain my Master's Degree in Social Work. I talked to a few people I held in pretty high esteem and all except one told me to jump at the opportunity. It was the course Bea had chosen to take and my cousin Marilyn as well but after talking to my dad who assured me that I could start teaching immediately as the city was in desperate need of teacher's and I'd be able to go right to Hunter College on Manhattan's East Side and get my masters after work. There was and still is no question that my father loved me but this was perhaps the worst bit

128

*of advice he ever gave me. The money that I would earn
teaching would then have to be used to pay for my
Masters Degree. But as I was unable to think enough to
make my own decisions when it came to governing my
own life I simply went with the old adage 'that father
knows best' and planned on returning home despite the
many objections from friends who wanted me to stay on at
Cal. There still remained another semester. I was getting
older and the kids now enrolling seemed to be getting
younger and dumber and watching from my hang out in
front of the Louis L. Manderino Library across from
Bea's house I reminisced on my three long years there.
I'd had some wonderful years, met some wonderful
people, learned to shoot dope and gone to jail there and
despite all that I was going to come out with a degree.
Going away to college had certainly brought me all that I
wished for and more. And to think that my only intent
when I got there was to get away from home. I felt like I'd
finally turned the corner and made something of myself
but the semester wasn't quite over and so I put off all
decisions until I'd finished up.
A.B. had stopped coming to see me altogether by now and
the winter of my senior year was not only cold but rather
lonely and everyone I'd started with had either dropped
out or graduated. Even my freshman bed warmers like
Bonnie ad Brenda had graduated and moved on and at
that moment when I knew that all was through Gary
came through and told me of a party up at Zulu.
Now Friday nights usually went one of two ways. Either I
had company and didn't want to be disturbed or I had a
test or paper due on Monday of the following week.
Either way the answer was the same and when people
banged on my door on Friday nights either because they
were underage and wanted me to go down to the bar and
order drinks for them or wanted to buy some weed the
answer was the same. No! Most of the time the TV or*

129

stereo would be blasting but I still wouldn't answer the door. But for some reason Gary knocked on my door and after looking out the window and seeing his car I opened the door. We ended up going up to Zulu, an all-Black apartment complex where college students resided off campus. Anyway I didn't really hang out. I'd already been through that phase and was content with the few friends I had but for some reason I went and met a few girls not from Cal.

They were young and from Pittsburgh and for the most part nothing to write home about. It was a typical Cal crowd except for this one lil chick who was off the hook. I could tell she was young and had been drinking but she was alive and vibrant and she caught my attention. I tried to talk to her and we conversed a little and from what I gathered I knew right then I had to have her.

From someplace called Chartiers City in Pittsburgh she was the cutest little girl I'd come across in some time. The only problem was she didn't seem the least bit interested and that only made her more desirable in my eyes. What appealed to me more than anything was the fact that she was bright. Oh I loved her smile and she had a body to die for but what was most appealing was that she was brighter than bright.

We spent a few days after I first met her at my apartment but nothing transpired sexually. She was young. I believe she was nineteen years of age although she insisted she was twenty-one, a virgin and that was fine. I had no plans to take her somewhere she had never been before. I liked her as a person. She was good company and she was alive. And that was enough for me. She was new and like a breath of fresh air she made me feel alive and wonderful. She was visiting regularly on the weekends now and when she did we did things that were new and invigorating and though I didn't have plans or intentions for her per se it was nice to have a friend and

*partner to do them with. A .B. and I had spent the last
few weeks talking on the phone and our division had only
grown wider but with Yvette now in the picture it didn't
matter too much anymore. No longer did I feel like an
old married man but felt the life slowly seep back into my
old tired spirit.*

*A.B. must have realized this or perhaps her sorors told
her that I was with someone new because she made it a
point to increase her phone calls and even made plans to
come up and see me. By this time I had crossed over
completely although I made sure I never told Yvette what
she meant to me. I was getting to be an old dog but it was
still puppy love to me but in a matter of a month or so I'd
be out of there and back to my old stomping grounds and
though I wondered at times I didn't see any future in a
long distance love affair so I enjoyed the here and now. I
still took her everywhere and introduced her to everyone
that meant anything to me including my family in
Uniontown and thereabouts. Still, I knew the New York,
New Jersey connection was a far more brutal contingent
and I wasn't sure if she or I would be able to handle that.
I was just happy to spend time with her in the days that I
had left before graduation. But what was odd about
Yvette was that in the three years that I'd spent at Cal and
the countless girls that I'd spoken about or taken over
Bea's house, Bea never said anything positive or negative
about any of them but it was obvious from the day she met
Vet that she didn't care for her. A.B. hadn't been a threat
and neither had Bonnie or Benita and Lord knows I was
crazy about Benita. But Vet was different and brought
about a different response altogether from Bea.
In fact, the last couple of weeks she stopped talking to me
altogether and made it a point of letting me know that I
had offended her by not letting her in one day when
Yvette was visiting. This was true but Yvette was new and
although I wouldn't admit it then I believe I was falling in*

love. I'd known Bea for close to three years and I'd never known her to switch gears like this. I was certain I hadn't changed. A.B. was my live in lover before I'd even known Bea but she had been no threat. Bea and I continued our friendship despite her. But things were changing now. Bea came by the apartment one day when Yvette was there and knocked. I heard her knock and wasn't sure who it was but I wasn't opening the door. I was enjoying Yvette's company and had grown tired of people constantly stopping by without calling or saying something. Nothing had changed but Bea took it as a personal affront when I didn't open the door and stopped speaking to me for a number of weeks. Being the closest person to me I was hurt by her reaction to my falling in love or at least seeking some happiness in someplace other than my select group of friends. I was in a transitional phase. I'd come out here to get my life in order and had pretty much succeeded in doing that and now I was preparing to go back and hit the big city, piece of paper in hand and see what New York offered me. Yvette being young and innocent was a nice diversion but I really didn't see any future once I left. I had long come to the conclusion that my father was right and that New York could offer me far more than a graduate assistantship at Cal. But I'd arrived at that decision for far different reasons. It was so far from everything I was used to and after three years I'd grown bored with it and all that Western Pennsylvania had to offer and except for Yvette I had no reason to stay but there were women everywhere so I could hardly let that dictate whether I stayed or whether I left. In fact, I now understood A.B. and her wanting to get away and not return.

Not long after that Yvette and I made love for the very first time and although I looked at every young woman in terms of sex I had grown to like her, (perhaps even love her), and this was the one place I didn't want to go.

*Feelings always swayed my decisions and most of the time
my emotions got me in trouble but in this case I stuck to
my decision and refused to let my feelings towards her get
in the way. One Sunday evening after she and I'd made
love and she left to go home I found myself thinking
about her even more than usual and made up my mind
that very day that one way or another I had to put some
distance between us. That being the case, I made it a point
to see every woman I could in order to get the balance
I'd lost back in my life. My son told me or I told my son
some twenty years later when discussing women in
general that women were like a cornucopia of fruits and
that when you have such a display of oranges and
pineapples and other assorted delicacies why would a
man that has access to all of these wonderful delights not
take advantage of all instead of settling for a diet of one.
Each of them brought a uniquely different flavor and
richness to the table and that is the attitude I had to get
back to. Of course Yvette had quickly become the
frontrunner and was unassuming but was canvassing my
heart with little effort. We hadn't made any type of
formal commitment to be a couple and I guess she didn't
feel she needed to. All she did was continue to be her and
I felt like I had somehow fallen in quicksand. The more I
wriggled to get free the deeper I sank. Anyway, (and
today I'm ashamed to say this), in an effort to believe that
no one woman lay claims to my life or no one had my
nose wide open and sprung, (in all honesty she did), I
slept with she, Bea and A.B. all in the same day. But the
funny thing was the next day when I awoke she was the
one still on my mind. It bothered me but I still had an ace
in the hole and that was that I was going back to Jersey.
I really didn't want to be in a relationship. What I wanted
was the fringe benefits of a relationship but I truthfully
didn't want the nagging accountability and responsibility
of being in a full time relationship. I wanted the*

*companionship and camaraderie and perhaps a tryst
every now and then but I didn't want any of that on a full-
time basis. I guess I was basically a loner but hated to be
alone except when I chose to and Yvette was getting too
close and taking away some of that sense of being a free
spirit. Not long after that I said my farewells to
California University of Pennsylvania and headed home.
Not long after being home I contacted my cousin
Margaret who was back in Jersey City after doing a stint
at Southern University in Texas. She and I were both
recent graduates and so we would give each other tips on
job openings in the city. She was a pretty prolific artist
and was seeking a job as an art teacher and so I steered
her to the Board of Education in New York City and she
was eternally grateful.
In the meantime I'd gotten a job teaching elementary
school in the Bronx just off the Grand Concourse and
walking distance from the house that Ruth built. It was
June now and school didn't start until September so my
dad got me a job as a tutor for remedial reading students
in one of the programs at Medgar Evers University on
Carroll Street in the Crown Heights section of Brooklyn. I
loved riding in with my parent's everyday on the Path
train from Jersey.
Claudia had gotten her degree at forty after she'd had Val
and was now working for some insurance company in the
World Trade Center and we'd drop her off there before
jumping on the subway and continuing on to Brooklyn. I
enjoyed being home and loved my new job. I was back in
New York and loved being there. It was fresh again after
my hiatus and my parents had obviously missed me. They
showed me all the new eateries and now that I had a little
change in my pocket I could hangout with them now
without being a burden. More than that I just loved being
with them again and working. Being a writing tutor was
right up my alley and I was surprised at how old many of*

my father's students were and how little they knew about composing a sentence, a paragraph, and a composition. My father was a patient man and took his time, assessing each of his students and picking them up where they were and taking each to the next level. He had been marvelous when I'd been young and observed him teaching junior high school and he was wonderful at this level as well. He taught me many things under his tutelage but one of the most important things he taught me had nothing to do with writing or remedial reading.

You see,I'd grown quite fond of a young lady named Tina who was all of four foot eleven, from the Bed Stuy section of Brooklyn. She was a cute little thing with a two-year-old daughter named Nicole. I met both and couldn't decide which one I liked more, the mother or the daughter. The jury was still out when my father noticed that certain twinkle that I used to get in my eye when a female turned my head and sat me down one night and simply stated that 'you don't shit and play in the same place'. I understood the analogy and squashed any future arrangements. Still, she and I talked every night and at length on the phone. In the meantime, Yvette had moved up to New Haven, Connecticut and was working as a bank teller. She and I would converse regularly but I made sure that I wasn't feeling as I had in Pennsylvania and I made sure she wasn't my sole means of companionship. There was no doubt that I was crazy about Yvette but I had just gotten out of a three-year relationship and I felt as if the world were mine for the taking. There were so many things for me to see, so many opportunities that awaited me that there was no way I wanted or was going to be responsible for someone elses happiness as well as my own. It was time for me to live, explore, make mistakes, fall down and then get back up and ride it again 'til the motherfuckin' wheels fell off.

*And I couldn't see doing this with someone holding on
for dear life.*

*If I wanted to go up to the Bronx and go to the Beer
Factory and sip beer all day then that's what I'd do. If I
wanted to go to see Rickie Lee Jones perform Chuck E.'s
In Love down in the Village then that's what I'd do. If I
wanted to go up to Greenwich, Connecticut for a day of
wine tasting then that's what I'd do. And that's exactly
what I did. Although when it came to Tina there were
restraints put on how fast I moved. But we found some
contentment in waiting and to be honest it only
heightened the thrill And whereas with Yvette I waited
patiently until she was ready because I knew that her
virginity was something special to her and I had the
patience of Job because it was always there and readily
available there was no doubt that when the semester was
over the first place Tina and I would end up would be in
bed. That was an absolute given. We flirted with the idea
of sex on the phone and when the semester ended on that
fateful day we met at her house in Brooklyn and ordered
out for Chinese. We were both cool though and played
off our wanting each other. An asthmatic she'd been to
see her doctor earlier that day but he refused to see her
without an appointment. So when I arrived we hugged
before she let me know that we needed to go to St. Mary's
Hospital so she could receive treatment for her asthma.
Arriving there I was appalled at the way people were
treated in the emergency room. A man with a gunshot
wound to the abdomen was left sitting idly and people
were running, screaming and cursing trying to get help
for their loved ones. There was a hospital strike at the
time and when Tina was finally called a tall brother
escorted her to a room while I stayed in the lobby.
Minutes later she came out upset to no end and explained
to me that she had undergone this procedure many a time
and this was the first time she'd ever been asked to*

undress to receive oxygen. Not knowing the procedure I sat there and listened while she went round after round with the hospital worker. She then told him that she would disrobe if I were allowed to sit in the room. As I had never seen her naked I was a little leery but had to go along with what my woman said. But the hospital worker wasn't having it and so she refused treatment and we walked home. Now it's a funny thing about New York. It's a land of opportunity. And walking back to Tina's house with my gold chains on swinging freely and my body language stating that I'm the man we were met with a group of young thugs hanging out trying to make a name for themselves. As soon as Tina and I walked past they started spewing expletives with the hopes of starting something so they could jump and rob us but Tina who had obviously been through similar situations before simply grabbed me by the hand and put a finger to my mouth to hush me and led me down the street. We arrived at her house and descended to the basement level where she and her daughter shared a room and sat down on the edge of the bed. The room wasn't much bigger than the twin sized bed and again I wondered how people were subjected to live under such conditions. Next to the bedroom was a rather large kitchen that was shared by the other tenants although by this time of night I never saw any.

Tina and I got comfortable and before I knew both she and I had undressed or undressed each other and our bodies intertwined so quickly and gracefully it would have been hard to tell either of us that this wasn't a match made in heaven. From the start it was passionate and after a time I rolled over gasping for breath and drenched in sweat, a broad smile etched across my face. Tina had been everything I envisioned her being and more and as I turned to hold her in my arms I noticed she was gasping for air as well but was having a hard time catching her breath. As I attempted to take her in my arms she smiled before sitting straight up and telling me to go into the kitchen and get her pills and some water out of the refrigerator. I promptly did so, giving them to her before returning to the kitchen to get her a glass of water. When I returned with her water I noticed that she'd spilled her pills everywhere and I began to worry. But there was little time for that as she instructed me to go across the street and call an ambulance. I dressed quickly and headed up the stairs, crossed the street and placed the call. I then headed back downstairs and helped her to get dressed. Her breathing was more labored now and I started to worry. It didn't take me long to get her dressed and upstairs and no sooner than I opened the door and led her out than the ambulance arrived and I was never so relieved in all my life.

The two Black EMS workers obviously accustomed to such crisis as these were cool and reserved and I immediately calmed down now that I knew she was in the hands of two capable professionals. They asked me what was wrong and I admitted that I had no idea but that I believed she was having an asthma attack and then I recounted the events that preceded my calling them. I then noticed that the other EMS worker was getting a large oxygen tank out of the ambulance and I immediately felt better but then there was a large hullabaloo about something or another and it became immediately clear that something wasn't right. When I walked to the front gate to inquire as to what the problem was I was told that they had the oxygen tank but they had locked the keys in the ambulance and the hose that attached to the tank and piece that fit over her nose and mouth as well. Again panic set in although they remained calm informing me that another ambulance was on its way. They insisted that I keep Tina active and told me to walk with her. I did this talking to her as calmly as

I could and walking her to the front gate and then back to the stoop. I prayed for the ambulance to come, as Tina was growing tired of the charade.

When no ambulance appeared after several minutes and tired of walking and trying to breathe Tina asked me to sit down at which time I did. She sat on my lap, putting both hands around my neck and said little, still breathing rather laboriously while the two EMS workers worked a hanger as best they could all to no avail. And then as if a Godsend another ambulance turned the corner and pulled right behind the other. I could have jumped for joy except that I felt a warm, wet feeling on my leg.

Glancing down I noticed the spot growing larger and spreading in diameter and then I heard a gnawing gnashing sound like I'd never heard before. It was Tina grinding her Tina together and I could hear them cracking, breaking and I screamed at the same time her head fell over on my shoulder and her eyes rolled back into her head. The EMS workers grabbed her and put her in the second ambulance and did their best to resuscitate her but she was gone.

When they'd finished pumping oxygen into her I hardly recognized her. She was bloated. After close to a half an hour of repeating the same procedure over and over again they pronounced her dead at five o seven that morning.

To say I was devastated is an understatement. I had nowhere to go and I couldn't understand why God would take someone so young and so beautiful. We'd just met. It was our first date. It was only the beginning and we had so far to go and so much to do yet.

I rode the subway for hours that morning. I rode from one end of the line to the other tears streaming down my face as rush hour commuters came and went oblivious to my pain.

After hours of trying to figure out what just happened I walked to the Path Station in The World Trade Center to

*start my last leg home. I don't know if I looked homeless,
pitiful or simply like a mark but a group of young thugs
stood on the platform a few feet away sizing me up. The
odds were not in my favor but it mattered little. I guess if
I'd been in my right mind it may have mattered but in the
state of mind I was in I didn't care how many there were.
The only thing I knew that one misstep and someone was
going to hit the third rail with me. Luckily nothing kicked
off. I guess they saw that I was crazier than they were
and decided against waging war.
I finally reached home about an hour later and knocked
on the door. My dad who had long ago grown
accustomed to me walking in at seven or eight o'clock in
the morning immediately knew there was something
wrong. And before he could ask I burst out with the fact
that Tina was dead and burst out crying. My dad was
nothing new to tragedy and had seen more than a handful
of his students die but despite his calmness I knew that he
had a certain affinity to Tina as well and had even taken
care of her two year old daughter Nicole on separate
weekends. Still, he remained my rock and took me in his
arms and held me until I could cry no more. My mother
felt my pain as well and cried with me. We sat down at the
kitchen table and went over the previous night. I had
little to say and after purging myself of all grief all I
wanted to know was why. When they couldn't answer
except to tell me that it was all in God's plan I retired to
my apartment downstairs where I holed up for the next
month or so venturing out only to go to the liquor store
walking the two blocks to Irvington where I'd purchase a
bottle of Jack Daniels. I'd then come home and sit at the
side entrance of the house with a wool hat and overcoat
on in July and rock back and forth. I don't know how
many fifths of Jack Daniels I drank but looking back I
would've been better off buying stock in the company.*

I cursed the New York hospital center, EMS workers worldwide, poverty, Nicole's deadbeat father who wouldn't give me custody and who wanted to know not only who I was but blamed me for giving her too many pills. But most of all I cursed God. I couldn't understand why he would take someone so young with so much potential, with so much to look forward to, in the prime of her life. I just didn't understand and it was so important that I understood.

My parents seeing that I wasn't coming around or dealing with my grief in a timely fashion put together a trip to Jamaica. They called it a graduation gift but I knew it was Black folks version of a shrink and grief therapy. Yvette was the only person I talked to these days. She'd moved to Connecticut with her sister and although we weren't as close as we'd been in Pennsylvania we were still close. I believed she fashioned me as her boyfriend and though we were close she never really pushed up or put demands on me like most of the women I knew. She seemed happy with the time we had together and although she wanted more time she never demanded it. She took the time we had and made the most of it. I had to be careful though. If I didn't or couldn't see her in a couple of weeks she would wear my ass out when we did meet. I knew I loved her and I guess that's what frightened me most about her. The other thing that frightened me about her was the fact that my mother who never liked any woman I brought home absolutely loved her and I knew if she had come to my mother as Dana had come with the fact that she was pregnant Claudia would have been renting the tux and getting Ms. Johnson to do the flower arrangements.

I never could quite pinpoint her allure, (and still haven't but that's another story we'll address at a later time), but she scared the hell out of me. It was funny but my last semester at school all I wanted to do was get back to New

*York to meet some sophisticated fly sisters and I certainly
did but it was this little Chartiers City chick upset my
whole world. I tried. I swear I did try and keep my
distance but I found myself more and more in her
company. She had an agenda all her own and I'm not
sure if it was to keep me supremely happy at all times or
to kill me. The jury was out then and is still out. I have to
admit she did make me happy but she had a new found
love and I'd wake up in the morning with her riding me
slowly sensuously and I'd go to bed with her riding bronc
screaming and hollering and pulling in the reins as she
came. I dealt with it and though I loved sex she rapidly
closed the gap taking me from novice to and old weather
beaten old geezer when it came to sex. There were times
thanks to Yvette that I even disliked it at times. But
following Tina's death I didn't have an appetite for
Yvette, sex or anything else.*

*So my parents packed my bags and flew my sister and me
to Montego Bay. Getting off the plane I wondered if all
my days of drug usage had finally caught up with me and
was beginning to show as we departed the airport and two
or three Rasta's approached me and asked if I wanted
some good good ses or some coke. I was more shocked
than embarrassed and wondered why with all the people
at the airport they would single me out. Checking into the
Holiday Inn in Montego Bay I was still wondering why I
had been picked out from everyone else. When after
much thought it still eluded me I placed my luggage in the
room with my parents. Now if you know Claudia at all
you pretty much know that she could travel the world over
but if she could save a penny by taking a greasy bag of
sandwiches or stuff twelve people in a hotel room then
she would and so here we were thousands of miles from
Jersey on a trip that cost I don't know how many
thousands all stuffed in one tiny hotel room. I didn't
mind much as I had no mind to stay in the room anyway.*

I was intent on knowing all there was about Bob Marley's birthplace and I only had a few days to find out everything there was to know.

I began my investigation with the outdoor bar where I ordered a double jack. Feeling no pain I wandered around the hotel and met a young man and an older woman about eighty who ran a record store within the hotel. They were both so open and friendly that I couldn't help but fall for them immediately. In the days that followed I spent more time with these two than I did with anyone else on the island. They were as curious as to what was happening in the states as I was about what was happening in Jamaica. They introduced me to artists I'd never heard of and although they acknowledged Bob Marley as one of the greats they nevertheless made it clear that although he was a commercial success worldwide he was not the man that Jamaicans listened to when they were sitting around with their sweethearts, lovers, and wives.

What they listened to when they were home with that special someone was Gregory Isaacs, and Frankie Paul. When it was time for clubbing it was Charlie Chaplin and Yellowman. I received and education in Reggae music and was never more grateful. I can't remember the young man's name now but he and I got along splendidly and I bought every album that he and the old woman recommended. We talked about the Rastafari's and the old woman gave me an education on the politics that governed Jamaica on Manley, (a proponent of poor people), and Seaga who could have cared less and was backed by the CIA and their interests in Jamaica. They not only told me of the places to go but also took me to insure that I see the real Jamaica.

I went up into the woods and went to shanties where I was treated like a long lost brother coming home. I had a few dollars but they wouldn't accept my money and fed me red snapper, and sweet, sweet, cassava and Red Stripe after Red Stripe. The food was grilled on large barrels and was nothing short of delicious. I wanted to take my parents but my mother had so planned according to what the travel agent told her were the best tours that it left little time for anything else. She knew she couldn't make too many decisions for me so I was basically left to do what I wanted to do. Valerie met Desmond not long after I did and he fell in love with her. After a few days I was convinced that he was going to be my brother-in-law. Val was somewhere around sixteen or seventeen and though we were as close as a brother and sister could be our age difference didn't allow us to swim in the same circles. She was clubbing hard at the time, rap and dance music was hitting, and there was a club directly across the street from the hotel. Desmond took Val and from what I understand she was in the dj's booth half the night. I don't know but that's what I was told. In the meantime, I met a cute little girl a couple of years younger than I. She had long Bo Derek like braids and a shape to die for. I don't know what the attraction was but her name was Val and she was also from New York and seemed to be enamored by me. She was young, too young to buy drinks at the hotel bar. I guess she was nineteen or twenty or something like that but she was ready for anything and everything. We sat in the hotel lobby and talked bout New York, and how much it differed from Jamaica and we both had to admit that the people here were, the very definition of abject poverty but where we had a house with a two car garage these people's quality of life was so much richer than ours. Where we were rich in material things they were rich in spirit. It was so noticeable in so many aspects of their lives that after a day or two I was already considering and looking into relocating and seeking a teaching position here. My parents weren't happy about the idea but I really embraced the idea.

Looking into it I found the need for teachers wasn't considered a high priority and my hope were eventually dashed. In the meantime, this lil' breezy from New York decided to continue to tag along and made me her confidante, tour guide, and whatever else she needed to make my stay in Jamaica miserable. I eventually introduced her to my parents who were glad to see I was once again in the mix. My sister Valerie who was moving a mile a minute and discovering Jamaica with the help of Desmond and a couple of other Jamaican guys who found her irresistible had already met Val from New York. Her only message to me was to be careful. My sister knew me and knew that I wasn't all that interested and I'm surprised she didn't advise her to run like hell or that her brother was no good and she was only going to get her feelings hurt. Val told many a prospective suitor this in her quest to protect women from my advances. In the meantime my parents were still doing the traditional tour thing and I really believed they loved Jamaica as much as we were but I'm quite sure they would have loved it even more if they had their children accompany them on their various jaunts. And so I talked to Val and convinced her that we owed Claudia and Frank an outing of their choice and we would tag along and put our own pleasure to the side for a day and join them. Claudia was elated to hear this and I must admit that I looked forward to joining them on the trip to Negril where we ate at a fairly nice restaurant; nothing like the shanties I was used to frequenting. After that we returned to the hotel and I made a quick run to speak to speak to all my peeps I hadn't seen and spent the last couple of hours on the beach sitting next to my lil breeazy from New York while she ordered Pina Colada after Pina Colada from some rasta waiter who worked nights and did whatever she asked despite her being underage. I guess he had ulterior motives but I knew that she had

145

ulterior motives as well and kept her focus on me. In the meantime, I kept my focus on the trip my mother had planned and took a rain check on her suggestion that I come up to her suite at the hotel and joined my family tipsy as hell. My mother arranged a trip up the river, (that's all I know about it but anytime you bring the trip up to anyone who's been to Jamaica they all know what you're referring to. Anyway she'd arranged for us to go up the river on this our third or fourth night there. I went outside to get some air and was out there when my boy Desmond passed by and blew some smoke with me. When I asked what it was he simply told me it was nothing special just a little sticky icky icky. I blew it and was ready. We drove to the bank of some river we're scores of people were lined up to board these narrow canoes. The smell of ganja was everywhere and I inhaled deeply. Desmond had given me a couple of spliffs and I brought them. I was going to spark one up somewhere as soon as I had a chance to ditch the fam but as soon as I got on the little canoe with the two Rasta's paddling up the river that shit hit me. I'd been smoking close to ten or twelve years and I'd never felt anything like this. I'd also been rather liberal when it came to marijuana. I never felt that marijuana was a gateway drug or anything more serious than having a social drink. But I changed my mind after that night. I tried to sit and watch the singers on stage and it felt like I had 3-D glasses on and they were almost sitting in my lap. It was all too much. I got up walked to the outdoor bathrooms for a brief respite and stepped into the stalls and was hit with nothing but smoke and got a contact that made me rush back to the boats where I waited close to two hours for the concert to be over and was on the first canoe out of there and headed back to the hotel room where I put my head under the covers and prayed for sleep or death whichever came first. I've been leery of marijuana ever since.

The next day my sister Valerie decided that she didn't want to go with Claudia and Frank on their daily excursion but mom thought we'd finally turned the corner and was happy to have us rejoin us on her Jamaican tours when Val came up with the idea of her feigning sick and needing me to stay in the hotel room and look after her. I had to admit it was a pretty good ploy and she woke up sneezing and coughing and I according to the scenario volunteered to stay and look after her. Ten minutes after they'd left I went to check to make sure the tour bus gone. When I returned to the hotel room to let Val know the coast was clear I found her fully dress and ready to go. We agreed to meet back at the hotel room periodically since we had no idea what time they were returning. As soon as I left the hotel room I ran into my friend Val looking as good as I'd ever seen her and there was no question about her keeping me to my word as far as her rain check so instead of breakfast we went and grabbed two chaise lounges on the beach and sat and watched as the Rasta's paddled slowly along jumping out every now and then to slice pineapples into slices with large machetes for hungry tourists lounging on the sandy beaches. But instead of us sharing a breakfast of fresh fruits Val picked up where she'd left off the day before ordering doubles of Jack Daniels with Pina Colada chasers. This was fine with me as Jack Daniels was one of my favorites but it was nine o'clock in the morning and by eleven o'clock I was pretty much inebriated. I guess this was her intention and when I told her how Val and I had duped my parents into leaving and we had to meet back at the room periodically she laughed and seemed inclined to do so with me. I didn't mind and we reached the room promptly. Of course, my sister was nowhere to be found and Valerie went about carrying out her plan from the previous night. Sitting on the bed next to me, she turned and kissed me long and deeply. Much as

I didn't want to feel her, know her, fall for her, the alcohol had thoughts of its own and I could feel myself rising to meet her, to feel her, to love her. All thoughts of my sister were now gone and I began to undress her. I could hear her moaning softly and no longer was there any thought of leaving my heart with her or the inconceivability of having another long distance love affair. I already had Yvette in Connecticut and that was difficult enough. And I was here now to get over a death and was still for the most part in the grieving process and really having or being with a woman for any reason wasn't of paramount interest but a naked woman in my presence was very difficult to resist. I began to feel the passion in my loins, my heart and my soul when I heard the key in door and grabbed my clothes and pushed her into the bathroom. My sister came in and tried to leave moments after getting there. I don't know if exactly what she was doing or who she had been hanging out with but I suddenly came to my senses and I knew she was my only hope. I sat her down and pointed to the bathroom door. My sister understood immediately and when Val's little hot ass came out of the bathroom she returned to the bed where she sat as if nothing had happened. It was a waiting game now. This cute young breezy had all intentions of waiting my sister out and my sister had no intention of leaving her brother victim to this breezy whose intentions were to get her ass in trouble. After a while she saw that my sister had no intention on leaving and soon departed. I wasn't totally opposed to sleeping with her but my emotions always became intertwined with loving someone and I didn't need that at this point in my life no matter how cute she was. And it always bothered me when women were more aggressive than I was and refused to let the scenario unfold in its own time. I liked to play the aggressor, liked to pursue and through it all liked the fact that there was a relationship, a bond and some sort of vibe between us. I'd had enough sex that it wasn't nearly as important to me as to why a woman felt compelled to engage and so I sat in the hotel room until I was sober and then headed out again.

My friend Valerie as always was now outside planning her next attempt at a tryst and we sat out in front of the hotel. No more than five minutes had passed when a young Rasta approached us. I had a few dollars left and was intent on buying Yvette and some other folk back home some wooden statues and other souvenirs so when he approached me around buying a gram of coke I politely refused. It still bothered me that they would pick me when trying to sell some drugs but the sound of some blow sounded good to me and she was all for it. Instead of giving him cash though I offered him the gold nugget I wore around my neck he seemed so infatuated with. The coke was good and we walked around in a euphoric frenzy for much of the day picking up a couple of hundred dollars worth of souvenirs in our travels. When I returned to add another few shopping bags to the one's I'd already accumulated I found Val in the bed sneezing and coughing and my parents there as well. They excused me for doing a little shopping and I headed back out. My shopping completed we went to the farthest end of the beach where we found two recliners and leaned back to catch what was left of the day's sunlight. Half an hour later the skies darkened and under the threat of rain, Val got up and went to talk to the waiter who appeared so fond of her and between the two of them they moved the orange cones signifying the end of the hotel property maybe a hundred yards or so closer to the beach so that we had our own little private beach. I saw this but said nothing as she returned with our usual Jack Daniels. That coupled with the cocaine and I was once again reeling under her spell. This time it wouldn't be quite so easy to avoid her advances and she made it

149

plain to me that I was going to give her some and she'd paid her man too much to cordon off the beach to let me say no. She told me how I'd teased her, how she'd wanted me from the beginning and how she wasn't taking any more excuses. I knew there was little to say and the time had come for me to own up to something I'd initially started. I was hoping that someone would wander by or that a boat would pass by and change her mind but there was no boat, no baby sister, no help in sight and she quickly pulled my pants down took the glass of Jack from my hands and began kissing my chest. Every couple of minutes she moved lower. I was dizzy by this time and soon found myself spiraling out of control. By the time she hit my mid-section I was done, finished but she was only getting started. Dropping her bikini bottoms she mounted me and rode me until I'd come not once but twice, screaming loud enough to wake everyone in the hotel and only stopping to revive my tired member so she could mount me again. It was as if she'd never made love or had sex before in her life and then it dawned on me as I looked down at myself and saw myself covered with blood that Val was a virgin and that I was her first. An hour or so later when the coast guard passed she admitted to me that it was the best she'd ever had. And laughing loudly then admitted that it was the only sex she had ever had outside of a kiss here and there. She admitted having relationships but when she refused to go all the way they'd all found a way of breaking up with her. Still, she refused to lay down with just anyone. And until she found a man she felt was her soul mate she had no problem refraining. But this was the way she expected, wanted, had visions of it being. And when we got back to New York we could pick up where we'd left off and eventually get married and have children. I was shocked. It wasn't the fact that she was a virgin. I'd had virgins before. But the fact that she'd planned everything out was what bothered me more than anything else.

She'd tell me that she was pregnant and later on follow that up with setting a date for our marriage. I'd gone through all this before with Dana. And I didn't mind this being her dream or vision for us. I just wish I had been considered and been informed in these decisions since they did include me. She later asked me if I believed in love at first sight to which I answered in my attempts to be man that I didn't exactly know if I believed in love. I could see this hurt her but a woman's funny. They can take the pain and remorse that comes with life and continue as if nothing at all has occurred. They are resilient and as young as Valerie was she had that toughness, that resiliency that took what I said with a grain of salt. She'd made up her minds and her convictions as well. I was to be hers.

Moments later she looked deep into my eyes and said 'take me lover' at which time I did. We made love all night on the beach and awoke in each other's arms. It was our first and last night together and when I awoke she was sobbing softly in my arms. I wondered if the inevitability of our union had finally hit home. I'd given her the marijuana Desmond had given me since she had no fear of taking it back on the plane. We said goodbye and exchanged numbers and addresses before going our separate ways. Looking back I missed that woman almost as much as I've ever missed anyone and I wondered if she were right about us being destined to meet. I only heard from her once after I returned home and that was by way of the mail. She sent me the weed I'd given her save a blunt and I don't believe I heard from her again. As much as I didn't like her little forays into sex and marriage I must admit she had grown on me to a certain degree.

The trip to Jamaica did me a world of good and when I returned I started at Community Elementary School 73X in the Bronx. The school was on a 165th Street; a stones throw from the Grand Concourse and Yankee Stadium. I could actually look out my classroom and see Yankee Stadium. The neighborhood was supposed to be rough but I was young and had no fear and had grown up in a neighborhood just like this one in Queens so the fact that everyone labeled it rough hardly mattered to me. There was a long hill that would make the long walk from the subway to the school excruciating but I loved stopping at the tiny bodega half way up it every morning to catch my breath. Here I'd order New York's breakfast specialty, a buttered roll and a cup of regular coffee and ten or twelve packs of Now & Later's and a bunch of other penny candies for my kids before heading up the hill to the school. The school itself an old dilapidated building that appeared more like an old factory than a school. It was a part of the New York Public School system but when the community decided that their children weren't being educated adequately they took control and voted to have some say in how their children were to be educated and thus it became a community elementary school. After being there no more than a week I could only imagine what the school had been like previously. My kids, who were all Puerto Rican and Black were dirt poor but like the Jamaicans, (who I'd just recently left), were all rich in spirit. Still they wore all the latest gear and fashioned themselves the next great rapper hailing from the city where it al began. I fell in love with them and their city ways and they brought me up to date on all that I'd missed during my college hiatus and I brought them up to date on the keys to survival and making it out of the ghetto of the South Bronx. I loved them and they loved me. And soon it became known that their was a teacher at the school that loved their children and cared about their welfare. I no longer had to worry about leery thugs eyeing me thinking I was 5-0 or sizing me up to rob me. Now when I walked down the hill at three o'clock it was' 'What's up Mr. Brown? How's Hector doing? Let me know if he's giving you any trouble and I'll tear his little ass up when he gets home. You just let me know.' They all had spots out there hustlin', scramblin', sellin' drugs but none of them wanted their younger brothers and sisters out there in the streets and they saw me as the hope and gateway out f the ghetto and gave me the ultimate respect for coming in to a place that had been forgotten and discarded and trying to bring hope to it's offspring. I loved it and loved my children for having such resilience to weather the mean streets of New York.

I can remember when I was growing up in Queens and wanting to be the toughest gangsta on the streets and one day sitting and reading Piri Thomas' Down These Mean Streets and changing my mind about the streets of New York. I followed that up with Claude McKays, Manchild In The Promised Land and was sure that the thug life was not meant for me. It didn't take Nostradamus to figure out the future. All I had to do was read those two books about young brothers just like me who wanted to be street and wanted to be hard and how their exploits led them upstate to jail to know that I for

one liked women too much to have all my rights taken from me and be exiled from all that I truly loved and all I needed was to spend a day, one precious day away from all that I loved and cherished so dearly.

It was this philosophy that I tried in earnest to teach my children that all that glitters is not gold and that the pursuit of wealth and gold is the direct path to Hades. It was my job to teach them that money was the root of all evil but through hard work, much labor and a philosophy of moderation instead of one of excess that they could find some peace and happiness in their lives. This I taught along with the ABC's and I must admit that for the most part this took hold. My students loved me. They loved me because I dressed the same way they did, listened to the same music they did, understood the trials and tribulations of our class which had to be a bit quieter than the other classes in the school simply because of our proximity to the library. They loved me because I understood growing up in New York City ghettoes, and spoke the same language as they did. They loved me because I wasn't the establishment. I was them and in their eyes I was a success. I had made it despite the odds and they knew that if I could make it out of there, then there was hope for them as well. Once I had their love, respect and undying devotion I knew that I could teach them anything. Their parents knew it too and there wasn't a day that didn't go by that there wasn't a parent standing outside my doorway at the end of the day. Some would come just to check on their child. Others would show up because the word had gotten out that I had their child's interest and welfare in the palm of my hand and was killing myself to bring out their full potential. They were there to give me license to spank or reprimand their child as I saw fit because they knew above all else that I loved my children and was not only passionate but sincere in my attempts to make their child all that they could be. My love and attentiveness was, however, not seen the same by all but it at least made me aware of what both parent and child had been going through prior to my arrival. For instance, the school library was next door to my classroom and so my class always had to be quieter than the others simply because of its proximity. But one day we were doing an activity around common and proper nouns and after days of literally pulling my hair out it clicked and I was tickled beyond belief that I had finally gotten through to them. I started tossing candy out for every right answer and shouted and yelled and they

154

followed my lead. It was time for celebration and I let it be known when this tall, stately Jewish woman who just so happened to be the school librarian tapped on my door. I wasn't particularly fond of her but was always cordial. Jews ran the Board of Education in New York and had for years. They had a saying that said when all else fails teach. I had a different outlook on their being in the classroom teaching our children. I sincerely believed one of the main reasons that the educational system in America wasn't and still didn't work emanated from slavery, which ultimately gave rise to the institution of racism. My theory is simple. It simply states that in slavery Whites thought that Blacks being able to read was dangerous. It would give rise to thought and thinking Blacks would question their own subjugation. And inevitably it would give rise to the thought that Blacks were equal. Following slavery and with the inception of segregation Blacks had their own schools where they were taught by other Blacks whose interests were the same as theirs, upward mobility. But when integration came we became jaded and thought that if we had the same books, desks and other resources we would then receive the same education. What in reality happened was White flight. White folks fled the public school systems leaving us with the dregs. White teachers who had little or no interest in our achieving academic parity and who instead of teaching simply warehoused our children with no other interest other than collecting a paycheck. That is not to say that there weren't White teachers who weren't receptive and sought to teach our children but it is in my opinion that the vast majority who I witnessed neither had the wherewithal or the interest to see our little Black boys and girls achieve academically. And my question to you is why would they help our children prosper academically when it would enable us to compete against their own children for employment and financial gain?

In other words, why would those in power and authority opt to even the odds with those they have been subjugating for four hundred years? Would they do it in the name of fairness' sake after four hundred years of considering us second-class citizens?

I truly believed, (and still do), that Whites have no more interest in us succeeding than they did in slavery. And the librarian in the next room let it be known just what she thought of my students when she came over to investigate. 'Look at Victor, Mr. Brown. I really don't see how you do it. Look! Look! Don't they remind you of little monkeys jumping out of their seats? I looked through the window of my classroom for the little monkeys she was referring to and saw nothing but my thirty some odd darling little heart throbs and realized that one of us didn't belong in this setting and I knew it wasn't me because I saw no animals and was right at home here with thirty some odd mini versions of me.

Both my principal and assistant principal were Black and in no time at all they taught me how to overlook these little Jewish princesses that skipped around the hallways acting like they were royalty and the rest of us were the hired help. We all knew that in a few years they'd either be retired or ousted. Most of them were here because of its proximity to Yonkers but it hurt me that they called themselves educators with their closed minds and closed hearts. And when I closed the door to my classroom I opened up a whole new world to children whose lives weren't nearly so wonderful when they hit those mean streets called the South Bronx. But here they could fill the warmth of Mr. Brown's utopia at least for a few hours a day.

There were other fringe benefits to teaching that I hadn't even thought about before I began. The majority of teachers were females, young women in their first or first few years of teaching and the majority were my age making for a plethora of beautiful women each having insatiable qualities of her own. I was seeing Yvette every weekend now and although we had never made a commitment to each other we were for the most part committed. My parents loved her and it scared me but I kept a look out and refused to admit that she had a lock on me. She did but I would have been the last one to acknowledge it. My kids were always taking bets as to whom Mr. Brown would choose and every time I would speak or make eye contact with someone in the hall they would up the wager.

It was damn near Thanksgiving and we still hadn't received textbooks for our classes and my principal grabbed me one day and had a heart-to-heart with me about the New York City Public School System and the politics behind it. He explained how the poorer neighborhoods, (the Black and Puerto Rican neighborhoods), were the last to receive resources and how we were lucky if we received anything at all. I was appalled and went home that evening and shouted my outrage to my father who calmly as ever stated that this wasn't anything unusual and then asked me 'who needs textbooks that are not reflective of our children anyway. They are giving you the freedom to create your own curriculum. Now go and look at the glass as half full instead of half empty and make the best of the situation.' And I did teaching math and science and history and geography all from a Black perspective. When it came to science it was all about George Washington Carver. When it came to history they learned all about slavery and Nat Turner, Frederick Douglass, Crispus Attucks, and John Brown. When it came to music they learned about everyone from Bessie Smith to Run DMC. That's the way I taught them and they learned. They learned with all the eagerness and gusto of a people proud to know about themselves.

My Aunt Lo wrote her doctorate dissertation on how children relate better and how they tested better when they were represented or better yet were able to see themselves or their likeness in basal readers and I believed this and put my theory into effect in my classroom. I must say from all reports that I must concur.

During this time I spent almost every weekend with Yvette in Connecticut. We were like young lovers and would go for walks hand-in-hand on the Green in downtown New Haven just blocks from Yale . We would stop at quaint little shops here and there and I knew I was falling deeper in love with her than I already was no matter how hard I tried not to. She'd prepare dinner for me and give me hot oil massages but not once did she ever ask me for any sort of commitment. I don't know if she purposely didn't ask because she didn't want me to the extent that she wanted to be committed to me or anyone. Not long after that I asked her to marry me. When she declined I was devastated. She gave me some excuse that her father would be devastated if she made that sort of commitment so early in her life. She stated that she had yet to go to college and experience things that she wasn't quite sure she could make me happy not bringing anything to the table. She asked to wait until she was fully mature and have the capabilities to add to that sort of commitment while ensuring me that I would later resent her becoming a liability to my dreams and aspirations. I'm not sure if I truly bought into Yvette's reasoning but I did recognize at that moment I needed a change and if I didn't do something quick I would become suffocated waiting on her. I have to admit though, I never believed and still don't believe to this day that her decision was meant to hurt me. I had to remind myself that Yvette was young and truly believed that her refusal wouldn't change anything and everything would continue as it has been. But I was devastated and decided that if there was no future with her then there was no reason to put my heart and soul into something and someone not going anywhere. I was tired and truly believed that absence makes the heart grow fonder and after no more than a couple of weeks I half expected her to come running back to me begging me to marry her.

That's what I thought. What happened though was altogether different from what I thought would happen. Yvette called but wasn't insistent on my seeing her and I wondered just how much she had invested in our relationship. There was no doubt that I loved her but I wondered if my emotional ties were mine and mine alone since she never professed her love for me. I guess I had always assumed. But once she was gone I knew just how much she meant to me. Still, I was firm in my resolve and the next few weeks tested my resolve. I don't know how many times I went to pick up the phone to call her but refrained. I don't know how many times my mother told me from the time I was sixteen that it was okay to fly solo and getting to know who I was as a person. And so I refrained. Sure, I was hurt that the only woman I had ever asked to marry me turned me down but I took her rejection as a positive motivator to better myself as a person and move on. Besides I had my career and that was more than enough to occupy any idle time I may have had.

Sitting in the teacher's lounge one-day daydreaming and second guessing myself around Yvette as usual I thought about the day she picked me up. I'd bought her roses and everyone at the school was curious as to who they were for since everyone in school wanted to know who Mr. Brown was dating since they had never seen me with a woman and by this time were all wagering to see who the lucky girl was. She showed up at three o'clock sharp in a

*full-length fur, fishnet stockings and heels. Most of my
students were in shock and after introducing her around
the office and seeing their faces I knew that she'd passed
muster. I was never so proud or so happy to say that this
was my woman.*

*Once in the car, she gave me another shock. She had
nothing on underneath. And though I had seen her nude
numerous times this thought reverberates in my mind
constantly.*

*In the two years that I'd known her she never made me
more proud than on that day. And now she was gone. I
kept telling myself that my moving on was all just another
stage in my life but damn it was painful. My best buddy
was gone. My thoughts were broken by Roy, one of my
teacher's aides who came in and sat with me. Like me
Roy was a basketball fanatic and where I would follow
the Knicks religiously Roy claimed to have played with
everyone from Nate "Tiny" Archibald to the All
American, Chris Mullin when he was at St. John's. We
loved to talk basketball but on this day it was just chit
chat. It was Thursday and Roy was curious to know what
I was doing for the weekend. I was in the midst of
making plans to go up to Syracuse for the weekend to see
Harriet Tubman's house and let him know.*

*My plan was simply to ride up there tour her home, which
was now a museum. My reason for going was two-fold. I
wanted to enrich my awareness when it came to my
heritage and I didn't want to spend another pining over
Yvette. What I needed was to be active and take my
mother's advice and get to know who I was and better
myself. But I guess that wasn't to be and instead of me
taking the train by myself as I first thought Roy invited
himself. Later that evening he told me that his wife would
like to accompany us and if I didn't have any objections
he'd drive. Talk about upset and that evening I told my
dad who just smiled and told me to tell him that I was*

160

looking at this time to do a little soul searching and that there were no hard feelings but I needed this time to be alone. I thought I had done just that but he'd ignored my pleas or privacy and not only invited himself but his wife as well making me the third wheel on a trip I had arranged. Still heated I made up my mind to go into school and simply tell him that I wasn't going. But instead it was he who approached me to tell me that he'd arranged for his sister-in-law to go so I wouldn't feel like a third wheel.

What had started as me going to Harriet Tubman's house to spend some quality time alone had turned into the Roy Stewart Family Reunion. I was now determined that I wasn't going. I didn't like the idea of him going to begin with, and then the addition of his wife made me the third wheel on a trip I arranged and now I was not only going with his wife but was set up on a blind date with his sister-in-law. If there was one thing I didn't do it was blind dates. I went home that night and told my father what had transpired and he laughed. 'So what are you going to do/' he asked. 'I'm not going.' I answered. And when the phone rang I simply picked up the phone and told Roy that I wasn't going. He talked for close to an hour trying to convince that I needed to go all to no avail. And when I hung up the phone I sat there smugly. Not only had I told him that I wasn't going but I had told him about his egotistical self and how he had ruined my weekend. He apologized and I put my head down on my pillow and went to sleep. An hour or so later, I heard my mother calling me to tell me I had company coming down. I opened the door up and who stood there but Roy. 'Ready to go?' I let him no in no uncertain terms that he'd wasted his time driving from the Bronx over to Jersey. I took him up to meet mom and dad and they seemed to like Roy and when he finished crying about how he had arranged for his wife and sister-in-law to go along for the ride I thought they were going to shed a tear. And when they finished teaming up on me I dropped my head and put my tail between my legs and climbed into Roy's car. An hour and a half later I wound up in Rosedale, Queens not far from where I grew up and met Cheryl Biggs. She was a cute girl in her mid-twenties with a cute ass and a sharp tongue. She was cordial after our introduction and offered us blackberry wine. We blew some smoke and we were off to pick up his wife in the Bronx. By this time, I was feeling no pain and jumped into the back seat and started a conversation with Cheryl. I found out she sniffed a little and asked Roy if he knew anywhere we could find a gram of blow so we'd have something to occupy our time on the drive up to Syracuse. Of course, he could, according to him he knew everyone from the mayor to Deniro and they all owed him something. Stopping in a part of the South Bronx that made Fort Apache look like the Hamptons we went up into one of the high-rises that still had a few windows left only to find the elevator broken. His cousin, of course, lived on the twentieth floor. Roy who substituted as the gym coach at school and moonlighted as a referee on the weekends was in great shape and likened the trek up twenty flights of stairs no more than his morning jog whereas I, on the other hand, saw this as God's way of punishing me for the ill I had done. We entered the apartment and was shocked to see them using ball peen hammers to crush up what appeared to be a kilo of cocaine into powder. Roy shook hands all around before introducing me. He then told his cousin what I wanted and his cousin simply picked up a rather large rock off the table, dropped it into a sock, which he then tied a knot into and tossed my way. 'There's a hammer on the table over there. You can crush it up there if you want to,' he said pointing to the table and looking at me. I thanked him and then grabbed a chair, and sat down and split the rock in half before crushing it into powder. We headed back to the car and I must admit that when we finally reached street level, (three or four days later), there was a rather large contingent of young men outside the front door. I have to admit that I was a bit intimidated. They were hard-core and it was obvious they were transacting business. We had obviously walked into the middle of their business but with no other way out I said excuse me and tried to make my way through when one of them bumped me. I tried to ignore him but he wasn't interested in me. 'What's up cuz', he said smiling and embracing Roy warmly. I breathed a deep sigh and walked to the car where Cheryl and Laurie were chatting and laughing at something or another. I hoped I wasn't the butt of their joke but slid in the back seat and opened my packages. I had at least three grams and it was good blow. It burned slightly and I felt it almost immediately. The shit was damn near pure and I passed the half-gram or so I had crushed into powder to Cheryl who sniffed daintily. She had what I liked to call 'coke etiquette' and I liked the fact that she wasn't greedy. The coke working, the conversation picked up and after awhile we both came to the conclusion that Roy was an ass for having thrown us together in such an uncomfortable situation. What was supposed to be a short ride turned out to be an eight-hour drive. When we arrived it was not only dark, but a blizzard was stirring and the house closed. Neither Cheryl nor I had prepared for anything more than a short jaunt and the money I'd brought I spent on the cocaine so when Roy suggested that the weather was too bad to drive in we both cursed him out. He assured us that there was nothing to worry about and that he would put us up for the night. The only thing wrong with that was that he put us in the same room. We were comfortable with each other but not so comfortable that we were ready to shack up together when we'd just met several hours ago. We sat there uncomfortable but cursed Roy out when we were lacking conversation. When it was time to go to sleep Cheryl made it clear that if I touched her she would cut my stuff off. I knew she was joking and I liked her. I liked the fact that she was cute but hard as nails—not like most women I knew. I knew that she was what the young boys called a ride or die bitch and at twenty-eight that thrilled the hell out of me. We went to sleep after an hour or so and never touched each other although we spent the entire night against our will locked up in the same hotel room.

No one was particularly in good spirits the following morning. It had stopped snowing, there were just flurries now and we piled in clean but the same clothes so we were feeling a bit grimy and not real talkative. We made it a point to drive by Harriet Tubman's house and stopped. Her home happened to be nothing but a small, one room cottage and I must admit that I was disappointed. I'd expected so much more. It wasn't open to the public and from what I could gather from peeking in the windows, it was rather sparsely furnished. I left there somewhat disappointed and wondered how she could have been in every textbook from first grade to eighth and yet this was all we could do as a country to commemorate what she meant to us as a nation.

I then thought that with all the slaves she led to freedom that if each had given her just a few pennies for her efforts how she could have lived so much better than she had. It was disturbing and these thoughts clouded my mind on the ride home. There was little else to distract me as everyone was tired and the only redeeming factor was that Cheryl gave me her phone number as I departed. The next day was Monday and after school was over I went home and gave her a call. We decided to get together the following day at Commuters Café in the World Trade Center and when we met we hugged and she passed me a twenty of sniff under the table as we drank drink after drink. It was at this time that I found out that she dated but wasn't serious about anyone. And she looked a whole lot better than she had the past weekend. She was still feisty and I liked that and decided given the opportunity I'd date her. She was street and I liked that as well. I was back in New York but always felt like I was always on the fringes. I was there but not apart of the city and I wanted to be home and apart of it more than anything else in the world. Cheryl was my connection with the city. She would make me feel one with the city once again. We spent every day for the rest of the week at the Commuter's Café, sniffing, drinking and learning each other. At night we'd spend hours continuing our date by way of phone. Of course I cracked and one evening I just took it upon myself to go home with her. We made love that day, the next and for several days never leaving the bedroom or the house except to go the bathroom. When we finally left it was to go home to Jersey and say hello the family. I hadn't bothered to let them know where I was going or even call them to let them know I was all right and neither had Cheryl and both families were in panic mode when we finally turned up. Cheryl's brother, a New York City Transit Officer had actually broken into the apartment in Queens and felt the toothbrushes to see if they were wet to see if she had been abducted and killed. And both families, thanks to Roy had been in contact and were worried to death. We thought we were in love and didn't take anything seriously and didn't know the meaning of danger so there worries to us were unfounded. My parents met Cheryl and my dad was cordial as usual. You had to read him to know how he felt about anyone unless he was just taken over by an individual. (In Y'vette's case there was no doubt he was feeling her), but in Cheryl's case, the jury was still out. Mom, however, liked her wit and feistiness.

165

*I brought every woman that I intended to have a
relationship with before them because I knew that they
had my best interest at heart and that they could see
things that I wasn't wise enough or mature enough to see.
But with Claudia's approval I decided to move in with
Cheryl and called Yvette who was still my best friend and
asked her to give me a ride over to Queens. It was a
ballsy move I know and I'm not sure she wasn't cognizant
of what was transpiring but she gave me a ride
nonetheless. I wasn't exactly sure about her love but she
was always there for me during this time. She still hadn't
agreed to marry me and so I pushed on. I moved in with
Cheryl and it wasn't long before I was back in touch with
Gary "G". He'd dropped out of school and was back
home living with his father not far from where I now lived
in Queens. I was still teaching but the school year was
coming to a close. I took two of my student s, (perhaps
my brightest and worst behaved), home with me and then
up to Yankee Stadium to see the Yankees play. I loved all
my kids but I think I loved Victor more than the rest. He
reminded me so much of myself. He was probably the
brightest of my students but it was Victor, my favorite and
my brightest that was the one and only of my students to
get left back. How that hurt me. I cried real tears, sad
tears for hours before sharing my grief with my dad who
consoled me telling me that in his many years of teaching
that sometimes happens. And then he made the comment
that was by far the reason for me still having some sense
of sanity today. He said simply that you can't save them
all. To anyone else that would have been an adequate
summation but I still couldn't understand why I, (the
chosen one), couldn't save them all. The commuting and
the New York lifestyle was killing me and Cheryl,
although a homebody for the most part wasn't helping
much either. That coupled with my principal, Mr. Cooper
telling me that I was coming back to teach third grade the*

*following school year with a class of forty-five was not I
wanted to hear at that point in my life. I decided to search
for something a little more convenient, (it still took me
close to two hours to get to work), and something a little
less stressful. I chose the welfare department and ended
up as a caseworker for the Bureau of Child Support.
I still kept pretty close contact with Claudia and Frank,
checking in with her everyday to see who I should have
been fighting or what injustice ha been enacted that I ha
failed to see.. I'm not sure I was ever in love with Cheryl
but I was certainly infatuated and it was easy at my age to
get the two confused. I loved the fact that I was back in
the throes of New York City life. I loved the culture, the
music, the language, the fashion that was distinctly New
York. I think this in itself would have been enough for
me but there was so much going on and I ha been away
for so long that I was marching at the quick-step just to
catch up. I was embracing everything that came my way
and even things like the vans driven by Jamaicans that
were quickly taking the place of city buses.
My neighbor Nigel drove one of these vans and I believe
he was one of the first people I met, (and probably the
worst person I could have met), upon moving to Queens.
We spoke in passing and after a couple of weeks he
started showing up at our front door asking if he could
borrow some alcohol. Well, alcohol was basically pennies
a bottle so we usually gave him the bottle and then just
added it to our next weeks shopping list. But I was so
naive as to what was going on that after his third or
fourth visit I commented to Cheryl that they must have an
awful lot of mosquitoes. Cheryl explained to me that they
used alcohol to smoke crack and I was shocked. I asked
her if she had ever smoked crack asked her what it did to
you and she told me that it didn't do anything to you other
than close your throat up but explained to me that it was
cool. When I asked Nigel he told me to stop by and he'd*

turn me on. I walked over and took one hit and fell back into the door. 'Damn' I said a big grin etched on my face. I had never felt anything like that and asked for another hit. No one else looked or seemed quite as happy as I seemed and although I didn't understand at the time I refused to let them discourage my newfound joy. I had a few dollars in the house and ran home to get it. I guess I spent a hundred and fifty dollars before going home. The only reason I left was because I didn't want to wear out my welcome. I had no idea how this day would change my life for the next twenty years. I went home and told Cheryl of my experiences and she didn't seem too enthused, (she never seemed too enthused over anything), one-way or another. Still, when I asked her if it was all right that Nigel and his girlfriend, Lecia come over and get high she agreed. Later that night they both came over and I put on a little music as if we were having dinner guests. Gary joined us a little while after they arrived and it soon became apparent that not only were we the hosts but the financiers as well. It was payday and I had a few hundred on me after paying bills and the crack took all of that. It was all new to me and neither Cheryl nor Gary told me the pitfalls of this new poison. I don't really think they knew. I felt the same euphoria I'd felt earlier in the day but I began to see the game for what it was. No one was really groovin' to the music and they all seemed like they were on a mission to find the Holy Grail. They were so intent on getting high; on getting that next blast that they forgot each other. I saw them drooling, all bodily functions gone, saw them attempt to steal from each other in plain sight and knew that this drug was like no other. There was little or no interaction between the people and after awhile I gave up trying to make conversation. The only thing everyone seemed to want was another hit and that required money. Neither Lecia or Nigel had any money. Gary had a few dollars but the brunt of it fell on

Cheryl who had a couple of thousand saved up for her vacation which was coming up in about a week. We'd planned on going away but she was caught up in the frenzy of this new shit and was dropping hundreds and beeping Ayon the dope man like there was no tomorrow. Minutes later he'd show up with another gram or two and everyone was once again sitting around waiting for the pipe to be passed. This went on for hour. I watched Nigel and Gary both of whom eyes were glued to the floor looking searching for anything that resembled a piece of crack even though there was crack on the table in front of them. It was so surreal. They were searching the floor for crumbs, Nigel was drooling and seemed unable to control it, Lecia was administering tiny portions of crack as if she'd bought it and Cheryl was spending like she was Fort Knox. The only two people that still seemed to be cognizant of what was going on appeared to be Cheryl and me. And although I enjoyed the high, after awhile it didn't appear that I could get any higher and I knew Cheryl was out of control and so I called an end to the party. Lecia who was still somewhat lucid and who had pocketed a gram was the first to leave, followed by Gary. But Nigel acted as if I hadn't said anything and when I asked Cheryl to go into the bedroom to let Nigel know that his financier had gone to bed and there was no more money he refused to leave. He got up as if to head to the bedroom and ask Cheryl for some money or to buy some more dope when I told him if he took another step in that direction that I'd fuck him up. He must've understood. However, not comprehending, his mind locked in on getting higher, he sat back down. Again I told him to leave, threatening him with no remorse when Cheryl came out of the bedroom and stated in no uncertain terms that it was her house and that no one had to leave. If I had been in my right mind I shouldn't haven't asked Nigel to leave. I should have left right then and there. I

169

argued with Cheryl but the crack had her and I'm not
sure if she understood that Nigel and Lecia were bottom
feeders feeding off her like leaches, no more concerned
with her rent, or bills than a man on the moon. But that
shit was good and for whatever reason she came to his
defense. I still put him out and spent the rest of the night
arguing with Cheryl who by this time had spent close to
fifteen hundred but probably hadn't seen more than three
or four hundred dollars of her investment and sat here
now arguing with me over holding on to the rest of it. I
figured she'd come to her senses tomorrow and so I did
my best to lie down and go to sleep when I heard the door
open and then a loud bang. Cheryl had allowed Nigel
back in and he and his already broken arm had tried
using the bathroom and had somehow slipped and fallen
in the tub. I knew there was no use in trying to talk sense
to anyone of them at this point and so I simply helped him
to his feet and once again to the front door. I enjoyed the
high but I'd been getting high off of one thing or another
since I was twelve or thirteen and in that entire time I had
yet to be hooked on anything. It just wasn't in my
makeup to succumb to a substance, any substance. My
attention span was fleeting and as soon as I got
accustomed to any one thing it was usually time to move
on to something else. But this crack thing was something
altogether different. I went to sleep and had crack dreams
where I'd wake up and there would be a big cloud of
smoke filling the pipe and it would disappear just as I was
about to inhale. Gary told me he experienced the same
thing and I felt good that I wasn't the only one but this
didn't put my mind at ease. It only scared me how a
substance could play havoc with my psyche long after I'd
finished and laid it to rest. Still, there wasn't anything
out there that had ever beaten me and so I continued to
smoke. Cheryl and I made about sixty thousand a year

had no real bills to speak of so smoking a little crack never really put a burden on us.

I loved my job as a caseworker for the Bureau of Child Support. My supervisor, a Black woman by the name of Janet Murell had about ten of us under her and was stately and elegant and loved her some Bert and this only made the hour or so journey to downtown Brooklyn each day that more bearable. She was dark-skinned, about five foot eight with a big wide flat nose, and a graduate of a historically Black college and an A.K.A. And like most of the A.K.A.'s I knew she carried herself with both pride and elegance. She was the epitome of what a Black woman should be in my eyes that I both loved and respected. Late at night I would fantasize about her but during the day it was business as usual. I spent most of my days interviewing clients who were welfare recipients. Being on welfare meant that they had to at least aid in trying to locate the absent parent, (usually the father), so I could refer him to court to help alleviate the state's payment of child support. I enjoyed this immensely as ninety-nine per cent of my clients were women although I always but always kept a professional demeanor and never hit on any of them. I didn't have to. I was in downtown Brooklyn where women were like bees and I presented myself like honey to entice them. I was making a good salary had little or no expenses so I spent a good portion of me salary on clothes. My boy, Jerome who started the same time as I did and was basically a chick magnet introduced me to Brooks Brothers and enlightened me as far as being professionally attired. I went from Adidas to penny loafers and from jeans to poplin suits. On warm days we stood out in front of New York Community College and tried our different approaches to get a young women's attention. When winter came we'd go down into the subways and rate women and see who could get the most phone numbers. I

171

*almost never won but held my own. One particular day I
met a woman, (I met several and even dated a few but this
one stood out), named Celeste who was a student at
N.Y.C.C. and we agreed to meet for lunch the next day.
She was cute and she knew she had really gotten
something when she chose me and from the looks of her
chocolate legs and thighs I knew I had stumbled on
something as well. I don't really know what she wanted
from neither me nor me from her aside from hanging out
in each other's company. But after meeting and blowing
some trees we met up with another couple, Ron who I
worked with and his girlfriend. Ron sat in back of me
and though he wasn't much older than I and we were in
the same line of work I didn't talk to him much. For
some reason he was just grimy to me. Anyway, it was
purely coincidental our bumping into the two of them but
they joined us for drinks and asked what we were up to. I
introduced Celeste and she let them know that we had
plans. She was always a lot of fun but she was a young
girl and after I did the introductions and told her that we
were co-workers and the way he slapped me on my back
and I joked with him I guess she thought I liked him.
Anyway, she didn't know the relationship between he and
I and to tell the truth with this being only our third or
fourth date I really didn't know her all that well either.
In fact, all I did know was that she was cute and had a
body that wouldn't quit and was inviting me with every
damn move she made. She looked good, we conversed,
and by the looks of everything we were gonna sex good.
Anyway, Ron was looking for something to do and was
leaning on us to come up with a plan that included he and
his when Celeste made it clear that she was taking me to
the closest hotel and love me down good. I was a little
taken back but was glad to know we were on the same
wavelength. Still, I didn't want or need any tag alongs but
Ron had other plans and told us where we could find a*

*rather cheap hotel in the area. Celeste ignored Ron for
the most part and had little to say to his anorexic looking
girlfriend and I immediately got the impression that she
didn't care for Ron or his lady but still took the
suggestion and after a few more drinks we hailed a cab
and made our way to the motel which was only minutes
from downtown Brooklyn.*

*Once there we checked in and I had to lend Ron a twenty
just to check in. Anyway, we bid Ron a quick goodbye at
the front desk and found our room and settled in.*

*Moments later we were both naked and moaning loudly. I
was dumbfounded by my own good fortune and had to
pinch myself when I saw her nude. It was one of the few
times I wondered if a woman actually looked better with
her clothes off than on. And in bed Celeste was a demon.
By the third go round I was breathing deeply and
wondering if I could hang with this young stallion. She
sexed me, loved me and then massaged every inch of me
before sexing me again. When she finally took a breather
and a smoke she turned to me, smiled and said, 'Can I
keep you?' I had all I could do to nod yes when there was
a knock at the door. Celeste and I both looked at each
other. Hell, who knew we were here? Could it be the
motel management? Had her screams of passion been too
loud? And then it dawned on us that .it was nobody other
than Ron. I had loaned him enough to get a room and he
had a bottle and I suppose some smoke so what else could
he possibly want? 'I was a little perturbed by the
intrusion and was at that moment sorry we hadn't just
told him we were heading home and left him at Happy
Hour. Still, I was cordial and cracked the door.*

*"Whatcha need man?' 'I was talking to my girl and we
was wondering if you two would want to switch. My girl's
wit' it. I was wondering if this nigga had lost his fuckin'
mind but was cool as usual. 'We don't get down like that',
I said not botherin' to ask Celeste and glad I didn't. Still,*

173

she asked me who was at the door and when I told her what Ron had proposed she hit the ceiling. In a way I was glad that we were on the same page but it was sometime before she finished her tirade. I left early enough to grab a cab and go home and change clothes for work. I felt good and liked Celeste a lot. She was bright, had aspirations and a slight Jamaican accent. She had a body to die for and a cute face and she was crazy about me. I was already having my druthers about Cheryl. Some weeks later, when we wanted to get high and had no money she beeped Ayon and went to the door with low cut lingerie on and her breast showing and made some arrangement to get some dope on credit. He gave it to her and I never knew what kind of arrangement had been made but my thoughts of fidelity were all but dashed. I continued to see Celeste and everything was looking up aside from the fact that she was becoming quite expensive. Neither of us had a place of our own so we frequented hotels when ever we got the whim and the notion and after awhile it was like I was paying another rent. She made several proposals but she was in no position to really do anything being a full-time student and all. We'd do go to her house occasionally as her father worked third shift but one day he came home early and made his way upstairs to his daughter's room to wake her up for school and decided it was a good time for a father daughter talk. I was under the bed by this time and every time he'd move I'd feel the weight of him on me and let out a slow deep breath. He was crushing me and that was good because I knew if he found me nude in his daughter's room he would have killed me. That was the last time I went to Celeste's house and not long after that I stopped contacting her. Her father and our not having anywhere to go to be alone were two of the reasons I stopped seeing her. The other and more profound reason was my growing addiction to crack cocaine.

My addiction was growing worse everyday. I went to bed high, had pipe dreams and woke up searching for it. I was now going to work for the sole purpose of acquiring money to get high. Nothing else seemed to matter anymore. I was up til three, four o'clock In the morning every night now, fiending, scheming and searching for ways to acquire money to get high or if I had a few dollars trying to flip it so I could get high. It was more than work and I spent my every waking hour making money only to see it go up in smoke. Work started to be a drag now and all I did was try to save face and avoid letting anyone know that I was on the pipe. It became harder and harder over the next several months and I found myself no longer going to lunch with Jerome but now going with Lisette, a recovering heroin addict. She and I would now cross the street and head to the park where we put our change or lunch money together to get a three dollar hit which in Brooklyn in the late eighties was like a twenty. We smoked it right there during lunch hour and spent the afternoon at our desks trying to play it off and avoiding co-workers. On paydays I wouldn't even bother to take the subway home. I didn't wait for Cheryl anymore but grabbed a cab right outside the building, hit the check cashing place, (the bank was too far out of the way), and then the spot and was in the house and puffed up before Cheryl even got off. I would then call her and ask her to pick up a few twenties on her way home and start all over again when she arrived. It was no longer fun and I finally understood why no one smiled or was in a good mood when I first started. It had basically taken over my life and I was only now starting to realize how much so. There was no doubt that I enjoyed smoking crack. I can even remember making the comment that if there was a heaven this was it. I'd even gone so far as to say if I had to make a choice between a beautiful sista offering herself to me and some crack I'd take the crack. And I meant it. That's how bad it had gotten. Now Gary and I talked on the phone both suddenly realizing how bad our addictions had gotten in so short a time. Gary had become more or less a recluse.

It was now June and he'd just reached a settlement of a little more than ninety thousand dollars from a car accident he'd been in a couple of years ago and had holed up in the basement of his baby's mother's house and sat smoking day and night. Every now and then he'd stop by and Cheryl and I quickly noticed the change that had taken place. Always neat and well kempt, his appearance had gone down hill rapidly and it was obvious that he no longer took pride in his appearance or what he wore. His clothes were ragged and dirty and he smelled as if he hadn't washed in months. I looked at him and swore I would never let myself get to that level. Cheryl, on the other hand, was really struggling with how bad Gary had become but never one to bite her words told him in no uncertain words that he stunk and told him to take a bath or leave. But instead of being offended Gary seemed to almost welcome someone suddenly taking notice of his rapid descent. He had really fallen and his newfound wealth had only hastened his fall. I have never looked down on anyone. I've always been a rather firm believer in fate and realized that this could have easily been me given different circumstances so I wasn't one to pass judgment. Instead I looked at this as a foretelling of what the future held for me. Still, the power of the drug made it hard for me to do anymore than obey its command.

A month or so later I was still in the throes of this drug when Cheryl informed me that she was pregnant. I was ecstatic about the prospects of a having a child and was glad it had come at this juncture. I think Cheryl had similar thoughts although she was never one to say much. But I think the idea of having a child gave us both hope

176

that I'd overcome my addiction. I still didn't believe that something as simple as a drug could alter my life and have such devastating consequences but all evidence suggested that that's exactly what was happening.
I became bitter, my thoughts jaded and everywhere I looked it seemed that this was what my world had come down to. Drugs... It's funny but when you're in the throes of addiction there are no straight-laced intelligent normal people. There are only those like you and lames. And as much as I chose and wanted to be normal I was now looking through jaded eyes and only saw the world in my terms. I was desperate now. I talked to everyone seeking help. I talked to those older and wiser. I talked to those that had traveled the same path. I even sought out the Nation of Islam as I had heard how they helped so many of my Black brothers who had been physically incarcerated or incarcerated as I now was—in the devil's clutches, hopeless with no way out. There were those who told me to put my life in the hands of Jesus Christ and with prayer and his blessing he would be my light and guide me out of this terminal darkness and I desperate to overcome this desperation, this trial, this tribulation gladly if not resolutely rendered myself to His will. But as my father used to teach me 'all things in time' andI guess it just wasn't my time because nothing I did would release me from the pain and heartache of this terrible addiction. When I felt I couldn't take anymore and all my hopes and dreams had been dashed I contemplated suicide and with butcher knife in my coat pocket headed for the swampy marshes surrounding LaGuardia Airport. Once here I sat on an old tree stump and asked God's forgiveness. I then asked Him why he had forsaken me. I received no answer to either of my queries and took the knife out. But I've never been what you may call a brave man and when it comes to pain I've never had a fetish or even a mild liking to it but I thought how I'd endured if not pain then

177

hardship all through my life in one form or another and was resigned to beating this monster if it was the last thing I did. But the fact was that this thing, this devil, this parasite that was living off me and devouring my very soul would not devour me nor the person I had become. The plain truth of the matter was that I liked me for me, for the person I'd become, for the things I'd overcome and if it wasn't God's will to take me from this earth then I wouldn't be leaving for any other reason. I regained my balance after another good long cry and headed for home trying to regroup on the long walk home, hoping and praying that there was no one at the house to entice me when I had only minutes before come up with a plan, a resolve to get me through the first phase of my self-imposed exile and rehabilitation.

I was bitter. I was angry at Cheryl who hadn't told me the whole story and had only given me a Readers Digest condensed and abbreviated version of this monster, this journey I was about to undertake. She was my Eve, cohort of the devil and the way I saw it she had fed me directly to him all the while telling me she loved me but exposing me to the devil himself leaving a bitter taste in my mouth. I hated the New York that I had returned to. It was not the New York of my youth where the warm summer skies of Queens used to envelope me and cloak my innocence with her warm rays. No, this was the coldest winter ever, the winter of my discontent and I wondered what the allure had been, what had made me race to return to this jungle that treated everyone one as its prey and was devouring Black folks left and right. Black men like me, strong Black men were falling and succumbing quicker than in any wartime era. I hated it but tried to regain some semblance of normalcy before the next tidal wave of the scourge I knew now as crack came riding through.

For awhile I exiled myself in my tiny bungalow and with a son on the way tried to focus all my money and efforts on his birth. On paydays I'd stop by Macy's or Gimbels and spend a few dollars on outfits and baby items just to have something I could see when the scourge hit again. One Sunday I even went so far as to purchase a floor model stereo component system I had seen in Macy's in Lefrak City. And being that it was a floor model I believe it was reduced from about fifteen hundred to somewhere around seven or eight hundred so I grabbed it. Problem was there was no packaging for it and so with the help of a taxi driver we threw it on a dolly, rolled it out of the store and threw it on the backseat of his cab still strapped to the dolly. When we arrived at the house Lecia and her crew were outside on the front porch scheming. My heart sank but having no choice the cabbie and I took it out and rolled it into the house. Cheryl seemed pleasantly surprised and after hooking up a few wires we sat in the living and enjoyed the smooth sounds of some smooth jazz I'd also picked up on the way home. The next day we went to work and for the first time in a long time I felt that our lives were starting to regain some semblance of normalcy and I felt the faint flicker of hope begin to rekindle itself inside of me. I thought of my father's words 'with hope a man is on his way to attaining some degree of success'. When we returned from work the following day we found the house had been broken into and the stereo gone. I was crushed to say the least but and even though I knew who the culprits were I said nothing. I'd basically had it and I believe Lecia realized and recognized that I had been good to her over the course of our friendship. She knew I was tired and at my wit's end when it came to how people changed and basically became animals when under the influence. Anyway she came over a day or so afterwards our house had been robbed and sat in the living room. She was remorseful

179

and a bit saddened by our loss. She acknowledged how I had been one of the few friends she'd ever had. I felt the love and knew that if Cheryl didn't put the fear of God in her she would have been quick to give herself to me. We'd been really close during our short friendship and she was only one of many that asked me why Cheryl was so mean. I didn't have an answer and as soon as she arrived home from work Lecia got up and left but it wasn't before she made this comment concerning the robbery. Lecia said, 'it's usually someone you trust most that will betray you'. I knew then that it was Gary who had robbed us and remarked this to Cheryl who was of the same accord. That night Lecia as promised stopped by the house at around one a.m. Her mother who owned the house they lived in was a major numbers runner in Brooklyn and was almost never there. She just happened to be home that night and one of the reasons, that she came over although she said it was because I always looked out for her and I was her only friend. Anyway, she must have had two or three eight balls, (amounting to somewhere around eight or nine hundred dollars in cash), in her possession and placed one in front of me. We smoked until the wee hours of the morning when she went back out and got some more.

Cheryl was asleep now and around seven thirty or eight o'clock in the morning there was a knock at the door. I, for one was always a little afraid of some jealous soul dropping a dime and the police knocking on the door so I didn't answer it. Lecia hid what was left of the cocaine when we heard her younger brother Jason calling her name. 'Lecia, I know you're in there and mommy knows you took her money off the nightstand. She's going to kick your ass. That's alright. You have to come home sooner or later.' I was shocked and worried now. How could she have stolen from her own mother and then jeopardized me by posting up in my house? I didn't say anything nor did she and after a while she made her leave.

Now, if that wasn't the final straw then all I had to do was wait a couple of days. The house seemed to be falling down around us and maybe God was sending me a message but I certainly wasn't bright enough to pick up on all the nuances. I went back to preparing for my newborn and this made Cheryl happy but it was the only way I knew how to keep money out of my hands and I did so as much for myself as the baby on the way. But a week later after returning from work the house was again in shambles and all of my baby's baby clothes and other items I had purchased for the last several months was gone. This time there was no inference as to who the thief was and everyone on the street pointed to Gary. It hurt me to think that he would do this to his best friend. I was the one who took him in when he had nowhere else to go and fed him 'til he got back on his feet but I realized the nature of the beast and just had to let it go. This after all, wasn't the Gary I had forced to go to class and let stay in my apartment when he had nowhere else to go. No, this was someone else I neither knew nor recognized. This was the kid who had come into ninety thousand dollars in June. No, this was the kid Cheryl and I witnessed walking through the C-Town Supermarket with an empty shopping bag pushing groceries off the shelf into his bag and dashing out of the store with them. Here it was early August and he was broke. He'd spent ninety thousand dollars in less than two months and had degenerated to the extent of stealing cookies and meats from grocery stores and robbing houses. The whole thing was pitiful and it just seemed like the whole city was turning into a drug zone. This was '86 and I had had enough. A week or two later my son Christopher was born. I named him after one of my favorite cousins, Jonathan Christopher who was on his way overseas on

*some covert mission with the army. He was an officer
and had done quite well for himself and was on his way.
Gary also had the nerve to stop by and hold my baby boy
but we really didn't see much of him after the robberies. I
guess he figured that if he didn't stop by then we would
have suspected him but little did he know that he'd
already been ratted out. During this time New York was
growing progressively worse and Cheryl and I were doing
our best to gather our lives together and doting on
Christopher only made it that much easier even though
we both still found the time to get high.*

*One day we were walking to C-Town to pick up a few
groceries and some formula for Chris when a car full of
Jamaicans rode by spraying the opposite side of the street
where the dope boys had a spot. The sound of automatic
gun fire was now a normal city sound and pieces of the
stores brick facing chipped off all around us. On that day
I decided that I'd had enough of New York.*

*I decided to leave New York that very day and called my
parents who were now in North Carolina to tell them that
I was on my way. They were aware by this time that I was
strung out after so many missed dates and lame excuses
that simply said that something was wrong with their baby
boy. I think the culmination came before they left for
North Carolina when it came time for the summer jazz
festival I'd attended annually at Jackie Robinson's house.
It had been moved to Senegal in Africa. My dad called
excitedly to invite me and tell me to get my money
together as we were going to Africa. He knew his son and
knew that I would too be excited but when I simply
informed him that I would have to pass because I was in
financial straits he knew something was wrong.*

*Informing me that it was a chance of a lifetime he offered
to pay and told me to meet him somewhere downtown to
pick up the forty or fifty dollars to procure my passport.*

I met him and no sooner had he given me the money for the passport I jumped back on the subway and headed for Queens where they had those large jumbo twenties and then to the house to get down. That was months ago. They'd flown over with jazz pianist Billy Taylor who was headlining this years event and came back with stories that made me both ashamed and feeling foolish for having missed such an opportunity. Still, no matter where I was in my life I knew that when I was out of sorts or losing the essence to my very being was that you can always go home and regain your balance and your center and I was tired of treading water and going absolutely nowhere so once again I headed home. But before I left and almost as if it was an omen Yvette called me. Now I wished I'd stayed with her but hindsight is always twenty twenty.

We rode around for a while as I tried to find a little something something before I left. It was my last harrah and I knew the time was soon approaching for me to leave New York and I was trying to enjoy my last days there. At least that's what I told myself in my attempts to rationalize my growing addiction. In any case, it was several hours before I ran into anything since there had been a rash of shootings to clear the existing spots. Jamaican posses were simply doing drive-bys to scare the already existing drug gangs who were setting up curb service all over the city and once they had a growing personnel or customer base the Jamaican posses would shoot 'em up scaring the sellers away or killing them then wait a couple of days and put their own people in place thus taking over the rather lucrative market. So, right through here crack was abundant and at the same time scarce. Anyway Yvette drove me while I searched until I found what I was looking for several hours later. I didn't have the heart to tell her that I was leaving. Later we made love in the living room and If I didn't know then or

183

had any questions it was then that I knew she still loved me.

Still, I could see the disappointment in her eyes that I had not just chosen Cheryl but a substance over her. What she didn't know was that I regretted my decision more than she would ever know. And as we lay there on the floor we heard a key in the lock and jumped and were dressed before Cheryl entered. It was a funny thing about Yvette but she was the only woman that could both command me and had such a hold on me that would make me defy common sense and logic to do something foolish and jeopardize my very existence. This wasn't the first time I'd done something stupid and irrational at her expense and wouldn't be the last.

A week or so later Dana, the Italian chick from my past called. It had been years since I'd seen her. She'd stayed in touch with my mother in an attempt to keep tabs on me and when I first met Cheryl she came over to Maplewood to my mom's house and even with Cheryl there tried to hit on me. When that failed she took us both out for drinks and then disappeared into the wind. But now here a week or so before I was too leave here she was showing up in Queens. Unlike Yvette she caught me on one of my off days where I was sober and lucid and of course broke so when she suggested we go somewhere I took her in her car mind you to long term parking at LaGuardia Airport where she made love to me and then asked me to make love to her. I did but not in the same way. I wasn't completely sure of what her goal was but being the person I am and trying to be hospitable I agreed for old times' sake and was completely unnerved when she let me know that I could come in her during our brief but notable tryst. Again and not to be inhospitable, I did and have never seen or heard from her again. I think she needed closure with the guy that made love to her for the very first time.

I can't remember who it was 'til this day that drove me to North Carolina but I think it was my friend Mary Hargrove. I'd met her cute little dark-skinned country ass when I was in North Carolina on a visit several months before and she and I had kicked it a few times and stayed in touch. She was from a little place outside of Fayetteville called Lillington where the houses reminded you of slave quarters complete with a potbellied stove and wooden windows with latches to keep the elements out. She came to eat at my parent's restaurant where I served as short order cook, (under Claudia's tutelage), waiter, clerk, dishwasher, server and delivery boy. After the few years back in New York and in the throes of and the streets and drugs I was glad to be at Claudia's side once again. She was no longer the warden or that evil demon although that bad gene hadn't subsided. Anyway it was while here that I met Mary Hargrove.

I found out that she had seven or eight brothers or sisters, a son named Corey and a husband that was incarcerated. She was working and just making ends meet and was a reserve in the army. And she loved to fuck. Now I was somewhere around thirty and have to admit that it took me a long time, (longer than most), to hit pay dirt and Yvette and Dana had experimented enough to take me to the professional ranks but I'd yet to meet anyone like Mary. There were no holds barred, no inhibitions, no fears, nothing when it came to Mary and sex. I'd found a teaching position and was once again in my element. I took the exam to teach Special Education, passed and was given a self-contained class which amounted to me teaching junior high or middle school Black boys who were said to have behavioral problems which I have to this day to recognize. What I found similar to my teaching experiences in the Bronx was very bright and energetic young Black males that white teachers had difficulty relating to and therefore teaching.

185

To me they were angels. So, life had come full circle. I taught then rushed to my parent's restaurant to lend a hand and worked at a live in position with the mentally handicapped on the weekend. If I had any free time I spent it with Mary.

She was always upbeat and easy to laugh and I knew what New York had to offer being the greatest city but Lillington despite its country façade had something to offer the world as well. I learned more from Mary than I had from all the women I'd known previously. I was no longer a scared little uptight Catholic boy and though I am not at liberty to expose her teachings as I'm afraid I may be infringing on her patent and copyright laws but trust me she turned me out. I smile as I compose this brief excerpt but Mary did more for my recovery and rehabilitation than anyone else. Of course some more knowledgeable than I will tell you that I simply substituted one habit for another but this I did gladly. Once incident that comes to mind is when she pulled up to my tiny apartment in Fayetteville. She had a tiny red pickup truck that she used to bounce around the country roads on and this particular evening maybe a day or two after I met her she asked me if I could use a ride home from the restaurant. She had a cute little red dress on and some heels, long straight black hair and some ruby red lipstick accentuating those full beautiful lips I came to know so well. I asked her to stop a couple of blocks from the house so I could run into the store and grab some cigarettes. Looking out the store window I could see her standing beside the truck and bending to her knees and then shoving something into her purse as I came out. As I started to get in she asked me if I minded driving. I asked her why when I only lived a couple of blocks away and was told she got better leverage this way. I didn't understand but got into the drivers seat and made my way home. Moments later I pulled up onto a hill in back of the church next door to my house at which time Mary zipped my pants, unbuckled my belt and straddled me with her back arched upon the steering wheel. 'I told you I get better leverage this way.' She rode me pulling at my penis with the lips and muscles of her vagina contracting each time. When she was finished riding we were both bathed in sweat and it was like that and every day afterwards for months to come. Each day it was a lesson in how to make your man come and want you even more than he did the day before and I learned my lessons well.

We were getting along well. I was still teaching and any off days I spent in the restaurant. I'd get there at seven thirty in the morning and may not get off until seven thirty or eight o'clock at night. And like I mentioned previously, on the weekends I worked in a group home for mentally handicapped adults. Between the three jobs I was able to afford a small place and I loved it. The only thing I really missed was my son Christopher. But I wasn't going to jeopardize my life by trying to live in New York for the sake of anyone or anything not even Chris. Sure, I loved my son but if I had stayed in New York I would have been dead and my son would have never gotten to know me. Cheryl was in constant contact and I knew she loved me and was certainly ready to join me and though I wasn't really feeling her and blamed her for my drug addiction I did miss my son. As the days went on I missed him even more but how many times had I gone six or seven months and slipped back into the throes of my addiction. I wanted to be sure.

The fact of the matter was that I'd not overcome my addiction I just replaced it with my addiction to women and North Carolina was like Pennsylvania. The women were beautiful, perhaps not as beautiful or as plentiful as the women in New York but then how could they be? There were eight million people in New York. But still they were plentiful enough and with the shortage of Black men in North Carolina I had a field day. Mary was my latest heartthrob and a couple of months after meeting her she had gotten to the point where she didn't think she could make it financially and told me she was considering reenlisting in the army on a full time basis and asked me if I would keep her son until she got out or better position herself for she and I to be married. The thought appealed to me. At this point in my life I really did not know the difference between love and sex but cherished both so I gladly accepted her proposal to keep her son. I also liked the fact that I thought I had won her over and she entrusted me to such an extent that she would leave her only son with me.

All that being said I did something that I did not usually do with women. I gave her my heart and soul and trusted her. A few weeks after she made this proposal she invited me to a barbeque at her house. I went and who was there but her estranged husband who she introduced me to. I was shocked, as she hadn't mentioned his being paroled anytime soon. I didn't stay long and moments after I walked into the house she called to tell me that there had been a change of plans and her husband would be keeping Corey while she went away and my services were no longer needed. Talk about hurt... Yet, I would be damned if I let her see my hurt and I continued to receive her phone calls and waited on her as if she were any other customer at the restaurant. During the following week she called me several times to talk and even get together. I declined at first but then she called to tell me that she wanted to introduce me to her sister, Theresa who was moving to Fayetteville with her two children from New York. Theresa was looking for a job and Mary thought that I might be able to help her so I agreed and told her to have her stop by the Big Dish and I'd see what I could for her.

Theresa was tall and ebony, with long legs and a pleasant demeanor and was as sweet as Mary but so much more. And after talking to her that afternoon and spending a little too much time at her table I invited her to stop by my apartment that evening. She agreed to do so and at seven or eight that night she rang the doorbell. We sat in the living room and sipped some wine and listened to music until the wee hours of the morning when I offered to take her home. She stood and gave me a hug and I returned the hug with a kiss. Deep inside of me I felt that it was wrong and then felt the pain of losing her sister. I'm not sure if I was consciously being vengeful or not and not sure if I wouldn't have done it if Mary and I were still together but I felt the passion. And took Theresa as if it were Mary and had her follow me into my bedroom where we made love several times before we fell asleep. I woke up a little earlier than usual the next morning to a feeling I had never experienced before as Theresa sucked my toes and then commenced to loving me some more. We spent the next week or two together rehearsing our roles until Theresa went home to Mary and professed her love to her at which time I received a call from Mary telling me how happy she was for Theresa but how hurt she was that I would have the nerve to sleep with her sister. She promised not to say anything to hers sister and knew exactly why I had slept with Theresa but asked that I not tell her hoping that Theresa would experience the same joy she had experienced with me. When I heard this I was hurt. I was hurt that she had no remorse when it came to me or felt any sadness or even contemplated how I must have felt over her leaving me with not so much as a hint of why. I never spoke to Mary or Theresa again and there's no question that Mary explained the situation to Theresa.

I settled into my life in Fayetteville and after awhile Claudia and Frank, now convinced that I was recovering

189

nicely and was back on track started talking about me taking on some other ventures as if having three jobs wasn't enough. They saw how happy teaching made me and even proclaimed that I was at my highest heights when I was teaching. They knew that my being totally engrossed in something was as important to my maintaining my sobriety as anything else. I was high strung and intense like Claudia and so after talking to the local editor for a Black newspaper out of Wilmington, North Carolina called The Challenger and her offering me a job to write a local column they pushed for me to take it. I did and my position with the paper grew. When I wasn't writing the sports section for The Challenger I was running it up to Laurinburg, North Carolina to have it printed. I was making a few dollars with my two full-time jobs, my two part-time jobs and the tips I made from delivering food and it was the latter that led me to my next little venture.

Up until now I'd been sharing my dad's car, which was fine with him since he was happy that the prodigal son had returned.

One day, however, on my way to make a delivery I passed a used car dealership and saw this shiny new car that caught my eye. I've always had a thing for the color red and this car shouted at me and literally said 'I'm the one for you.' As soon as I saw it I knew I had to have it. It just so happened to be a two-year-old, red, BMW. I don't know why it appeared so appealing to me but the moment I saw it I had to have it. I then went to my boy and banker Deryl Gant. Deryl was vice president of First Union Bank in Fayetteville. I told him about the car and asked him what my chances of getting a loan for it. He replied that my chances were pretty good and even better since I had saved a few thousand since I had been there but he'd like to take a look at it first. I had no problem with Deryl giving it the once over since he and I hung out together and dated a couple of the same women, (even though Deryl was married), and even lent me his car, (he had a Saab), to g on a couple of dates with. So, I know he wouldn't steer me wrong in approving or disapproving the loan. He was constantly telling me that I needed to buy a car just so his wife or customers tooling around every night with a different woman wouldn't see him. (People want to know a high profile person in charge of their finances is not some flippant player). So, Deryl saw my getting a car as important to him as it was me. I, therefore knew he wouldn't steer me wrong.

Claudia, on the other hand, saw that car for what it was worth and told me in no uncertain terms that a red car would only bring me headaches. And although Valerie, (who was now attending North Carolina A & T University), Deryl, and Dee Hardison, (the ex-NFL football player all exchanged cars with me regularly in attempts to stay incogNegro and keep our creeping after dark on the down low it brought me nothing but problems. Cops would stop me on a regular basis and ask what I did for a living. Women would inevitably give up the goodies and then ask to borrow the car. I was even audited by the IRS after a taxman came to the restaurant and saw me, the deliveryman, driving a brand new Beamer with an apron on. I guess it never dawned on anyone that a Blackman could work his ass off to achieve things in life.

Still, I was glad to be off drugs and be heading in another direction with my life. Yet, I was becoming a little concerned that my life consisted of little more than sexing women and working. I needed more. And so when Cheryl asked me if she could join me in Fayetteville I agreed. I was never so glad to see anyone in all my life. She'd brought my son and Christopher was at once a fan favorite, a celebrity, a star. Everyone fell in love with him

191

even Claudia who blamed Cheryl for her son's addiction
and stated that Christopher was not her grandchild.
In the end she became Christopher's biggest fan and
supporter. And where his grandfather and Aunt Valerie
loved him from the start his grandmother was slow to
warm to him. Cheryl was working at McDonalds within a
week of arriving in Fayetteville and freed up some more
money for me but once again the same problems erupted
and we were once again at each other's throats. Chris
spent much of his time at the restaurant driving his little
yellow and red car and bumping into diners constantly.
And I knowing that he was in good hands, started staying
out more and more. I picked up hours at the group home
and when lights went out for the residents at around ten
at night my real job began. Instead of bringing women
home I now brought them to the group home where I
maintained a small apartment off from the main house
and away from my clients.
Not long after her arrival Cheryl found a position with
the Fayetteville Police Department with the major crimes
division as a secretary and was now working two jobs.
She eventually gave up McDonald's and joined the rest of
the family at The Challenger newspaper as a receptionist.
And being that she was working two jobs and I working
four we put Chris into The YWCA Day Care Nursery.
The director was Sheila Hopkins a very sophisticated and
preppy young woman and graduate of the very prestigious
Bennett, all Black girls college in Greensboro, North
Carolina. She was like no other young lady I'd met and
from her penny loafers to her plaid skirt she was friendly
and warm and I liked her. I invited her to the restaurant
first for lunch and then to the group home where I swore
I put on my best theatrical display to come off like a Black
Clark Gable. And even though I knew one of her favorite
attributes was the fact that she was a born again
Christian I was intent on having her. When she first

192

arrived all had gone well but after the first kiss and a little massaging of her breasts and clit she gasped and when I went to grab a glass of water as she requested and I returned I found her gone. I knew that she was weak and knew that she was feeling me and in the coming weeks my pursuit of Sheila was relentless. I had become a pretty good judge of women by my early thirties and almost never went for thug qualities or ride-or-die bitches. I had that in my baby's mother. Instead I went for nice girls, girls who had grown up with the same values and ethics that I had grown up with. I always wanted a woman that was as close to a saint as I possibly could get. If Mother Theresa had been available she would have been my number one pick. They say every man wants a lady in the living room and a whore in the bedroom and I guess that's the way I was for the most part. Sheila was certainly a lady. She had a faint lisp and it made her even sexier but she had some deep seated issues but when one first met her she was the consummate professional. But what intrigued me most of all was what was behind her holier than thou, good girl aura. We never talked about anything other than the politics of the day and I found this little dark-skinned woman bright and refreshing. She wasn't the most voluptuous, with drop-dead looks but I've never been a man that put a whole lot of stock in something as fleeting as physical appearances.

I used to tell Val when choosing a mate that you'd better choose a mate that you can roll over and talk to after a night of great love making because sex takes all of fifteen minutes but a marriage, a union takes a lifetime so I have never equated sex with a relationship although I have fallen into deep lust on several occasions. And Sheila intrigued me. Both well schooled, well heeled, she was also so reserved, that she appeared to me an enigma. And always curious I had to know her and part of that something I had to know was how she was behind closed

*doors. Half of my intrigue was the challenge of seeing if
I could seduce a woman. And a woman devout in her
beliefs to abstain from sex was a challenge for me. When
the opportunity finally arose I couldn't wait. And trust me
the wait was worth it. This woman who had been hiding
behind the cloak of the Lord had so many deep seated
issues and was hiding from the deep-seated hurt she had
experienced in her various experiences with Black men
that she had consciously made a decision, (like so many
of my Black sisters are forced to do), to refrain from men
and give herself over to the Lord Jesus Christ. I
understand the thinking and the logic that drives this
thought but given the opportunity to experience an
emotional and physical love from a sincere and faithful
man—given the opportunity to be loved—mind, body and
soul I guarantee she will. And in my eyes this was the
case with Sheila.*

*All those years of pent up aggression and anger that were
masked by her being 'saved' came bursting through with
all the passion and hunger of one incarcerated for far too
many a year. And when she started she couldn't stop.
I'm not sure which it was but she was good for showing
up in a London Fog late at night when she was sure no
one was home with a bottle of wine. After drinking the
bottle of wine she would place one leg over one arm of the
chair and the other leg over the other arm, undo the belt
of the London Fog letting it fall to the sides exposing her
nakedness before inserting the neck of the bottle as far as
it would go and then wait for my reaction before plunging
it in again and again until she was sweating profusely
and convulsing over and over with orgasms. Other days it
was cucumbers or other fruits and vegetables she had in
the fridge. And still on other days she'd ask me to spank
her or choke her when we were making love.*

*On rainy days she insisted on throwing on nothing more
than a pair of boots and making love in the backseat of*

194

her tiny Hyundai as she braced her feet against the backdoor of the car and scream at me to fuck me harder with each thrust. When she'd come and was sore and raw she'd find a way, (even with the limited space), to turn over on her knees, her face in the backseat and tell me to the same to her from behind—only harder.

Now I've been writing for some time now and I must admit that there have been quite a few references to different women and I suppose I'm guilty of substituting one addiction for another but I think it is important to note that my addiction wasn't from cocaine to sex but I was an addict in search of love. What I wanted was a partner that would love me and stand by me but no matter what I did I could never find that person. I don't know if my standards were too high or too low but for some reason whomever I met found me lacking in some way. Each time I would walk away with a bitter feeling as if love and happiness were somehow just not meant for me. I can also say that I fell in love with almost all of the women I spent time with but for some reason it just wasn't meant to be. Still that didn't mean that I didn't continue my search to find Mrs. Right and it wasn't long before I met Laura. She was a tall young lady about six feet or six foot one and very attractive with light brown eyes and legs for days. Funny thing about Laura was that my mother met her first and called me over to meet her. Seems she was a dancer at Big P's up on Murchison Road. Her stage name was Candy. Everyone knew her and she could hardly eat her lunch in peace. She and my mom hit it off at once. Claudia had a way with all the strippers, bookies, numbers runners, gangsas, crooks and people on the seamier side of life.

Both drug boys and drug addicts loved Claudia I don't know if it was because she kept it real or that they recognized that bad gene . Anyway Laura and I were introduced and being aggressive she came in the day

*following and made sure that I was the one that waited on
her. She bought a piece of peach cobbler and we chatted
briefly, (I chatted briefly, she asked a million and one
personal questions), before she left to catch her bus. My
mother was impressed when Laura told her that she
stripped instead of going on welfare. It didn't take much
to impress Claudia. I wasn't of the same accord but said
little when Claudia informed me of this.*

*After several days of coming in showing large wads of
money she asked me what I was doing after I got off
work. When I said nothing she asked me to pick her to
pick her up at Big P's when she got off work but asked me
not to come inside. And being that there was a ten or
fifteen dollar cover charge I had no desire to go in.
Anyway, I sat outside waiting quietly when she came out,
a swarm of guys surrounding her. I wondered what all
the commotion was about and watched one young boy rip
a fifty-dollar bill in half and tell her that when she was
ready she could have the other half. Seeing me she got in
and told me to drive. I did and when I'd gotten no more
than a block away from the club she burst out in tears
and told me to take her to a motel I knew well right
outside of Fayetteville. We made love or better yet she
made love to me and told me to take her home. It went on
like this for a couple of weeks but I soon grew tired of
carrying Kleenex's to meet her and left her alone.*

 *Cheryl and I were still a tough go of it and after one such
argument she moved out taking Chris with her. It was a
little over a month when I saw Chris again and this only
happened by chance. I was making a delivery to social
services when this little boy ran up to me yelling 'daddy,
daddy'. I looked down to see it was Chris and was visibly
shaken. Cheryl and I talked and I broke down and told
her how much I missed my son and she agreed after a day
or two that we could try again. I don't know what drove
us apart from the outset other than I never forgave her*

for turning me on to crack cocaine or warning me about it. I guess everyone must take responsibility for their own mistakes but I couldn't think of a person that professed their love for me that would have allowed me to or suggested that I do crack. Now in her defense I'm not sure in nineteen eighty-six that anyone knew the destructive power of the drug but why anyone would allow a loved one to try something, a drug was beyond me.

Still, I loved my son and so I said what needed to be said and accepted her prerequisites although I knew that it was only a matter of time before the shit hit the fan again. There was really nothing either of us could do. I know now that even if I wanted to make it work I wouldn't have been able to change the way I felt about her.

It wasn't long before I heard from Yvette again. And I'm not sure I knew what it was but I was convinced even though I loved my baby boy that perhaps I'd made a mistake in not waiting for Yvette. I think I'd come to the point even though I'd made an effort not to ever have any regrets that maybe I should have married Yvette. She made me feel good, we had a lot in common and the bottom line was that we really and truly liked each other as people. She was bright and I found that intriguing in itself and she was open and giving if at times too loving but there were no walls or barriers between us. She'd call every two or three years to see how I was doing and I was always glad to hear from her. Most people had a reason and a season but whenever she called my heart would commence to doing jumping jacks and despite being in a relationship she took priority. And as it would happen Yvette called not long after Cheryl had arrived in Fayetteville and moved in. Yvette had a way of calling not to ask but to inform me that she was coming and did so on just such an occasion one week in the late summer. Well, one thing I'd gathered by now and that was when Yvette called the best I could do was grab the nearest thing to me

197

and hang on until the typhoon blew through and then when all was said and done to go take a count of how many bodies had been scattered about and how much damage had been done. It was like one of those storm trackers when all was said and done or like someone from FEMA assessing the damage. And like a hurricane there was no way to stop it or control its movement. At best all one could do was to assess the damage in the aftermath and then try to clean up the mess it had laid in its waste. The only problem was that she didn't create the damage. It was just her pronouncement that she was coming that caused me to rip up all that I had painstakingly built and allow her to visit for a day or two. In that day or two upon her arrival I would put everything on hold or cast it aside even though it had taken me months and sometimes even years to build. Yvette was my Delilah but instead of losing my strength, I'd usually lose my mind and burn all bridges upon her arrival. She was my Eve and she was the poison fruit.

My God could have drawn me a map of the way to righteousness but if Yvette had told me to follow the other path then Lord knows I would have taken it. Now that's not to say that she proposed or instigated me doing any of these things. It was just the effect she had on me. I can remember her coming and staying in the Comfort Inn. I didn't stay there with her but frequented it enough that I may as well have stayed there. And then when she'd run out of money and had no place to stay I turned to Cheryl and told her that Yvette was in town and didn't have anywhere to stay. When she took the attitude of oh well I became livid and informed her that Yvette was staying there and if she didn't like it she could leave. This didn't do well for the longevity of our relationship or strengthen the bond between us but I didn't care. Yvette came and stayed for a day or two. We spent every minute of every hour together and as soon as Cheryl went to sleep we made our way into the bathroom and made love.

It was funny though when she left it was a year or two before I heard from her again. And it was always that way. She and I loved each other but I was like a time-share property to Vet. I was somewhere to go, to get away that was safe and dependable. And when she had gained her stability and was fine I wouldn't here from her again. Not long after that I found myself strung out again. (Yvette claimed later that she was only interested in checking on her first true love and seeing if he had regained his balance and his form but each time she came she found me still out on a limb and she wasn't having it. Still, she hoped and prayed that I would get myself together and return to the guy she had once known and come to love.)

I was shooting cocaine now as well as smoking it and things were now as bad as they had ever been. I was tired. I was tired of living with Cheryl, tired of working the long hours at the restaurant, tired of running the streets, I was just tired. A couple of days later I stopped by my neighbors on my way home from work and my neighbor, Egypt was having some type of get together. Egypt was always having some type of party and there were always plenty of drugs. He was a heroin addict but shot cocaine when it was available.

That night I witnessed a young White boy about my age who had just copped an eight ball of cocaine. The coke must have been good 'cause as soon as he shot it he hit the wall, his back arched and then he slid down the wall, eyes fluttering before he hit the floor. I watched his body go rigid as his lips turned purple. I could tell he was dying and watched the remainder of the room hide their drugs in lieu of the police coming. Egypt was cool though. After rustling through the pockets of the kid overdosing and stealing his cocaine, Egypt proceeded to give the man mouth-to-mouth resuscitation and revived him. The man grateful, sat upright, the color restored itself to his lips and face. He sat there for several minutes until he regained his clarity and then began searching his pockets. When he didn't find his drugs he started accusing everyone in the room. I left at this time wondering how he could possibly wish for more drugs after he'd just o.d.'d and been blessed with life.

It wasn't long after that I admitted myself into rehab where I spent thirty days and felt a rebirth. Once again, I wanted to start over and saw this as a new beginning. My family was very supportive and was there to lend me support. A day or so prior to being released I had a family counseling session where my family was invited and told of the expectations they had for me and the expectations my family was to incur to help me maintain my sobriety. One of the things that were mandatory was not to make alcohol easily accessible because after many days of therapy it was the general consensus that alcohol was the trigger. Everyone agreed and vowed not to offer or purchase and be cognizant when I was around that they shouldn't indulge and I sincerely appreciated their acknowledgement of what triggered my addiction and their efforts to refrain—everyone that is but Cheryl—who was adamant that she wasn't going to stop drinking because I had to and refused when I asked her not to buy it or bring it into the house because I had to refrain from drinking. That in itself was a strong statement that she hardly cared for my well-being and I should have taken this as a cue to move out but instead I ignored her and chalked it up to her continuing state of being arrogant in her ignorance. Now I don't want any of you to think that I'm using Cheryl as my scapegoat, when it comes to me using Cheryl's my reason for all that happened to me in my life. Cheryl was not the reason for my continuing relapse into drugs or the fact that in my search to find a woman that fit all the requirements that my mother had in my life. That is not so. It was my responsibility to find both sobriety and a wife or girlfriend that would allow me to grow and be both a man and responsible parent for both myself and my son Christopher. I will readily admit that. But I must say that in my quest to do so she was not the most amiable or supportive person to accompany me on my journey. Still, I knew that without her she would take my son and Lord knows if I cared about anyone, I cared about Chris. He, after all was the most positive person I had in my life. There was also the fact that I was born to one of the strongest Black men I have yet to come to know and he had instilled in me from the very beginning that a good, strong Black man that indulges in activities that may result in the creation of a child has an obligation to see it through and raise and provide for that child and this I intended to do despite my disease and addiction.

It was four or five years since I'd been introduced to crack and here I was still fighting the battle to overcome its hold on me and while in rehab was told that it was a battle I would have to fight for the rest of my life so along with crack, and Cheryl and the rest of my demons that had taken up residence in my life I fought.

It was not long before I was drinking right along with Cheryl and although I didn't indulge as she did everyday I was now what you might call a functioning alcoholic, drug addict and womanizer. But I had hardly given up hope that I would someday overcome all three, (although I didn't have the slightest idea of how to accomplish any of them let alone all three). The only thing that I could think of was to immerse myself in all three and do my best at reconstructing a world that I'd once known and that meant me indulging myself in things that had had a positive effect on me and things that I loved to do and those things ways centered on my love for the arts. I

201

loved reading, writing, (although I never thought I was especially good at it), and music. And it wasn't that I had negated any of the three it was just now that I became even more engrossed in all of them. So I read and looked for things in and around Fayetteville that were of interest to me. And although Fayetteville was a military town, (Fort Bragg being the second largest military base in the United States boasting eighty thousand troops), there was always some type of activity designed to entertain them. On top of that there were plenty of events hosted by two of the south's many historically Black colleges, (Shaw and Fayetteville State University). Many of the faculty from both colleges frequented my parent's restaurant and after awhile came to know my families' interests in afro-centric happenings and events. The Challenger newspaper also kept us very well informed on the African American activities within North Carolina. So, when Mandela was arriving in Atlanta and my parents decided to arrange a bus trip to see him I was there or when Wynton Marsalis was performing in Fayetteville I was there. It continued on like this and anytime the newspaper was to cover musical concerts I was there. I was privy to meet and interview such people as Chuck D., of Public Enemy, Eric B. and Rakim, Doug E. Fresh, Kool Moe D, Biz Markie, and even sit down in Ice T's hotel room which was an experience in itself because he forecasted the L.A. riots of nineteen ninety two a good year before they ever happened. (And they talk about Nostradamus). It was all a wonderful experience in itself but I think the two experiences, which had the most profound effect on me, were meeting two of my heroes.

At Fayetteville State, I had the opportunity to sit in a room of perhaps ten or twelve historians, scholars and college professors to listen to a lecture given by Dr. Ivan Van Sertima. Now you and countless others may ask who Ivan Van Sertima was and I do not pretend to be the most knowledgeable person in the world and was perhaps less knowledgeable than you but I had the good fortune to have two things happen in my life purely by coincidence. One is that I moved into a townhouse next door to the U.S. Flea Market Mall on McPherson Church Road in Fayetteville. The second thing is that inside the U.S. Flea Market Mall were a group of Muslims intent on providing knowledge to ignorant Blacks like myself. A young Black brother ran it by the name of Adam Biya and every Saturday morning I would go and pose a question to brother Adam. (One was all it took). Forty-five minutes later, I'd walked away richer for having made his acquaintance and a large volume of something scrumptious and delicious for the upcoming week. One of the people Brother Adam introduced me to was Ivan Van Sertima who not only theorized but gave veritable proof that Africans settled Mesoamerica long before the Spanish did. I believe the book was entitled "They Came Before Columbus" and I found it fascinating. (It still remains one of my favorites.) He also wrote "The Moors" about Hannibal's conquest of Spain and the resounding effects it had on everything from pigmentation to Spanish architecture.

Thanks to Adam I read all of Ivan Van Sertima's books and when I found out they were bringing him to Fayetteville State I was literally the first in line to procure tickets. When I sought someone to share this once in a lifetime experience I couldn't find anyone but not to be deterred I went alone. It was not the first time I'd attended an event that appealed to me alone but I was saddened that Blacks had no interest in their own history but would wake their children and force their children each day to attend a lecture on how the White man in all his barbaric cruelty conquered this land and set up shop with our ancestors as his forced labor force. To the contrary, the discovery of Mesoamerica, on the other

hand was done with little or no violence and when the
Africans left, (according to Van Sertima), the Mexicans
or Indians built pyramids and huge stone replicas of the
Africans as a tribute to these men who they came to love
and respect. (I see no huge stone busts of Washington or
Christopher Columbus adorning our shorelines).
It's nevertheless a wonderful story and must read for
African-American boys and girls but a story discredited by
all the White historians of note.
I thank Adam Biya for enriching my life. I appreciate the
fact that he gave me tiny bits of knowledge surrounding
but more importantly he introduced me to one of my
strengths without actually knowing he did so. What he
did was whet my appetite as far as telling me a little bit
about my heritage and history and never telling me the
full story but just barely enough to make me thirst for
more knowledge on the subject and letting me sell myself
on buying the book. I don't know how many thousands
of dollars I must have spent with him but I can say this.
Not one dollar spent do I regret.
There's another small story I'd like to tell you about that
occurred to me during this time and changed my life.
Despite all the negatives that occurred in my life during
this time and prior to I must say that my parents still had
the utmost love and trust in me that I would one day
overcome my affliction and I will forever be indebted to
them for their support.
In the meantime, I worked long, and hard for my parents
at the restaurant and every spare minute I had I would
walk two doors down and visit Larry's Press Box. Larry's
Press Box was a baseball card shop and though I had
little knowledge of the card business I was a fast learner
and being a sports enthusiast this was right up my alley.
To make a long story short, cards were big business in the
early nineties and Blacks always being the last to know
had no idea of the investment possibilities or the money

that could be had if they played their cards right. Larry King the owner of Larry's Press Box took a special interest in me when he found out that I wrote the sports column for the local newspaper. He was a big booster for the Duke Blue Devils basketball team and donated enough that when the team flew out of town for away games Larry King flew right along with them.

Anyway, he was a millionaire and my mother ingratiated us to him when she did a feature article on the front page of the Challenger. But he and I had a different type of relationship. I was a Big East basketball fan and he was a staunch supporter of Duke and the ACC and so we had some rather heated debates. He even tried to sway me to becoming a Duke fan when he bought me tickets to the Duke LSU game. I took Cheryl who for some reason was insistent on going although he only had one ticket. I'd bought into all the hype surrounding Shaquille O'Neal and guard, Chris Jackson, (who later went on to become Mahmoud Abdul Rauf and went on to become an NBA star). When we got to Duke's Cameron Indoor Stadium I was shocked to find I was the only Black in attendance aside from the players on the Duke basketball team and a lone cheerleader.) The crowd was raucous and unruly and Shaq had three fouls in the first couple of minutes and the crowd, which was all white called him everything from jig-a-boo to an ape. Of course LSU lost. I was shook and although I'd encountered hostile environments before nothing compared to Cameron Indoor Stadium. I couldn't envision Larry being a part of such a racist group but I never mentioned it nor did he.

What he did though was introduce me to the world of cards. Now Larry was a millionaire. I have no idea of how he amassed his fortune but he was presently working as the city's surveyor. He'd purchased a building much as my father had done and renovated it and turned it into Larry's Press Box where he sold sports cards and other

sports collectibles and memorabilia. I soon learned the
business since Fran, a young white divorcee with two
boys worked there and she and I became fast friends. I
liked her and she thought there was no one funnier than
I. She was a beautiful person who had been sold a bad lot
in life and at thirty-four or thirty-five was still quite
attractive. Her husband had long since left her with two
sons eight and ten years of age and through it all she had
remained upbeat. Larry had taken her under his wing
and taught her the business and she in turn had done the
same for me. Anybody that knows me knows that I have
an obsessive-compulsive personality and when I became
obsessed with cards it was for all intensive purposes a
wrap. I read about the card business and everything
associated with it and learned the business in a matter of
months from top to bottom. I spent every extra dime and
every tip I made on cards now and Larry seeing my
enthusiasm started schooling me on the business as well
and even gave me investment tips on what I should buy
for quick dividends. I listened and learned well. I bought
boxes of cards for forty dollars and three months later the
boxes I'd bought were worth a hundred and twenty
dollars a box. I followed the hobby the way a Wall Street
broker follows NASDAQ. I knew when it was time to buy,
time to sell the only thing that eluded me was when it was
time to sell where would I and could I sell at. I'd been
stockpiling cards that Larry had been giving me tips on
for who knows how long. Cheryl who had no interest in
my card hobby or anything else I was doing only
remarked how my cards were cluttering up the place and
the fact that she was losing closet space to cards.
My mother always open to something new started picking
up packs of cards from Wal-Mart and my good friend
Sheila noticing my enthusiasm starting seeking out
venues for me to open a card shop in. I was leery of
starting my own shop because I just didn't have the

confidence to open one. Not long after that Larry suggested that I join his sports card club three evenings a week. When I showed up he introduced me to the club members, (all of whom were white), and after a few weeks I noticed that their knowledge base was no more than equal to mine. Soon after that I began to travel to pick up items different than what Larry sold. And to make sure I was not equal to anyone I began to attend the hobby shows held around the state and most of the card shops in Virginia and South Carolina. Before it was over I knew most of the card show owners in Virginia and South Carolina on a first name basis and being that the sports card business was predominantly white I guess I stood out like a sore thumb. Nevertheless, I had moved to the head of the class in my knowledge of the card business and Sheila's words rang out loud and clear. It was time for me to venture out. If no one else was supportive and encouraging she was and when she told me that she'd found me a spot in a flea market for two hundred dollars and volunteered to pay the first months rent there was no saying no. She knew I had a problem with drugs but she had such faith in the other me and saw my passion and love for cards that she believed that if I put the effort in the shop that I put into collecting then there was no way it could fail. But something preempted her advancing me the money and that was Larry. 'Til this day I see it as a blessing sent straight from the Lord. One day I was visiting with Fran and trading her lunch for some packs of cards when she received a call from Larry requesting to see me when I stopped by. I waited a few minutes then took the elevator up to his office where he was on a business call. He pointed to the chair opposite his desk and told me to have a seat. When he finished on the phone he leaned over the desk and stared me straight in the eye and asked me if I knew he had a Larry's Press Box in the US Flea Market Mall. Fran had alluded to this sometime earlier so I knew he did and nodded affirmatively. He then told me that he'd gone up there to check on it and told me just how dirty and nasty it was. He also told me that his workers weren't taking proper care of it and where it should have been making money hand over fist in actuality it was losing money. He then asked me since I lived next door to it if I would go there on Saturday and clean it up and vacuum it and make sure that it was it was in pristine condition and to take inventory of what was in the shop. Since I appreciated all that he had done for me in teaching me the card business and given me tips on what was hot and what was not there was little I could say. I didn't fully understand why he asked me but I gladly accepted thinking that this was one way in which I could show my gratitude.

I went home that evening and told Cheryl what Larry had asked me to do and asked her if she would help me on Saturday morning. I went to sleep that Friday night thinking. Larry knew I had a penchant about cards and couldn't understand how if he thought his workers were stealing from him why wouldn't the thought cross his mind that I might do the same. Of course, he'd walked in on me several times manning his store downtown when Fran would call the restaurant saying that she had to run an errand or pick up one of her kids from school and I'd been there alone. It was like leaving rats as security guards in a cheese factory. But I didn't steal.

Anyway, Cheryl agreed to help me and on Saturday we went about the task of cleaning the shop. Larry had one of the bigger shops in the mall but it only took us about a half an hour to do inventory. When we'd finished Cheryl plugged the vacuum in and began vacuuming the rug. There was a two thousand dollar ceramic bust of Pete Rose adorning the showcase and the chord accidentally wrapped around the statue and it hit the floor and shattered into more pieces than I care to remember. My

208

heart dropped and I cringed. What could I tell him? Did I
have to tell him anything? Should I tell him tell him I'd
taken Cheryl with me and she did it?

In the end I drove downtown and went up to his office
and simply told him that I had knocked it over and it had
broken. Hell, I thought he must have had close to ten
thousand in inventory that certainly wouldn't make or
break his day. But instead of him responding to the
broken bust Larry simply looked at me and said after
looking through the inventory and pointing to a
particular set of cards. 'These are my son Brandon's. If
you can would you bring these to me?' In all actuality, I
thought he was going to give me the set of cards he'd
picked out. They were worth about a hundred dollars but
he caught me off guard when he said, 'Bert you can have
everything in the store if you agree to pay the rent. What
I'm trying to say is that the store is yours. The rent is five
hundred dollars a month and is due next week." I grinned
excitedly and accepted his offer gladly although I had no
idea either what I was gonna do with it nor how I was
gonna keep it supplied. But Sheila was almost excited as
I was and kept telling me it was no problem and urging
me on. Both my mother and father were ecstatic as well.
And all else ended for me. I was teaching middle school
now in Raeford North Carolina and loving it. There was
no more crack cocaine in my life. I had a son who I
adored, two loving parents, a very loving and supportive
girlfriend who couldn't do enough for me, a career that
ultimately satisfied me and a hobby that consumed any
extra time I had. I was loving my life now.

I was teaching at West Hoke Middle School in Raeford,
North Carolina a small country town known for its turkey
factor. If you didn't work at the turkey plant chances are
you didn't work. It was the only employment there and
most of my students' parents were employed there. The
majority of the population was Black and the remainder

*were Lumbee Indian. These were Native Americans who
had been there since the time of John Smith's arrival and
as the story goes when John Smith went back to bring
back more settlers and returned he only found markings
on the trees but no settlers. As the story goes and despite
popular belief it was the Lumbee Indians who
incorporated them into their throes and hence you have
the only blonde, blue-eyed Native Americans I know of.
My students were the descendants of these first colonists.
It's a funny thing though the resemblance to Blacks these
Indians had. It's been long said that any part Black blood
you were Black. (Just ask Tiger...) The Lumbee Indian
feels that same wrath and has been permanently relegated
to the back of the bus. The projects of the South Bronx
were like the Hamptons compared to the shanties they
lived in. Poor wasn't even the word for them.
I had a friend Gail who I used to carpool with who grew
up in Johnstown, Pennsylvania and was as disoriented
and at a complete loss with poor urban children as
anyone I have ever seen. She was White and though I
have gone through hell and high water at the hands of
some Whites I must say that there are Whites who are
better at dealing with aspects outside and foreign to their
culture than others.
Gail had obviously not been exposed to poor people other
than White folks and it came through loud and clear.
When I first introduced myself to her she was at first
taken back. But after some time and my principal, Mr.
Langdon sending her to my classroom to observe and pick
up pointers on classroom management, she came to know
and respect me for my teaching expertise. What Gail
wanted more than anything else was to be a teacher. After
getting to know her somewhat she admitted that as a little
girl growing up in White America that was all she wanted
to be. But her traditional learning gave her theories and
curriculum but somehow left her far short when it came*

time to address our urban youth. When it came time to
build a rapport, hence a relationship with children she
was at a loss. The kids viewed her as Polly Purebread, a
White woman who had grown up on whole milk and
Wonder bread where they had grown up on Wise potato
chips and Nedicks orange soda for breakfast. There was
just too much of a division for her to bridge the cultural
gap and fuse the great divide and therefore her desire to
become a teacher would have been better served in her
hometown of Johnstown, Pennsylvania where everyone
resembled her than in this backwoods town of urban
poor. Still, I could see beyond the obvious and saw a
woman interested in making a difference and tried to help
her bridge the gap between her ignorance and lack of
empathy towards her students and her self. I did the best I
could to help her . Every evening we would go to Darryl's
or Chili's restaurant on our way home and grab some
buffalo wings and a couple of drinks and rehash the day.
I was older than she and perhaps that made a difference
but everyday she would find the glass half empty whereas
I would find it half full. It helped that I had Chris who
was extremely bright, (and my previous teaching
experience and working with inner city kids), so it helped
me to have a little more tolerance and understanding of
where they were coming from. But Gail had no inkling of
this or the mindset of inner city kids or the world they
lived in. But since someone chose her to fill a void and
teach my children I thought that she should at least be
somewhat aware if not adept at doing so. It was painful
going and I swear there were times that I just wanted to
toss in the towel. I wondered how someone could be so
blissfully ignorant. She grew to love me and was
appreciative of my helping her.
On occasion when I was busy or had something on the
agenda and didn't want to overburden my parents I'd ask
her to baby-sit Chris for me and oftentimes she would

211

return, face red and flushed, trying to catch her breath, and fuming. When I asked her what was wrong she'd go into this long tirade around what Chris had done or told her and though it wasn't that serious I'd reprimand Chris and be howling inside. (Believe Chris was a pistol.) But at the same time I had to ask myself if a thirty-year-old woman had trouble controlling a four year old what possessed her to think that she could handle middleschoolers who were perhaps the roughest population of students there were. The answer I received at the start of each school day when Mr. Langdon would bring me several of her students and ask me if I would allow them to sit in my classroom for the day.

My classroom was made up of the school's most severe behavioral problems—in other words I had bright Black boys that had been the victim of racism and who at thirteen or fourteen had basically decided that White folks in authority had nothing to say to them. I was a Black male and had endured all the same things and let them know it and whereas they saw the whole situation as hopeless I inspired hope. As in the Bronx they became mine. Gail, on the other hand, was neither willing to embrace or call these children so different and foreign to her anything more than her students with special needs. There was no attempt to guide them as people, there was no respect or love or caring and they knew this and refused to show her any type of respect. Many times over the course of the school year I prompted her to find the good qualities in her students and glorify these qualities. But she could find no good qualities, (even when I pointed them out specifically), in her students and so instead of creating a mutual affection there was constant friction that reached the boiling point and simmered over daily the result being that after awhile I simply included several of her students into my lesson plans. My principal recognized this and changed my designation from Special

212

Education Teacher who teaches children with behavioral problems to a cross-categorical designation so that I could teach all children with special needs, (or better yet the children no one else wanted in their classroom). After a while I took pride in the fact that no one else could handle these children but me. And when Mr. Langdon held our monthly staff meeting and had me stand up and made the comment that he wished he had the time to make an instructional video on how to manage a classroom and use Mr. Brown's class with some of the worst kids in the school as an example I thought I'd died and gone to heaven.

I had a self-contained class, which meant that my kids were mine and mine alone for the entire day. Not only weren't they able to change classes with the other students but they were basically separated from the rest of the school population like lepers.

Outside of school they mingled with the rest of the population and word soon got around to the other kids about Mr. Brown and it wasn't long before I had kids I'd never seen before knocking on my classroom door asking if they could sit in for reason or another. Teaching has always consumed me. As I told you earlier I have an obsessive compulsive personality and thanks to Lerone Bennett Jr. who wrote Before The Mayflower and of course Van Sertima's They Came Before Columbus I knew our contribution to America and despite what had transpired since our arrival here I felt it my responsibility to my Black boys to elevate them to the level that we had once been. I had their attention and respect so the rest was easy. Still, there were several of my students who had to learn to better conform to authority.

Weezas was one of those kids. He lived with his grandparents; was spoiled rotten and he was bright. He was probably my brightest student but at thirteen he was on probation for something involving a little White girl. I never did get the whole story but Weezas had a lot of anger when it came to White's and any time someone White attempted to redirect him I knew I'd have to find him and reel him in before it elevated and he cursed them out. It was funny since I stopped by his house several times after school to get a better understanding of where he was coming from and why he was so angry. His mother who was a sweetheart lived with her parents, as did Weezy. His father did not live there but from what his grandparents told me his father had another family two doors down and would come visit them yet never stop and even say so much as hello to Weezy. The coming and goings of his dad used to eat Weezy up. Yet, he was too bright to just let go so I made a deal with him. The deal was as follows. If he could control his temper and not curse anyone out for two weeks I'd take him home for the weekend. And for the next two weeks I didn't hear a peep out of Weezy. I took him home and spent the entire weekend with he and Chris and they loved it. I took them to the movies, the card shop that I now called Chris' Bullpen, and to the restaurant of their choice. They loved it. His grandparents were ecstatic and told me that all Weezy talked about in the weeks that followed was his visit to Mr. Brown's house.

Following the visit and knowing that I had at least twenty little Black boys in more or less the same position, I knew I had to do something and do it quick so I got some of my more supportive parents and some of my friends together and decided on an all night basketball tournament. Mr. Langdon who was always trying to involve the parents was thrilled. We had close to fourteen or fifteen pizzas, I rented some movies for those who weren't interested in playing basketball but wanted to be there anyway. Local businesses also donated twenty or so cases of sodas. They loved it. Gail was invited but didn't come and couldn't understand why I would give up my weekends for those kids. I'll tell you though they were good before the all-night basketball tournament but afterwards there wasn't a thing that I couldn't have asked for. They knew that I considered their lives as important as my life and I cared enough to postpone my immediate gratification to make sure that their futures were focused and on target. Weezy had gone out of his way to personally strive to do his best and his grandparents seeing the turnaround met with me once or twice a week to bring me small tokens of their appreciation. They had little problem in the way of Weezy's behavior now and were so appreciative that I never had to go shopping for fresh vegetables after that. In fact I only received one negative phone call after that concerning Weezy and in all actuality it was really not a problem. You see the connection between what was cool and what was in all emanated from BET which is designated the home of rap and hip-hop and in the early nineties all the young Black men were going beltless and busting a sag. To begin with in order to wear the style correctly one had to purchase their pants either a size or two too large in the waist so they were able to hang low around the hips. And from what I understand Weezy had begged and begged his grandmother to purchase him some pants so he could be in style and sport the latest fashion. But his grandmother who knew nothing of busting a sag wasn't willing to have her grandson going to school 'looking like no fool wit' some big ol' pants that don't fit' and so she refused to buy him any and so she called me. Weezy not to be denied had another plan. Now Weezy's grandfather was a mountain of a man standing about six foot three and weighing somewhere in the neighborhood of about three hundred pounds and he was a farmer. Anyway he was out in the fields long before Weezy left for school and with no man at home Weezy took his grandfathers extra pair of coveralls donned them and decided to wear them to school. It wouldn't have been so bad but Weezas stood no more than four foot eleven and his grandfather's overalls simply engulfed him. I caught as soon as he got off the bus and in enough time that the main body of kids hadn't had a chance to set into him. I took him home and had him change clothes but aside from that incident I had little or no problems out of Weezas. I said all that to say that BET was and is one of the most influential and negative influences on our children today. After having grown up in New York and then returning after college I contend that television in the absence of parenting can be very influential. BET brought gangsterism and the art of being a thug to every backwoods town across America. But in places like Raeford, North Carolina it wasn't a case of having to do something gangsterish or thuggish out of some necessity like having to eat it was just some wanna be mentality that gave them the idea that if it came out of New York then it was cool. Fashion evolved the same way. Drugs, objectifying women, fast money and fast cars were glorified while intellectualism and education were for all intensive purposes were put on the back burner. I hardly think this was a mistake. Since our arrival in this country education for Blacks has never been a priority for the powers that be and as long as we are ignorant, uneducated, and in the dark we pose no threat. I tried to explain this to my students and some understood what I was saying in full. Others got bits and pieces and still others didn't comprehend at all. Weezas was one of the one's that had a hard time comprehending. He had a fixation about being hard, about being tough, about being street, but I didn't condemn him for that. I believe to a degree that that's inherent in all little boys as they enter adolescence.

In a lot of societies the older males usually take them through this stage or passage of rights but here there was no right of passage because all too often there was no

216

*positive adult male role to guide them through this stage.
And so therefore the next logical entity was television and
the young Black men that resembled them adorned in
hundreds of thousands of dollars in jewels, and
surrounded by everything that America considered a sign
of success. So what if you had to stand on the street and
sell poison to your mother, or your sister or your little
cousin. That was the key to being a man, a*

*playa, and a balla. So what if you risked a bullet, or jail,
or your life. Hell, you could get killed crossing the street
during rush hour if you weren't careful. But hey if you
struck it rich like Tony Montana or Jay Z or Biggie then
what? You'd made it!
Weezy had this mentality and no matter what I told him
about the pitfalls of his way of thinking he just didn't get
it so I asked what he had planned for the Christmas
vacation before asking him if he wanted to go home with
me to New York City with me for the holidays. He jumped
at the chance. I then presented the idea to his
grandparents who seemed as anxious as he yet did not
offer to help at all with the train fare. Cheryl was glad to
be going home and so were my parents who were
accompanying Val, who had only recently married a
soldier from Fort Bragg named Joe. Jose was a
paratrooper from Los Angeles of Puerto Rican descent.
My father bought them house as a wedding day gift a
block or so away from their own home in Fayetteville but
it seemed like no sooner than they got married he received
his orders to relocate to the Bronx as an army recruiter.
A few days before Christmas, Weezy, Cheryl, Chris and I
took Amtrak up to New York. Somewhere, maybe an
hour or so into the ride Weezy started getting a little antsy
and after walking up and down the entire length of the
train Weezy came back to me and asked me for a couple
of dollars. I knew his grandparents had given him a few*

*dollars for spending change but he considered me his dad
and all day sucker so I gave him a five and he
disappeared again. After being gone an hour or so I
decided to make sure he hadn't gotten in any trouble and
found him in the lounge car playing poker with a group
of older gentlemen. I checked all around to make sure
they didn't mind him sitting in and though a couple didn't
seem too happy about his presence they were pretty
insistent about his staying. An hour or so later he
returned with a fistfuls of dollars. Weezy had to have a
little over a hundred dollars or so and he was beaming.
After giving me my five dollars back he returned to the
lounge with Chris who he had adopted and bought us all
food and drinks.*

*Arriving in New York we stayed at Jose's house out on
Sheepshead Bay. Here we stayed and got acclimated to
life on an army base. On the third day we went in to visit
Jose at his office in Washington Heights also known for
its' large population of Dominicans. Dominicans are a
beautiful people. They're a mixture of African, Spanish,
and Indian and in my opinion one of the prettiest people
to walk the earth. They're also known for having their
hand deep into the cocaine cartels and they've almost
single-handedly taken over the trade in Washington
Height making it an extremely dangerous place to be after
the sun goes down. I took Weezy to Jose's job and after
spending some time with him my father, Weezy and I went
downtown to give Weezy his tour of Manhattan. He loved
it. He loved the people, the crowds, the excitement, the
hustle and the bustle and all of the things that drove me
away from this meddling, mess of madness. On the way
back uptown to pick up my dad and Jose from work we
disembarked at our subway station late as Weezy had to
take in and examine every little thing and so any chance
we had to get out of the Bronx before nightfall was all but
history. So we ran up the subway stairs and Weezy*

*always cognizant of what the b-boys were wearing saw
three coming down the subway stairs and a smaller teen
heading up and out of the station. But the three going
down had obviously noticed something about the younger
lad that caught their attention and they cornered him.
Weezy who was curious turned to stop and watch when I
grabbed him and pulled. They were obviously robbing the
younger boy of his gold and sneakers and it was nothing I
wanted to be a party too. It had happened never
happened to me in all of my yeas but I'd learned from
watching that it was best to stay low key and quiet and it
would be soon be over. You might go home angry at your
loss but the important thing was that you would go home.
It was just all-apart of the city life and although you never
really got used to it you accepted it for what it was and
kept it moving. It was a great teaching moment but I
wanted him to think bout it. I knew he would bring it up
later and expect an explanation. Still, I promised myself
I'd let him dwell on it. But no sooner than we walked into
Jose's office and were in the midst of Jose and my father
Weezy blurted out, 'Mr. Brown, Mr. Jose me and Mr.
Brown just seen this kid get robbed.' Jose smiled, 'You
stay around here long enough you're gonna see a lot of
that.' Weezy respected Jose. Jose had grown up in
central L.A. a Puerto Rican in the land of Blacks and
Mexicans, in the land of Bloods and Crips and seen a
little bit of everything by the time he was in his late teens.
He'd been chased by this gang and that and now in his
late twenties was like me and wanted no parts of any of it.
The army had been his way out and he had jumped at the
chance to leave all of that behind. My dad just looked
away. He had seen his fair share of the seamier side of
New York as well and like me had grown tired of it and
had moved south. It was only new to Weezy and he had
been shook. The kid being robbed was not much older
than he and he was having a hard time dealing with it.*

219

And though he didn't say anymore I knew it had left an indelible imprint on him. Jose and my father put their coats on and Jose locked the office up. We stepped into one of those cold winter evenings New York is so well known for and there weren't many people still on the street and we headed to our subway home. Walking along one of the Bronx' side streets we came upon a group of Black and Hispanic young men. As we approached them not knowing who we were reached up and grabbed their gats from on top of the steel rollaway doors. Seeing this Weezy grabbed my hand and started pulling and pushing me to cross the street. Both Jose and my father redirected him while I tried to pull him back, masking my own fear at the same time. 'Don't do that!' I whispered at the same time. He was frightened and when we were amongst them everyone said what's up and continued walking. I breathed a deep sigh of relief and then chuckled to myself. Weezy overheard me and asked what was so funny. His hands now clammy from fear hardly saw any humor. 'The roughest toughest kid at West Hoke Middle School is suddenly afraid of his shadow.' I said now laughing aloud. He saw no humor in it and suddenly let go my hand. On the train Weezas turned and looked up at me as if to ask for an explanation but I had none to give. I guess we have all gone through the same thing, the fear, the not knowing, the streets and all that came with them. I don't know if that fear ever goes away but I explained what I did know to him. In the streets it's basically you against them. If you fear for your life then give them what they want. Your life means more than whatever you're trying to keep. But never show any outward signs of fear like trying to cross to the other side of the street. Then you're admitting you're afraid and you're inviting an attack. And then I asked Weezas if he still wanted to be gangster and thug. I asked if he still thought he was hard. He rode home the remainder of the

220

*way quiet, fixated and it was at that point that I knew the
money I'd spent to bring him to New York was nothing
compared to the growth and education he'd received. I
could have stood in front of his class and gone on for
days spouting and proselytizing about the evils of the
streets and how BET corrupts the minds of little Black
boys and it wouldn't have had nearly the same effect as
that fifteen or twenty minute ride to and from the Bronx
that day. Some years later my mother called to tell me
that she met Weezas grandmother in Wal-Mart. He was
now attending the University of Tennessee, was a
sophomore and had made the deans list. Tears come to
my eyes just writing about it. I only wish I could have
had the opportunity to affect more students in the way in
which I did Weezas and I may have. I just don't know.
New Years Eve came and Cheryl and I found ourselves on
a flight to Freeport in the Bahamas.
Arriving in Freeport we debarked and were ushered to a
limo, (which in all reality was a large van with limo
written on the side). We entered the limo on New Year's
Eve heading for the hotel. Before we'd gone a block there
was a thunderous noise like an explosion and I felt the
vans forward progress stop and go skidding sideways. A
woman drunk beyond belief had hit us. The impact of the
two cars colliding did nothing for her inebriation. I was
unhurt and unmarked. Cheryl, however, had a deep gash
in her leg that required seven or eight stitches. When she
attempted to get the information on the woman who'd hit
us she was asked if her name was Sue. She replied no
and the police officer at the scene who was now at the
hospital stated that all Americans were named Sue
because that's all they sought to do. She was released
and later transported to our hotel room where a fruit
basket and bottle of wine awaited her with a Get Well card
attached. She was comped a hundred or so dollars in
casino chips and I had a little over a thousand dollars to*

gamble with and we limped across the street into the casino and spent New Year's night gambling in a packed casino. I didn't win but found my hands getting clammy the same way they did when I was about to take a hit from the pipe. I didn't like the feeling but stayed there pulling the one armed bandit for half the night trying to hit and win the jackpot. I never saw a glimpse of Cheryl during our time there. Eventually we'd meet back in the room when we were spent. The men from the islands couldn't do enough for her and waited for her and greeted her like she was some type of queen making herself known to the commoners. I, on the other hand, was content to lie out on the beach and sip Jack Daniels and read. Well, I was content to do that until the day Cheryl came down to the beach and informed me that the book I was reading was upside down. That being true I still loved lying on the beach pretending to read. Cheryl was in heaven and I was content knowing that she was. We returned home and it was back to the humdrum reality of our daily lives. I'd left the business of running the card shop to Robert and Nilsa, a Puerto Rican couple that had a townhouse maybe a block or so from ours. I'd known Robert for a little more than a year and liked him. He was young and personable and helped out when the shop got especially busy so he was the logical choice when we went away. Sheila manned the smaller shop across town and had her hands full with that. She was complaining that I didn't spend much time with her anymore or the shop and I agreed. The shop she manned paid about seven hundred a weekend and took care of both rents but after the rent and other expenses were paid it was often difficult to restock the smaller shop or perhaps Sheila was right. Maybe I had taken it for granted and her along with it. I don't know but when I returned from Freeport I found that most of my inventory was missing and there was no money to account for the loss. It was obvious that Robert had stolen a good deal of merchandise or sold a good amount and pocketed the money. I was livid and spoke to my father and advisor on matters such as this. I spoke to him because where I had a temper and always believed in extremes like I need to hurt or kill this motherfucker he would make a more rational logical decision. You must recall I still had this bad gene. I guess his faith always provided him with the right thing to do. He believed, like I, that money was the root of all-evil and then because this had done nothing to dispel my anger he brought up and incident that had affected me greatly only a few weeks before. Cheryl had taken Chris to the pool in the apartment complex to go swimming. I guess Chris was about five years of age and somehow in the blink of an eye he'd gotten out into the deeper water and he'd almost drowned. I thought about the blessing he'd bestowed on me through Robert and as angry as I was with the loss I'd just taken I knew that all I could do was regroup and try to resupply. I knew it would be difficult since I had traveled to three or four states to amass my collection. Still, I was determined to start over and despite the loss which make have come to two or three thousand dollars I'd been smart enough to start a little nest egg just in case of emergencies such as this and though I knew I'd have to hit the road hard I was determined that I wasn't going to let anyone put me out of business. I hadn't lost my love for cards or the hobby but I'd certainly grown tired of what I had to go through to remain in business.

Trust me I ran into a lot of Whites that looked at the card hobby as a business exclusive of Blacks and one of the few bastions where they could go and hide from Blacks. For me to not only be apart of the hobby but to own two card shops was tantamount to a crime in a lot of people's eyes. I wasn't naive to any of this when I took over the business from Larry but I didn't look for it to be any different than any other venture I would have engaged in *that was White owned. But in 1992 when cards were big business and all the rage, the stakes were higher and the general consensus was that a Black man shouldn't have this store. I knew this and refused to let them beat me. Still, I felt the pressure. The weight of carrying two stores, trying to maintain a stable relationship with the mother of my child, and a career teaching disadvantaged children that needed more than the traditional classroom time was a bit more stressful than anything I'd expected but I went about it with all the passion and zest that I'd invested in everything I did.*

In a month or two everything was back to normal but it had taken its toll on me. Sheila had all but given up on me and was planning on leaving Fayetteville. She told me that she'd grown tired of Fayetteville wasn't making enough money, (who was), and was just ready for a change. I knew that she was being truthful in part but I also new that a large part of it had to do with the relationship between she and her mother. It seems that when Sheila was a child or better yet a teen her mother dated on the regular and Sheila felt neglected. Since then, (and Sheila was in her thirties now), she had a thing with her mother not wanting her. Now here she was once again running guilt trips on her mother, telling her mother that she hadn't been there when she needed her and now asking her to put her up in South Carolina until she found a place of her own. Her mother resided wither boyfriend in a studio apartment. He received rent free for being the janitor of the apartment complex they lived in. Even though there was barely room for the two of them Sheila moved in. She stayed in contact and for once she seemed happy if not satisfied. On the one hand I was glad for her but as with women I had a relationship with I studied them so as to get to know them better but also to get to know myself better and how to interact with them. One thing I knew about Sheila was that there was all this repressed pent up anxiety due to her mother and her childhood and her wanting what every woman I knew wanted and that was a good man and a wholesome fulfilling relationship. She repressed it for the most part but it has always been my belief that if you apply pressure in one area it will find some other area to let go of that energy. Someone stated that for every action there's an equal and opposite reaction. I certainly believed to this to be true in Sheila's case and although I was sorry she felt the neglect of abandonment by her mother I was certainly glad it manifested itself in her. In the bedroom all her pent up aggressions, and twisted thoughts of neglect exploded and any issues of abandonment came out fast and furious and turned into all kinds of freakish behaviors and I absolutely loved it.

Without Sheila I soon grew lonely and there was no one to turn and share my thoughts with. Sheila was always mature, low key, a rock when I needed someone to lean on, and now she was gone. It wasn't soon before I was dabbling again and not long after that I received a new threat.

After teaching and then helping my parents out at the store I'd drive and pick up odds and ends for the store. There were five or six other stores in Fayettevile all of whom sold the same things as far as the hobby was concerned and I knew that but I had to bring something that set myself apart and kept customers seeking something new. I did this with high end, must have collectibles and I soon had a customer base that looked just for those items. Sales were up and competition was little or none. I'd carved out a nice little niche for myself when Perry came along. At first I thought he was no more than a customer but after several weeks of getting there first and buying up all of my high priced items I realized that he had an ulterior motive working. And after meeting down at Larry's with all of the other hobby shop *owners I soon realized that I wasn't the only one being victimized by Perry's buying sprees. At first I welcomed his buying but when my loyal customers came in each Saturday morning and my finest items had been depleted I was in somewhat of a quandary. I couldn't refuse his purchases and I knew that a bird in the hand was worth two in the bush. If I didn't sell to him there was a chance that I would be stuck with an item and he never questioned my retail prices, which were marked up considerably. The problem was that when he finished shopping my store looked like a Sunday night at closing, the shelves empty. Now when customers came in on Saturday mornings they wondered if I'd lost interest or was going out of business. Not seeing what they wanted they usually turned and walked away. In time everyone was asking who this Perry was. None of us knew but we were all speculating. I did everything I could to stay afloat but we soon realized that there was no way we could deny him the right to buy or curb his greed. We eventually found out that he had an Asian woman bankrolling him and his intent was to bring us all to our knees and then open his own colossal store. Most of us were first time business owners and had only gotten in because of our love for the hobby. Business acumen was not our claim to fame.*

After months of this agonizing, nail biting, effort in futility he came in and made me an offer to buy it and all the merchandise in it. I sold it and dove deep into my addiction. Not long after that I quit teaching and called Sheila. She was still living with her mother and her mother's boyfriend but was saving her money and planning on moving out. I called her and told her that I was knee deep and not doing too well and she was elated. Not elated that I had once again succumbed but elated with the chance of us being together again. I loved her. There was no doubt about that. She was sexy and bright but I didn't have myself together to the point where I could maintain a relationship and especially with one as needy as she and I knew that if she accepted my request to join her in Charleston then the first thing that she'd say to herself is that I'd finally come to my good senses and decided to leave Cheryl. The crack addiction never bothered Shelia. I'd stop by her apartment on the way from a night out hoping, praying, wanting, fiending, and she would bring me in, sit me down and delve into my inner psyche trying to find out where my mind was. Once she did she'd let me have my way. If I needed her in the physical sense she was there for me. If I needed her in an emotional or intellectual way she was there for me. If I just needed to cry and vent she was there for me. She never got upset or frustrated but was always patient and calm. I not only liked her for this but also appreciated it immensely. Still, I had no real interest in marrying or entering a relationship other than perhaps a friendship with her or anyone else. I guess it goes back to the fact that I couldn't strong arm a girl to go with me in high school. And I wasn't trying to lock lips with a woman for a lifetime when I could become intimately involved with a woman now and share the experience of loving her and letting the relationship run its course without making an empty commitment to loving someone for a lifetime when I lived for the moment.

Most, (if not all), of the women I came to know wanted the lifetime commitment and although it never really became a matter of substance it was always an issue. It never became more important or put our relationships in jeopardy because I had a very simple philosophy on marriage that simply stated 'that all things in time', and if it's meant to be then it'll be and let's just let the relationship run it's course and when the time comes I'm sure we'll both know it'. A few times I did reach that level where I thought I was seriously ready for marriage.

Sheila was one of the women I often thought I wanted to spend the rest of my life with but at the present time I just wanted to get out of Fayetteville and away from all the bad karma that seemed to be attracted to me and was intent on smothering me.

Not long after that I grabbed the few thousand dollars I'd amassed over the last couple of years and along with Val and Jose drove down to Charlestown, South Carolina. Charleston, with its weeping willow trees adorning both sides of the narrow streets and southern plantations is perhaps the most beautiful place I've ever visited. Its quaint old historic beauty was so utterly serene and peaceful that I was quite taken by it the moment I got there.

Sheila was ecstatic to see me and quickly pulled me into the fold introducing me to mom and Max. The first week or so was like old times. Sheila acted like my arrival was the second coming and though I wasn't feeling really good about up and leaving and starting over once again there was hope. Cheryl was financially stable so I knew Chris would be looked after but I still had this strong belief that you can feed and house a child without necessarily nurturing a child and when it came to parenting my son I not only had my doubts but knew that I could do a better job so I had my druthers about leaving Chris but my addiction left me little choice. My parents, on the other hand looked on it as a Godsend. The fact that I was leaving Cheryl gave them hope for their son. According to them she was the sole reason for my addiction. And though I don't attribute my addiction to her and try to take full responsibility there is still something that sticks in my craw when it comes to Cheryl playing a role in my addiction.

Not to belabor Cheryl, my addiction or the fact that I was leaving my only son behind I found Charleston to my liking and in no time at all had become quite at home. I

228

*especially liked going downtown where the African
women would come in on the weekends from the Gullah
Islands offshore. It fascinated me how just minutes
offshore of the mainland these African women had
maintained there African language and culture despite
being thousands of miles away from Africa. Proud they
cared less about the Americans who made up the
mainland and seeme only interested in selling their
African wares to tourists who much like myself were in
awe of how they had maintained their cultural identity.
Colorful bars and quaint businesses lined the streets
around the market and was always bustling as people
moved to and fro soaking up the rich southern sun. The
weather was always warm and mild and made it ever so
conducive to living there.*

*Max was the custodian for an apartment complex with
two large lakes out in front of it and it was not uncommon
to walk out and see slow moving alligators either entering
the shallow waters or making their way on land. Max
was an outdoorsman so he was in tune with the whole
nature bit. I, on the other hand kept a baseball bat by the
door and a phone to call the fire department, the police
and EMS if one of them looked in my direction. Sheila's
mother was in tune to this outdoorsy shit too and Sheila
so intent on getting the long lost love from her mother
jumped right on the bandwagon. When I arrived these
Negroes did not see me as the cool kid from New York
City but more like this week's guest on Bow and Arrow.
And when I got there they went about purchasing me my
own fishing rod and gear so I could go out on the boat
with them and do a little deep-sea fishing. Now if you
remember back to my tales of the Marines you should
know that I am a land lover by nature. And the Black
folks I know aren't particularly fond of boats or water,
(especially after recollecting on the cruise that brought
them here). But here in the South they are quick to jump*

*on the bandwagon and someone mentioned deep-sea
fishing and now they are all out on the Atlantic trying to
catch marlin. The thing with my people is that they don't
own forty or fifty foot yachts though. In fact anything
from a rowboat to a homemade raft seen on HGTV will
do and Sheila's family fell into that group. Well, I
weaseled my way out of that little outdoor venture and
settled on going shrimping and crabbing which was to my
way of thinking a little safer, (you stayed on shore to
shrimp), since all shrimping and crabbing consisted of
was tying a chicken bone to a piece of string and throwing
it two or three feet off the bank of the river or putting
some bait in a metal cage and throwing it off the shore
both of these appealed to me. Meanwhile you fished
while these delicacies were getting caught in your snare.
It was all great fun and after an hour or two you might
even find yourself in the midst of a seafood dinner all at a
cost of a couple of dollars for some chicken necks. All in
all it, was good fun and good dining too and made up the
majority of our entertainment while we lived there but in
weeks we both were working and found a charming little
villa minutes from downtown Charleston. Life was good
then. We enjoyed each other's company and would sit
around and talk for hours and joke and laugh about
anything and everything that came to mind. When there
was little else to talk about we'd search through the
entertainment portion of the newspaper and find some
remote jazz café and sip wine and listen to the music until
the wee hours of the morning. It couldn't have been any
better and not one to look a gift horse in the mouth I just
thanked God and kept stepping but with every rainbow
there is always some rain and things had been going a bit
too well when Sheila started inquiring about things that
could only damper our arrangement. Things like
marriage... She wanted to know if I was happy and
countered that she was happy and wanted to know why we*

couldn't be happy for a lifetime together. The mere
thought of anything for a lifetime, (which was the same as
forever to me), was like doing acupuncture in an open
wound and so I backed off a little. Then there was the
fact that we needed transportation and she having family
in Charleston made arrangements with Bubba to lend us
a Chevy to use at our, (actually it was at her discretion),
before I arrived and I don't know what kind of cousin he
was or what side of the family he belonged to but this
cousin Bubba became somewhat agitated when I moved
in. In any case, we used this car and I feeling good but as
is my nature always wanting more met a White woman in
a grocery store with a few of my mentally handicapped
clients and she got to exclaiming about how patient and
well I worked with them. Turns out she ran a mentally
handicapped facility in someplace called Summerville,
(which I later found out was only a stones throw away
form Charleston). Anyway, she offered me a job right
there on the spot and I later accepted. The facility she
ran was more or less the same as all the rest with one
exception that was to be my downfall. There were forty
some odd other employees. And they were all women...
This wasn't in itself bad and probably wouldn't have been
an obstacle to most people but it certainly was to me.
Here I was in a relationship with not only my best friend
and my lover who had taken me in when I was down and
out and now I had the temptation of forty women, most of
them single and all of them Black waiting on someone
who really didn't know what he wanted out of life.
In any case, I was placed in a home with a young lady by
the name of Laura who was tall and as wild as they come
to be my trainer. That weekend she felt me out trained me
and told me that after the clients were gone to sleep then
anything goes. And with that said she pulled out a fifth
and we sipped until we were both fast asleep. The next
weekend we did the same only this time from a hotel room

*right outside of Charleston. The weekends were the first
time Sheila and I had been apart since I arrived and she
was more than a little curious to know what had
transpired. I told her the first weekend and may have put
a little too much emphasis on Laura's training because
no sooner than I walked in the door the second weekend
she asked me, 'You fucked her didn't you?' It was
obvious I had and in all reality she didn't appear too
angry. But what surprised me, (and I don't know why
anything Sheila did would surprise me), but her
questioning was not why I had or how did I feel towards
Laura but instead centered on how I did it and was it
good and then asked me if I would fuck her the way I
fucked Laura. She even asked me if she screamed... It
was all a bit much but I did as I was commanded and to
my surprise after that day there was little mention of it but
I started noticing differences in her attitude. There was
no doubt that something was going on that was causing
her significant anguish but never one to tell I could only
imagine what she was going through. Not long after I'd
come clean about Laura I came home only for her to tell
me that she'd slept with Bubba and that he'd taken the
car. The house looked like it had been hit by a hurricane
and I wasn't sure if he'd beaten her or just had sex with
her. What I did know was that she'd made it a point not
to let me know too much and unlike her I wasn't about to
ask for details. A few days later, she and I went
downtown and I commented on a well-dressed gentlemen.
We were in a large crowd there waiting for a jazz concert
to start and I was just making idle chatter, nothing
serious. As I looked over the crowd I grabbed Sheila's
arm and said, 'Look at her. Doesn't she look nice?' The
elderly woman of about sixty wasn't elegantly dressed, the
epitome of class and I appreciated people that took forth
the time and put forth the effort to stand head and
shoulders above the crowd. Sheila didn't see it that way*

though and started yelling attracting the crowd's attention for no apparent reason. 'You wanna fuck her don't you. Go ahead and fuck her then. That's what you wanna do. Why don'tcha just fuck her then.' At first I took her seriously and tried to make sense of it and then I realized that her problems were a lot more deep seated than I wanted or had time to deal with so I just let it go and walked back to the car where I sat trying to make sense of what had just happened before heading home.

Not long after that I moved out and up to Summerville where I found a nice little one-bedroom apartment in an adults only community. It was by a very wealthy, elderly, White couple that I came to know and respect. I continued to work at the group home and made some very close friends. Sivitra Lighty was perhaps my best and closest friend during this time and replaced Sheila nicely as my new advisor and confidante without all the hysterics and drama. Sivitra was a big woman who carried herself well. She had a pleasing personality, an easy smile, and an infectious laugh. We had engaging conversations on just about anything and everything and she like I were caught in the crosshairs of our lives neither of us knowing exactly where we were headed. What I liked most about Sivitra though is that she was honest and quick to give me the heads up about the women I worked with. She had a boyfriend or so she said she did but she was one of the few women that put no demands on me and when she was free we'd go out and eat or take in a movie or just make love. I liked that about Sivitra. She was independent, had her own life, her own apartment, was used to making on her own and independent of a man and harbored no ill feelings or negative vibes when it came to what she wanted, when she wanted it and never had any qualms about the meaning of the relationship. We were friends. That's where it began and ended. When other females were around she simply acted like we were the best of friends and if she thought she was intruding she made her leave. Sivitra never stayed long anywhere anyway. I guess that was just her nature. She kept busy and I believe that by keeping busy she never gave her mind the time to think or dwell on what things might have been. They were all intensive purposes what met the eye, no more no less. And she endeared herself with me and everyone else. Of course there were those that speculated that she was doing more than just dropping by to say hey to a friend but she looked good, out dressed the rest and was oblivious to the gossip. When I tired of the gossip on who I was sexing that week or what plans they had for me or who was next in line and the normal catfights that women became embroiled in Sivitra would feel for me and take me out or bring over a bottle of wine and we'd sit and mellow to some jazz over a bottle of Merlot until I'd fallen asleep in my recliner with her softly massaging my back and then she'd be gone. I might hear from her the next day when she called to check on me but that was it. Funny thing was though that everyone liked her and at the same time they were all jealous of her. When I confronted her about this she just laughed in her high pitched shrill voice and said she knew but it wasn't worth the time trying to figure others out she was much to busy doing her to look back at all those trying to catch up. I guess we rode the same wave and that's why we got along so well. To this day I don't really know.

By this time I was working three jobs and not just maintaining but doing the damn thing so well that those in management started hearing about me and I started making a name for myself in the front office. Still, the amount of hours was beginning to take it's toll and rumors were beginning to bubble about how I was looking for a little something less stringent. I was too. And had decided that I either had to cut down my hours or quit altogether. On paydays I hardly had a chance to do anything other than pay my rent and rush to my next job. And a day off was like a rain shower over the Sahara Desert so few and far between were they. Not wanting to lose me management called me in one afternoon and offered me a position as a job coach. The job was nothing to write home about but the salary was. At first I didn't understand it but after it was explained that company morale had risen and where the workers were not apt to move and keep their clients moving I kept mine moving. You see it was the only time I had for myself and here I was in a new place trying to take it all in and yet never having any time because all I did was work so I flipped the script and made my clients part of my welcome to Charleston committee and so if I was curious they to were curious. We visited museums, historic sites, plantations, and conservatories... You name it we did it and after awhile the clients began telling other staff and their families and pretty soon my fellow staff members were checking my agenda for the weekend and began to follow along or initiate their own outings. And being that a good many of them knew more bout Charleston than I did I followed them when it interested me. Soon word got back to Ms. Thomasina Alston, (the finest woman in all of South Carolina), and she made me a proposal that I gladly accepted. I'd seen Thomasina around from time to time but like Sivitra she was aloof to say the least and had an uppity air about her that almost said she was too good to speak to anyone that wasn't management or at least making six figures. But I ignored this. By this time I'd slept with most of the staff and I'd only been there a little over a year so as fine as she was and as bourgie and standoffish as she appeared to be I was hardly flustered by her demeanor. Well that's what I thought. After she proposed the raise and change of positions I sat there while she went on about one of my clients who had a *crush on her. George was a highly functioning mentally handicapped White of about thirty years of age who had a crush on Thomasina. (I must say that if George was in any way handicapped his handicap hardly affected his sight) Thomasina was built as well as any woman I have ever known or been in the company of. And ended up taking both Thomasina and George to the restaurant. To make a long story short, George had a crush on Thomasina and everyone knew it and he'd been asking her out for the longest time. But in her eyes she did not think it appropriate for her to go out on a date with a client and so she asked me if I'd chaperone. Now as I've expressed to you previously I didn't have a lot of free time working three jobs but I was of the same mind set as George and figured what harm could an hour or two do in the company of this goddess. So, I agreed. What happened, however, was that I became the chauffeur, picking up both Thomasina and George and escorting them to the restaurant. She'd gone home and changed and was wearing a white flowing dress in the manner of Marilyn Monroe, no stockings, and a pair of white espadrilles. Her hair was close cropped and she looked like an African queen. She as always looked good and she knew it and if she didn't George certainly let her know, stuttering and drooling all at the same time. I really and truly thought he was going to come right there but I couldn't say anything because I with all my suave and cool debonair wasn't far behind him. Seldom do women shake me up to the point that I'm speechless but after a couple of shots and a pitcher of beer I still found myself unable to speak. I watched and listened and felt a little more comfortable after seeing a couple of people I knew. It just so happened that the restaurant was a huge crab shack right across from my apartment complex and was a frequent watering hole for me. Their specialty was an all you could eat crabs for sixteen ninety-five so I virtually lived there. When we were finished and had taken George home Tommy, (as she liked to be called), suggested that we go have a last drink before calling it a night. I humbly obliged and when it was time to leave I asked her where her car was parked only to find out that her oldest daughter had dropped her off and taken the car. This wasn't what I wanted to hear as I was feeling the Jack now and waited for her suggestion. I wanted nothing more to be rid of this woman with her fancy talk and highbrow demeanor but instead she asked if I was in any shape to drive. I told her no hoping that she'd call herself a ride home and I'd be done with the whole she-bang. Instead she suggested that I stop by my place and grab some coffee. Usually if this suggestion is made from a woman that I'm attracted to the wheels start turning but this was a whole new level and I knew that the waters were deep and I was in over my head and was at best scared. But I did as was told and took her up stairs and let her make a pot of coffee. Three years later she was still making that pot of coffee. After making love I don't know how many times and how many ways there was no one else. She was at the top of the food chain, elegant and wordly and I knew that I had stepped it up. But with me clean and holding down two jobs and in demand there wasn't much anyone could tell me.*

Sivitra would come by now every now and then but there was nothing other than conversation anymore. And she'd laugh at how all my freedom was now gone since Tommy entered the picture. I was on lock. No longer did my female friends call from downstairs to let me know they were on their way up. No longer did women just stop by. And I must say to her credit that she never did more than give them a friendly smile and present herself as cordial and friendly. It was just something about her. Tommy had that certain something that would make men accompanied by their wives just stop and stare and other women cringe and head for the hills never to return but I never questioned her because she was enough.

Of course, and this I truly believe, there are people who have good hearts that are never meant to be in a relationship. I truly believe this and for the longest time I believed I was one of those people. If marriage and longevity are the keys to happiness I just don't believe that I am one of those that has the qualifications. Perhaps a year or so went by and I decided that Chris would be better off with me and so I went and got him and brought him back with little or no resistance from Cheryl and Tommy thought he was the greatest thing in the world. She had three teenage girls and had always longed for a son so she went about adopting Chris as her very own and oft times I 'd have to fight to spend a little time with my own son. But she and her girls loved him and were always begging to keep him so I let her. Besides I was a first time parent and she was five years older than I and had raised three where I had raised none so I listened and learned. When I tended to be too drastic in my approach she was always there to temper my anger. Later that year I had a daughter with Cheryl on one of those rare trips to take Chris to see his mom. When she was born I went and got her as well. Her name was Nicole. But as I have stated previously it just wasn't meant to be.

My father who was so pleased at how I had finally gotten myself together and was now playing Mr. Mom to a son and a daughter came down to see if the rumors were true. Like every other female Tommy enamored him and I guess he was as proud of his son as a father could be. To him Tommy was a stallion, a thoroughbred, a looker and he appreciated her being there for me but even more he appreciated her caring for his grandchildren who he so adored. Tommy couldn't do enough for Frank and took him everywhere she thought he wanted to go. If he thought too loudly she was off and running trying to fulfill his every wish. It made me feel good that she would work so hard to try and please him in her effort to show me how much she loved me. I was in love and would have certainly married her and been content to live the rest of my days right there in Charleston but Tommy was still married. Her husband was incarcerated and she never but ever mentioned marriage. I wondered about this but never approached her around the subject. I knew she was concerned about our age difference and the fact that she had three daughters and a nephew she was caring for but I never looked at them as a problem. I was making good money between the three jobs and had the mindset that there wasn't anything that I couldn't do so I didn't count her children as a financial burden. And I loved them all. Still, I never brought the proposition of marriage up. Christmas was approaching rapidly and my father's only concern was the enormity of the Herculean task that I had undertaken. Three jobs and two children even with help was a lot to take on. But I had the attitude that I'd wasted too much time flirting with drugs and so if nothing else I had to make up for lost time. In a sense I was driven but at last it was in a positive direction and I think Frank knew that. Yet he still hated to see his son struggling so. Thomasina was taking Chris to daycare in the morning and dropping me off at work unless she had to take her kids to school or had to work. When she did my man Jabril would stop by in his cab and make the rounds dropping me off at work and then taking six year old Chris to daycare and then picking Chris up and then me from work in the evening. A young white couple that lived across the apartment complex would babysit Nicky. They were so good to her that she would cry when I would come to pick her up in the evening. Looking back now I must admit it was a bit much. On Christmas I woke up with eyes as wide as any child anticipating Santa Claus' arrival, (I had a sneak preview), to see my family's joy of

239

*the Christmas I'd planned. Chris excited raced into the
kitchen to see if Santa had eaten any of the cookies he'd
eaten any of the Oreo's he'd left out for him the night
before. He was shocked and a bit taken back to find that
half the plate was gone before proceeding into the living a
smile as wide as a football field etched on his face and
then seeing all the presents raced to wake his
grandfather. I went and changed Nicky and brought her
from her crib into the excitement and she crawled under
the tree not knowing what all the hub bub was about. I'd
made sure that my father had everything that he never
needed and was content to lean back and pat myself on
the back and just soak up their happiness when
Thomasina knocked on the door and asked for my father.
He returned and placed a set of keys in my hand.
Thomasina grinned and handed me a small package.
Taking it I kissed her, thanked her, and had Chris grab a
garbage bag of gifts for herself and her girls. She
promised to return later and invited Frank over to her
place for Christmas dinner, which he gladly accepted. No
sooner than she left he picked Nicky up, grabbed Chris by
the hand, (no easy task getting him away from his toys),
and took me outside. In my parking space, which had
been vacant aside from Tommy's car, was a brand new
red, Dodge Shadow. 'Just trying to make life a little
easier for you son.' I was shocked. Days later he left and I
was never so grateful. My relationship with Thomasina
continued for a year or two and I'd grown accustomed to
her coming over on Friday nights after work and frying
fish and drinking beer. That was our time together—just
the two of us. The topic of marriage never came up and if
there had been anyone around that time that I would have
considered marrying Thomasina would have been my
logical choice. She made me happy, made life easier and
made life worth living. Chris loved her and I couldn't
have asked for more. My addiction was in the past, a*

240

distant memory and there was nothing but hope for the future. There was no need to dabble and sip the juices of women, I had the woman of my dreams and if she'd have me then I would be glad to call her mine for the rest of my life. My conviction steadfast now I decided to ask Thomasina to marry me and there was no better time than Valentine's Day.

Valentine's Day morning I woke up earlier than usual, took the dozen red roses from the refrigerator, packed Chris and Nicky in the car and headed for Tommy's house. I felt good pulling up in the driveway and rushed anxiously to the door. Her daughter answered and I immediately knew there was something wrong. But hey what could be so wrong? After three years and with more thought than I'd given anything in my life but I knew this was the right move. I asked if her mother was home once more and she still stared at me as if I were a mere figment of her imagination before looking at me as if she were ready to cry and said, 'My dad's here.' I was stunned. I stood there speechless, unable to move. Tommy hearing the noise finally came to the door and stood there looking at me looking almost as shocked as I was. The only thing I noticed was the large, red and purple passion marks on her neck. Handing her the roses I muttered, 'these were for you.' I turned and walked away. My mind was a jumble of thoughts as I drove home. I stopped at the liquor store and bought a fifth of Jack Daniels. At home I cracked the bottle and sipped half of it before the morning was over. I don't know how I managed Chris and Nicky as tears streamed down my face. I do remember Chris asking me if I was alright before asking me if he could have some ice cream, and cereal, and candy, and popcorn and pop tarts and everything else he knew he wasn't supposed to have and when I entered the kitchen to wash my face there sat my kids in a pile of pudding and God knows every type of sweets known to mankind. I saw

*them but was too shattered to do anything other than cry
some more before playing Sade on for the fifth or sixth
time.I was crushed.*

*A week later, I took my kids to their mother while I tried
to regroup. I tried to regroup. But the mere thought of
Tommy and the tears would start flowing. I picked up
what was becoming my routine and bought a fifth of Jack
and headed home. I was drinking every night now but it
was hardly enough. I remembered seeing a club that I
used to pass by on my way to work. By now I knew when
there was something going on and I knew the boys
standing out front were doing something. I pulled up and
several ran up to the car. I chose one and tasted the
product. It was definitely that hard white cocaine and the
first time I'd even considered doing it in two years.*

*I bought five rocks, paid my man and pulled off. No
sooner than I pulled off I saw blue lights in my rear view
mirror. At this point I didn't give a fuck. I eased all five
rocks in my mouth and eased the car over to the side of
the road. When I looked up there were four other police
cars pulling up. My heart was in my mouth. I knew I
was busted. An officer told me I'd straddled the line but I
knew that there was no probable cause but they'd
probably seen me pull up at the spot.*

*After checking my license, insurance, and registration
and searching the car and finding nothing I was released
with a ticket. Truth of the matter was that I'd let one of
the rocks drop to the floor of the car when I was putting
them in the mouth and they had overlooked it. I was so
shook when I got home that all I could do was sit in the
living room. I wanted to know how things had gotten so
bad in so short a time. But they had and now the days
were evolving so slowly it was like watching paint dry. I
sat and smoked until the sun came up. The smoke was
good and I found myself lost but serene. All my thoughts
of Tommy were now gone but the pain and loss remained.*

242

A day later, Thomasina came by the house. She had her own key and for some reason she took the liberty of letting herself in. I was still so incapacitated that I didn't bothered to move or get up. I just stared at her and I must have put the fear of God in her because she took one glance at me and ran right back out the door.

I don't know what she saw but she later told me that I looked at her in a way no one had ever looked at her before. She said she saw something that said I looked as though I wanted to kill her. I did but I didn't know it showed and I certainly wouldn't have done anything to jeopardize my own self. But not less than a week later I packed up as much as I could fit in my car and headed back to North Carolina.

The change of scenery did little for my state of being. In fact, I was even more depressed that I had to return and leave my independence. I soon found a position as a group home worker on third shift and was fine with that as I didn't want for much and had little desire or motivation to do anything else other than try to get straight again. During this time I did little and one night in my effort to stay awake at work I picked up a paper and pencil and began to write. The next night brought the same and any time that I found a few minutes I found myself writing, continuing the saga of Sylvia Stanton, the new love of my life, my heroine. I enjoyed my new pastime almost as much as I did anything and soon my new passion engulfed me. I went to bed writing, woke up writing, ate writing, made love through my writing. I had other things going on but everything played second fiddle to my writing. It was my therapy. I had charges pending and I was facing a hundred and ten years for sending away for CD's that were advertised on the back of the Parade section of the Sunday newspaper. I always had a passion for music—any type—and when I saw the opportunity to purchase thirteen for a mere penny plus the shipping and handling I jumped at the opportunity. Hell, I worked and could fulfill my commitment obligation or so I thought so I enrolled another nine or ten times under someone else's name. They called it mail fraud. I called it the opportunity of a lifetime. I even bought bookshelves to house all my new CD's and it was going good and I was starting to enjoy life once again when the police rolled up to the house like I was Osama Bin Laden and I was public enemy number one. There were cop cars and detectives. In fact, there was everything but the S.W.A.T. team on hand for me and my CD's. I held Chris down on the floor just in case they started shooting. Instead they knocked and I of course didn't answer and waited until they'd all left and then I drove my son and myself over to my mother's. I later went downtown and turned myself in. I was fingerprinted and let go on my own recognizance and spent the next year wondering how much jail time I would receive. I have no fondness for being incarcerated. I have never been very fond of men so it was not my wish to be incarcerated. And the mere thought of ten years on each count scared the beejesus out of me and the only way I knew how to not drive myself crazy with worry was to write. So, it was both therapeutic and relaxing to me. I finished the book some months later. I paid my lawyer five thousand dollars for him to assure me that I wouldn't do any time but each time I went to see him he was anything but reassuring stating that he didn't know but was waiting for the right judge to hear my case. Little did I know that the good ol' boy network worked in such a way that a lawyer had a certain affinity to certain judges and could almost guarantee whether you did any time or not. I know if there were kickbacks or what but when I went up in front of the judge he announced the charges. There were people in there being charged with everything from possession of crack cocaine to homicide. But when

244

*the judge read my charges and then said that the
maximum sentence for my offense was a hundred and ten
years the entire courtroom gasped in disbelief. I sat there
with my mother who didn't flinch and I gained strength
from her. And then the good ol' boy network of judge
and lawyer and D.A. huddled and when they broke up I
knew that the whole thing had been a farce and they were
just going through the whole act. Seven years probation
and ten thousand dollar fine was the verdict. I was put on
intensive probation where I had to go and see my
probation officer once a week for the first year and once a
month for the remainder of my probationary period. My
probation officer didn't understand why my sentence was
so harsh and relaxed my probation as much as he could
but he could have relaxed it totally. I was now a
convicted felon and could not obtain a job. My teaching
career was over and anytime someone saw felon on my
application I could basically throw the towel in. I had a
son and daughter to raise with no chance for income but
not to be outdone I moved my family to Greensboro.
Valerie had gone to college at North Carolina A & T and
I had been there on several occasions to visit her and
loved it. And so with our meager belongings I moved my
family to Greensboro and immediately set out to find a job
and make it once more. It didn't take long for Cheryl and
I to locate jobs with K-Mart distribution Center. We both
worked nights unloading trucks and it paid the rent but I
wanted more and so I found a job in a Black owned group
home. Within a year I'd risen to the title of Program
Director for the company. I enjoyed the position although
it kept me busy from the time I got up 'til the time I went
to bed and often woke me up when I was asleep to go out
and tend to one of my crazy or frequently disgruntled
teenagers. In more instances than not I'd bring my hell
raisers home with me and put them in a spare bedroom so
I wouldn't have to go searching the projects at three or*

245

four in the morning for them. This way, at least I knew where they were.

The toll of working two full time jobs was taking it's toll on me by this time and I opted to leave K-Mart after six or seven months. I had a plan though but putting it into effect would take a little start up money and all the money I was making was going for bills so I grabbed a little part time job at a local curb market and ended up loading watermelons and other produce from a truck in my spare time. It was hard but I'd never been a stranger to hard work and I was motivated by my dream of once again owning my own business. To this day I still believe that the most fulfilling job one can have is when he's running his own business and calling the shots. To me there is no greater joy than when one controls the plight of his own destiny. After a year or so I'd saved enough money to realize my dream and found a small flea market and opened a booth. The card business now a thing of the past I started shopping at yard sales and collecting anything and everything that I thought would have a significant retail value and that I could turn over quickly for a profit. I did well but I soon recognized that even though my merchandise was nice and under priced Whites refused to shop with me. Nothing that I could do would allow them to spend their money with me so was their hatred. So, I quickly revamped my selling tactics and redesigned my whole schemata so that everything I sold was ethnocentric and catered to the Black buyer. I found a distributor in Florida that wholesaled Black music and I started an account. I found an Indian distributor in New York that sold brass. And I picked up Black books straight from the publisher and wrote to well-known Black artists who sold prints to me at way below market value. I saw my sales rise and my customer base grow to the point where I was no longer just making ends

246

meet but beginning to live lavishly and in the fashion that I was accustomed to once again.

Chris and Nicky were growing up and I loved them both to death. Chris spoiled was as mischievous as I was growing up. I'm thinking he had that bad gene too. My mother called him loquacious which I thought was putting it mildly. The boy talked constantly and stayed in trouble at school. My father chalked it off to his being bright. The teachers, however, were climbing the walls. It didn't bother me any since I considered myself ADHD without the formal diagnosis. I took him everywhere I went and he would get into the car talking and still be talking when we arrived back home. Nicky, on the other hand, proved to be Chris' alter ego in almost respect. Quiet and reserved, my pudgy little girl was quiet and stayed by my side most of the time. I adored them both and was somewhat adamant about being father of the year if there is such a thing.

The years following were much of the same. I was dinking now and even began mainlining cocaine but that was short-lived. I was too afraid of all the things that were associated with the needle. There were Aids, those God awful ugly track marks and the constant threat of overdosing so I just left it alone and stuck to smoking my life away. Life went on as such. I smoked, drank, and dated on the regular.

As the years went on I noticed how crack changed people. Observant, I'd always studied people. What became fairly obvious to me was that crack changed people. It turned them into animals. Crack was an exercise in survival of the fittest. I saw so many shiesty moves amid schemes that it made me wonder if crack wasn't the devil himself. I saw people hurt, maimed, shot and emasculated. And I thanked God for Claudia and Frank and the morals and ethics they instilled in me. I saw men—big, strong, hard men drop to their knees in front of other men for a hit of

*crack. There were women, on more than one occasion,
who would beg me to suck my dick for a crumb. I saw so
many things that I had a hard time fathoming that it was
easy to become bitter but I had the ability to switch
between the two worlds and there were just too many
beautiful people I encountered on the other side to let the
world of the crack addict make me bitter. I hated
everything associated with it but I loved the drug, the
high, and the thrill of the streets. As I got older it became
all but routine and I was growing weary of the chase—the
chase for the pot of gold at the end of the rainbow, the
almost getting caught and getting away, the idea of
getting shot or killed. I just got tired but still the addiction
remained not releasing me from its hold.*

*And then on December 15th, 2001 as I sat in a crack
house, just as I'd done countless times before it happened.
My boy Abdul, an African who thought I could do no
wrong had given me his car and four or five cases of
movies and asked me to sell them for him. I'd made my
rounds, hitting Greensboro, Winston-Salem, and
Burlington and made somewhere around six or seven
hundred dollars and hit the spot when it was over.
Everything was in high gear when I arrived. I bought an
eight ball from one of the ballas that stepped through. I
took care of the house and went into the backroom to get
high. The house asked if I wanted some company but as
usual I declined. I had a thing about crack ho's. Having
a mother, a sister, and a daughter all of whom I cherished
I hated seeing a woman demean herself for a substance.
Still, and as much as the house tried to stop anyone from
entering there's always someone who is fiending and will
stop at nothing to get in. A cute little breezy finally and
somehow made it in and offered herself to me for a hit. I
had a mother, a sister, and a daughter—all of whom I
adored and I knowing that this was someone's mother or
sister or daughter couldn't allow her to bring herself to*

248

*this point for this shit so I declined and turned her on
anyway. At around seven o'clock in the morning, the
house now quiet, money gone I said my goodbyes and left.
When I arrived home I showered threw on some
sunglasses packed the car and headed for the flea market.
It was Sunday and I knew that it was gong to be slow.
Sundays always were and so I sat and tried to come down
when the phone rang. Cheryl called crying and I knew
something was amiss. She who never let emotions show
could hardly talk. When she did all I could get from
between her sobs was, 'Dad just called. Your mother
died.' I don't remember too much after that. Somehow I
drove home. The closest person to me was now gone and
all I could think of was that she was gasping her last
breath while I was smoking mine away. It's something I
still have trouble talking about but it was the turning
point of my life.*

*A couple of years later at my father's request I published
that book which lay dormant in my closet for years. A
moderate success I went to London and Paris for a couple
of months and then to Mexico City for another month or
two and loved every minute. London was especially nice.
Here where in the country that initiated the slave trade I
for once in my life felt free of racism. It was as though a
weight had been lifted from me and I enjoyed not only the
long and sordid historical past but the Brits
intellectualism as well. People just seemed so much
brighter there and in touch with what was transpiring
around them and in the world in general whereas we
Americans were ignorant of the workings and under
workings which affected us a s a nation and as
individuals. It was never so apparent as when President
Bush was elected for his second term in office and the
London newspapers reflected the sentiment of Londoners
as a whole. It read, "How Can 51 Million Americans Be
So Dumb.' I read it and cringed but not simply because*

Bush had been re-elected but because America had been duped again. Great Britain was only the second country I'd visited and just like the first time I hated returning home.

On my return I remarried and moved to Pittsburgh. Remember Yvette? I now work as a psychiatric tech in an insane asylum. Chris and Nicky have grown into pretty successful young adults despite it all with Chris receiving a four-year academic scholarship to the University of North Carolina. He graduated two years ago and is currently living in Virginia. Nicky is a freshman attending North Carolina A & T. This is my life.

Made in the USA
Lexington, KY
10 July 2014